MARY CURZON

MARY
CURZON

NIGEL NICOLSON

WEIDENFELD AND NICOLSON
LONDON

TO ALEXANDRA NALDERA

O matre pulchra filia pulchrior –

CONTENTS

ILLUSTRATIONS

[vii]

ILLUSTRATIONS

Between pages 164 and 165

The author thanks the following for permission to publish the illustrations listed: Lady Alexandra Metcalfe, 5, 7, 9, 14, 15, 17, 19, 20, 21, 22, 23, 24, 27, 28; Mrs Middleton Train, 1, 2, 6, 8, 10, 12; the Chicago Historical Society, 3, 4; Weidenfeld & Nicolson Ltd, 13 (photo: A. F. Kersting), 25; Library of the India Office, 18; Popperfoto, 26; Derbyshire Countryside Ltd, 29 (photo: Sydney W. Newbery). The portraits of Mary Curzon by Lenbach on the front of the jacket, and of Lord Curzon by Laszlo on the back of the jacket, are both the property of Lady Alexandra Metcalfe.

ACKNOWLEDGMENTS

GEORGE CURZON, Marquess Curzon of Kedleston, has been well served by his biographers. In 1928, only three years after his death, Lord Ronaldshay published his three-volume *Life of Lord Curzon*, which remains an indispensable guide to the whole of his career. In 1934 followed *Curzon: the Last Phase* in which Harold Nicolson described Curzon's period as Foreign Secretary, when my father was a member of his staff. Thirty-five years later we were given Kenneth Rose's *Superior Person*, a scintillating book based on deep research into Curzon's life before he became Viceroy of India at the age of thirty-nine, with an Epilogue which traces more shortly his subsequent career. Finally, in 1970, we had *Curzon in India*, a two-volume account of his Viceroyalty by David Dilks. I have drawn heavily on the information contained in all these books, and been guided by Mr Rose's bibliography to many others.

This book is about Curzon's first wife, Mary Leiter. Lord Ronaldshay read the large correspondence which she and Curzon maintained from their first meeting until her death, and made some use of it in his biography. But he did not see the many other documents, including her early diaries and her letters to her family, which through the generosity of the Leiters were added to the Curzon archives many years after her death. In the 1960s the whole collection came into the hands of Curzon's surviving daughter, Lady Alexandra Metcalfe, and the Library of the India Office had them bound in some fifty volumes as a gift to her. It is on this splendid documentation of her mother's life that this book is based. Lady Alexandra invited me to write it, and she has read

[ix]

it in typescript. Although the opinions expressed in it are mine, not hers, she has suggested a few amendments which I have been glad to accept. Her helpfulness, constant encouragement and frequent hospitality have made my task a very happy one.

I was fortunate to have in the United States the help of Amy Henderson, who dug deep into the archives of the Chicago Historical Society, American newspaper files and libraries at Washington, to discover the facts about the history of the Leiter family and Mary's early life. When I visited the United States in 1976 she was able to put into my hands the product of her extensive research, and led me to many sources of information I might otherwise have missed.

Apart from Lady Alexandra Metcalfe, I am indebted to several members of the Curzon and Leiter families, particularly Viscount and Viscountess Scarsdale for allowing me to examine the archives at Kedleston; and to Mrs Middleton Train, Mrs Marion Oatsey Charles, and Mr and Mrs Thomas Clagett, all of the United States.

Among others who have helped me are Kenneth Rose, who read the first half of the book in typescript; the staff of the India Office and London Libraries; the Historical Society of Chicago; Richard Kenin of the National Portrait Gallery, Washington; Sir Philip Magnus-Allcroft; Mrs Susan Mary Alsop; Mr and Mrs Donald Hess, who lent me their flat in Tangier, where much of this book was written; and Jane Lancellotti who typed it.

FOREWORD

'IGNORANCE', wrote Lytton Strachey in the opening sentences of *Eminent Victorians*, creeping up catlike on the scholars, 'is the first requisite of the historian – ignorance, which simplifies and clarifies, which selects and omits, with a placid perfection unattainable by the highest art.' He did not mean us to believe a word of this. A biographer's ignorance is never bliss. Far from clarifying, it confuses and distorts. If omission is selection, it takes a clumsy and haphazard form. We cannot know, and do not wish to know, everything about a person's life, but there are central things that we need to know and are often denied. Imagination must come to the rescue, extending the known to the unknown.

I can say with confidence who Mary Curzon's parents were: Levi and Mary Theresa Leiter. Where and when she was born: in Chicago in 1870. I can outline her girlhood there, and her education, and describe how she emerged from it to find herself in Washington, a belle, a star, and then went to Europe, which she conquered too. I can explain how she came to marry George Nathaniel Curzon in 1895, and became Vicereine of India at the age of twenty-eight, occupying the highest position which any American, man or woman, has ever held in the British Empire. I can relate how she bore three daughters, and nearly died in 1904; then did so, two years later, aged thirty-six, mourned in three continents.

All this I can and shall tell, with whatever details her letters and diaries, the newspapers and biographies and memoirs, have preserved. But Strachey's gift of ignorance does not sieve these

records with 'placid perfection'. It does so with wayward careless-
ness. I cannot name for certain Mary's many suitors, and must
guess with what conviction she rejected all but one. I do not
know how big a part her father's fortune played in Curzon's
decision to court and marry her. I know, as he did not, that at
first she was unhappy and homesick in England, but not whether
the prospect of the Viceroyalty excited more than appalled her,
since her letters were reticent on the subject and her diaries were
written for other eyes to read. I am not quite sure how far Curzon
sought or relied on her advice, nor to what extent, in their most
private moments at Calcutta and Simla, she gave it. Was Balfour,
was Kitchener, in love with her? I would like to know in what
proportion Curzon's need for her, and hers for him, determined
her return to India after her near-fatal illness in 1904. I do not
know exactly, why so young, and why so suddenly, she died.

How can one penetrate these mysteries except by guesswork?
Every biographer adopts unconsciously some of the devices of
fiction to explain whatever is undocumented. His basic materials
may be solid wood or stone, but he adds to them lightly with
plaster or putty to render his vision whole, his model unique. In
this book I have carried the process a slight stage further. I have
speculated occasionally upon her states of mind. In adopting this
method (which in a more formal biography might be considered
unpardonable), I hope that a truer portrait of Mary Leiter may
emerge than one pieced together from the scattered bits of
information that happen to have survived.

ONE

CHICAGO

THE Leiters came from Leitersburg, near Hagerstown in Maryland, just south of its ruled border with Pennsylvania, the Mason-Dixon line. The family gave the village its name by the simple act of founding it. In 1811 Andrew Leiter purchased 400 acres of open land from his father and divided it into fifty-three lots, retaining for himself the most desirable site by the river-crossing, where fifty years earlier his grandfather had built an isolated stone house which still stands. It remains the most substantial house in the village, elegant in its Georgian derivation, strong, honest-faced, with a balcony running the length of its posterior wing. The village climbs from the river to a crossroads which forms the centre of about fifty houses varying in size from cottages to miniature mansions, most with porches, some clapboarded, some brick, some stone, neat in themselves and neatly grouped. Above the roofs and scattered trees rises the white spire of the Lutheran church, where the Leiters worshipped and some are buried. Many of the present inhabitants were born there, for they are farmers and small tradesmen, tied to their inherited land and occupations, and the village has changed little in size and character during the last 100 years, the main road from Hagerstown to Gettysburg bypassing it to skirt the foot of an Allegheny spur.

Andrew Leiter was a blacksmith. Although he founded the township, he was an inefficient man of business and died insolvent. He came from a sturdy stock of pioneers. One can trace his ancestry back two generations only, to a Jacob Leiter (in his Will he signed himself Lyder), who in about 1727 emigrated to Pennsylvania from the German part of Switzerland. He was not a Dutch Calvinist, as the American *Dictionary of National Biography* confidently states, and as Levi Leiter and his children always believed. The tradition may have arisen because Jacob, like most emigrants at that period, embarked for America at Rotterdam. Nor was he Jewish, in spite of the recurrence of many Semitic first names among his descendants. He was a Mennonite, the Protestant sect, Swiss by origin, whose members often referred to themselves as 'a peculiar people', dedicated to a simple farming life and the avoidance of worldly pleasures. The ultra-conservative subdivisions of the sect still refrain from voting in political elections, will not send their children to school beyond the elementary stage, are opposed to such simple conveniences as rubber tyres on their horsed vehicles, and have banned from their homes radio, television, washing-machines and even family photographs. Jacob Leiter found the Mennonite tradition, added to the hardships of frontier life, too austere. He left the church, became a Lutheran, moved from Pennsylvania to Maryland in 1762, and built his fine stone house.

He quarrelled with his elder sons, and divided his property between the two youngest, one of whom was another Jacob, Andrew's father, and the other Abraham, the village miller, who was Mary Leiter's great-grandfather. Abraham had nine children, of whom the eldest, Joseph, was the first Leiter to achieve any eminence beyond his village. As a young man he was apprenticed to George Ziegler, a local carpenter and cabinet-maker, and in 1828 married his daughter Anne. He had little formal education (one term's schooling, it was said), but read widely, and was intelligent, hard-working and successful, creating from nothing a large practice as an architect and contractor. Many of the buildings still standing in Leitersburg were erected by his firm. For fifteen years he was President of the Planters Mutual Insurance Company of Washington County, Maryland, and in 1846 was elected Democratic representative for his county to the Maryland House of Delegates. A portrait of him survives. It shows a handsome man with a firm brow and level eyes; a kindly

man, one guesses, and a natural leader. He was Mary's grandfather. She never knew him. He died in 1862, eight years before
she was born, and his wife a year later.

Joseph and Anne had four sons, of whom Levi Ziegler Leiter,
Mary's father, was the third, born in 1834. The other three
remained content with modest occupations and seldom left their
village, while Levi seems never to have revisited it in his adult life,
and bequeathed to it only one memorial, a Ziegler cemetery,
which now lies almost derelict behind a low brick wall, where
self-seeded saplings encroach on the gravestones of his mother's
family.

Levi's education has been described as 'liberal', but it can have
amounted to little more than what the local school, built by his
father, could offer, supplemented by what he heard and read at
home. The surrounding countryside encouraged an open-air
boyhood, the river at the foot of the stone house being its most
enticing feature. Levi, however, was no Tom Sawyer. Lonely,
industrious, critical, ambitious, he soon made up his mind that
Leitersburg held little for him beyond childhood, and at the age
of nineteen, with parental encouragement, he left his first job in
the village store for the town of Springfield, Ohio, where he
worked for a year in Peter Murray's store and lodged with David
Leiter, his father's cousin. In 1854 he went to Chicago, and
obtained employment with the firm of Downs & Van Wyck,
merchants.

Chicago at that time was the phenomenon which, in different
guises, it has never ceased to be. Its population was already
40,000, but only twenty years earlier it could hardly have been
termed a village. The first permanent habitation was an outpost
fort built in 1803 and rebuilt in 1816, but a soldier passing through
the area as late as 1827 noted that the civilian population
numbered only six or seven American families, with a small
camp-following of half-breeds and vagabond Indians. As the geography of the expanding country became clearer, Chicago was
seen to occupy a nodal situation on the frontier. It lay at the most
southerly point of the Great Lakes system, accessible equally by
land and water, and on the main overland route to the West. It

[3]

was the point where the lakes approached closest to the navigable waters of the Illinois river, which led in turn to the Ohio, the Mississippi and the Gulf. A port could be formed at the mouth of its little river, the only one for many miles around Lake Michigan. It was the natural commercial centre of a territory, thousands of square miles in extent, which contained some of the richest agricultural soil in the world and was filling rapidly with settlers.

In 1833 the speculation boom began. The core of the future city was marked out in rectangular lots which sold for $100 apiece and multiplied in value 150 times within three years. Roads and shipping-lanes, and soon canals, railways and the telegraph, converged upon Chicago from every direction. By 1850 it had become a metropolis, and the first grain-elevators, slaughtering and meat-processing plants, lumber yards and factories, began to rise on the border of the lake and river. Chicago became the market for the wheat, livestock and timber of a vast province, and sent out to it the agricultural gear and machinery, the household goods and clothing, needed by the fast expanding settler population of the plains. With all the bustle that this involved, the rearing-up and tearing-down of temporary buildings, the rapid making and disintegration of fortunes, it was the most exciting place in America. Its architectural historian, Thomas E. Tallmadge, describes it as 'a charming white and green city', white with the pinewood and porticos of the Greek Revival, green with trees and long strips of lawn. Its drawback was the mud, 'the deepest, blackest and stickiest that the world had ever seen'. Much of Chicago was built on a semi-swamp, and until the 1860s no sure method was found to anchor the larger buildings or solidify the streets, which oozed with slime and sewage. Tallmadge's richest anecdote is of a man seen struggling up to his armpits in the mud of State Street. When a friend called out from the sidewalk, 'Do you want any help?', he replied, 'No thankee, Sir; I've got a good horse under me.'

Levi Leiter was twenty years old when he arrived in Chicago in 1854. He had had some commercial training from his father and in the two stores at Leitersburg and Springfield, and at

Downs & Van Wyck he began to learn the business of large-scale distribution. He stayed with them for a year, and then moved to the bigger firm of Cooley, Wadsworth & Co., wholesale dry-goods merchants. At about this time, another youth of the same age, Marshall Field, joined the firm. He came from Massachusetts, a farmer's son who had served four years as a clerk in a country store, and like Leiter reached Chicago with overflowing ambition but no money beyond what he could earn. His starting salary at Cooley's was $400 a year, of which he saved half by sleeping in the store. Quiet, serious, good-looking, aloof, 'silent Marsh' desired no social life: he thought only of work and money. He was one of Cooley's salesmen, travelling the villages of the hinterland with his cartload of samples, winning orders by his knowledge of the trade, his courtesy and his memory for names. Leiter was the firm's office-clerk, soon promoted to book-keeper and accountant, outwardly a more dynamic man, bushy-whiskered and irascible, with unquestionable integrity and an outstanding gift for finance. The two young men formed a close friendship, and planned together how they could rise from the back-rooms, the gig-carts and the mud, to become their own masters. It took them eight years. By degrees Cooley raised their salaries to $2,500, and then offered them a partnership, with John V. Farwell, a third member of the staff. On Cooley's retirement in 1863, the three of them took over the assets of the business as Farwell, Field & Co. Levi Leiter was the junior partner.

So far their progress had been steady, but for Chicago not remarkable. Field and Leiter could have ended their days in modest affluence, with a house in Lake Forest, a carriage to drive there, and a wholesale store of moderate size to direct. The turning-point came at the end of 1864, when Field quarrelled with Farwell, and simultaneously Potter Palmer, founder and owner of the greatest wholesale and retail store in the West, offered to sell it to Field and Leiter on very advantageous terms, leaving $450,000 in the business until they could afford to repay him. Field was initially able to raise $250,000 and Leiter $120,000, mainly from bank loans. The firm of Field, Palmer & Leiter came into existence in January 1865, and two years later, when Palmer had been wholly repaid his share out of profits, it became Field, Leiter & Co., the firm which today, as Marshall Field, is to the United States what Harrods is to England.

The inspiration behind this highly original business was neither Field's nor Leiter's, but Palmer's. He was Chicago's first merchant-prince. Founding his store in Lake Street in 1852, he began by catering for the modest needs of settler families, and continued to do so on three of its four floors. He soon realized that in Chicago itself there was a growing number of customers who could afford something better. He imported from New York, and then direct from Europe, the latest fashions in women's clothes, furniture, carpets and bibelots. 'Dry-goods' were now to include luxuries. Palmer's retail floor became the parade-ground of Chicago's society. His quality goods were not only the best but the cheapest, since he bought direct from the manufacturers, and introduced the system, then considered commercially suicidal, of allowing customers to take goods home on approval and return them for a full refund, without argument, if they were found to be in any way unsatisfactory. Palmer was the first to say that the customer is always right, to allow women to change their minds. 'Give the lady what she wants' became the firm's slogan, and the title of its most recent history. Customers were to be treated with courtesy, and the store was to be decorated with a lavishness unimaginable in their own homes.

In 1868 Field & Leiter moved from Lake Street to State Street, the heart of the city, where Palmer built and leased to them a six-storey, marble-fronted building, in which gas-jets illuminated walnut counters spread with a rich display of silks and satins, sable-trimmed coats, black and white astrakhans, Persian cashmeres, point-lace shawls, and hats and dresses direct from Paris. Inside the main entrance was a 'greeter', trained to remember by name customers who might not have been there for years. Women were to be addressed as Madam, not 'my dear' or 'lady' as elsewhere, and the conventional introduction 'Have you been waited upon?', which sounded subservient, became 'May I help you?'. There were rest-rooms with attendant maids, a children's nursery, a writing-room, a tea-room, even a sick-room for customers suddenly taken ill. The atmosphere was one of gentility, leisure and mutual trust. Each customer left convinced that she or he had been welcomed individually. For the staff it was a friendly and well-paid place to work in. A job at Field & Leiter carried prestige. What has now become normal in all great stores, was then extraordinary.

The two partners were men of very different temperaments. Marshall Field was the super-salesman, Levi Leiter the financial director. Field supervised the store, Leiter its administration. Their partnership did not run easily. For days on end they would not speak to each other when they disagreed on policy. The wholesale side was doing six times more business than the retail of luxuries. Why, asked Leiter, should they not scrap luxuries completely, and confine the business to wholesale? Field, the senior partner, refused. The fame of the retail side drew the country traders to the wholesale. He wanted a shop; Leiter a store. Field's attention was focused on the growth of the city; Leiter's on the growth of the West.

Rumours of their dissension, and anecdotes to illustrate it, began to circulate among the staff. There was the society woman who returned a cape the day after a ball, insisting that she had not worn it. It was so expensive a cape that the matter was brought to the attention of Field himself. He took her word for it, but found, after she had left with her refund, a lace handkerchief tucked into the sleeve. His comment was characteristic: 'If she says she didn't wear it, she didn't wear it. But I guess we'd better send her back her handkerchief.' Leiter, on the other hand, was once seen striding towards his office when he noticed a visitor with greying hair and a jet-black moustache. 'What do you want, sir?', he asked. The man replied that he had come to order some goods. Leiter retorted: 'No you don't. Your moustache is dyed, and you are obviously an impostor.' On another occasion a young assistant who had sold $800 of goods brought the order to Leiter for approval. 'No sir, you cannot have these goods.' 'But I am going to pay cash!' 'That makes no difference. Your credit with us is bad.'

These stories must be treated with caution. They are quoted

from *Give the Lady What She Wants*, which was published many years subsequently, when Field's name was the only one generally remembered, and it alone was the patronym of the store. But they indicate the tradition. Leiter was seen retrospectively as the partner who protected the business, Field as the partner who generated it: Leiter as the watch-dog, Field as the purring cat. Of course it was not so simple. The West was then notorious for gamblers and non-payers, and Leiter's strict credit control and genius for financial management carried the firm through all its early crises, the Civil War, the slump of 1875, the fires which gutted their premises twice within six years. He was a prodigious worker, his personality dogged, tenacious and suspiciously observant, but although in business he was peppery and could bark unpleasantly at subordinates, in his personal life he was gentle and retiring, unless he had been drinking (which he did not do to excess), when he became contentious and his voice loud.

It was not until 1866, when he was thirty-two, that Leiter married. His wife was Mary Theresa Carver, a daughter of Benjamin Carver and Nancy Lanthrop Fish, and a granddaughter of Judge Samuel Fish of Norwich, Connecticut. The Carvers were fond of claiming descent from John Carver, leader of the *Mayflower* Pilgrims and first Governor of Plymouth in 1620. The tradition would have been a fine one but for the inconvenient fact that the Governor had but one child, who died in infancy at Leyden before the Pilgrims embarked. Nothing is known for certain of the Carver ancestry except that they came from Utica, New York State, and moved to Chicago in about 1855. Benjamin was first employed as a secretary and cashier at the Marine Bank, and later rose to a higher position in banking. In 1895 he was named by the *Chicago Tribune* as one of the influential citizens of the North Division. Levi Leiter certainly did not choose his wife because she was rich or influentially connected.

Before her marriage at the age of twenty-one Mary Theresa was a school-teacher. There was nothing discernible in her later character to demonstrate the fact. Some people called her good-humoured, and she could be, but to most she appeared bold, proud, ignorant and selfish, ambitious to make for herself a great social position without the intellectual capacity to sustain it. Mary was loyal to her mother, but it cost her some effort. Once she described for Curzon Mrs Leiter's character as 'calm, strong and sensible', and then went on:

There is a high moral tone to all her infantile stories, which I remember well as a child. I am afraid I am not made of such strong fibre as she is. She would show absolute composure in an earthquake, and always accept the inevitable without a shadow of discomfiture. She is self-centered, which I suppose is natural to anyone with such absolute self-confidence, and all our talk seems to revolve about small episodes in her existence. . . . She is peculiar but magnificent.

She was a firm believer in Christian Science, convinced that physical well-being depends entirely upon an effort of will, and her manner was correspondingly extrovert, even jovial at times, demanding constant entertainment, in search of which she would flit from Chicago to New York, from London to Paris. But she could turn unpredictably severe, when her 'high moral tone' caught up with her ebullience, and her victims were usually children, servants or women of inferior means. She had no natural wit, but was considered eccentric in a rather engaging way, due chiefly to her lapses into malapropisms, as when she exclaimed, 'At last I am back on terracotta' on landing from a stormy Atlantic crossing, or when she announced that her husband would be attending a fancy-dress ball 'in the garbage of a monk'. The best joke of her life was probably inadvertent, when she protested that a public urinal which was to be erected outside her Washington house would be better sited in P Street.

The Leiters had four children, a son and three daughters. Joseph was the eldest, born in 1868; Mary Victoria came next, on 27 May 1870; and then Nancy ('Nannie') and Marguerite ('Daisy'). Mary's birthplace was 924 Indiana Avenue, Chicago, between 19th and 20th Streets, in the then fashionable residential district south of the city centre and near the lake. When she was one year old the family moved nearby to 60 Calumet Avenue, a new marble-fronted brownstone mansion built to their own design. Neither house survives, for the district underwent a transformation at the turn of the century and is today largely industrialized. In its heyday it was as grand as any in the United States. Carriage-ways wound through gardens to porte-cochères of pretentious magnificence, and each house, in competitive ostentation, flared at the roof-line into turrets and cupolas, the Gothic vying with the Renaissance. None was complete without its ballroom and orangery, and the smaller rooms could be charming, as one can see from the reconstruction of one of them in the museum of the Chicago Historical Society, richly carpeted and curtained, the furniture upholstered in red, central chandeliers glinting in the light of coal fires. The rooms suggested security and ease, a refuge from the turmoil of commercial competition that had made their creation possible.

The district was spared by the great Chicago fire of 1871, because the wind blew the flames away from it. Mary was sixteen months old when on 8 October the fire started in a cowshed a dozen blocks away, and raced north and east through the wooden houses towards the iron and stone of the city's centre. The wind carried sparks and blazing timbers across the widest streets, and the fire was soon completely out of control. The great heat generated gusts of air from new directions, and the flames came not in steady thrusts which could be predicted, but in twisting waves which often turned back on what had so far been spared. As soon as the fire had entered a building through its cellars, windows or roof, it rose or descended within seconds to engulf it all. Many of the most modern buildings had been certified fireproof, but none could withstand heat of this intensity. Even if the outer walls stood intact, the iron joists melted, and floor after floor collapsed into the furnace below. The firemen's hoses were wholly ineffective, as the high wind blew the jets of water into spray as soon as they left the nozzles, and by 3 a.m. the waterworks themselves were wrapped in flame. Attempts to blow firebreaks with gunpowder were overtaken by the reach and carry of the sparks. The noise, one eyewitness wrote, 'was like nothing so much as the united roar of the ocean with the howl of the blast on some stormy rocky coast'. The fury of the fire, as of invading Cossacks at full gallop, created panic among the people. 'Mobs of men and women rushed wildly from street to street, screaming, gesticulating and shouting, as if just escaped from a madhouse.' Some saw their chance to drink themselves senseless in saloons, others to loot, for what property could be considered private when everything would soon be destroyed? Most fled to the lakeside with whatever they could wheel or carry, and stood waist-deep in water, as once the citizens of Pompeii and London, to watch the destruction of their city. An area of $3\frac{1}{2}$ square miles was totally ravaged, 300 people died, and 100,000 were rendered homeless. At least it was on a scale with Chicago's pretensions. 'It is the finest conflagration ever seen', wrote one reporter, 'the greatest and most brilliant apparition of the nineteenth century.' The rest of the country gloated: 'Again the fire of heaven has fallen on Sodom and Gomorrah.'

The Field & Leiter store on State Street was one victim of the great fire. An attempt was made to save it by dowsing the walls and hanging wet blankets across every window, but the building became untenable when the water failed, and the last man had scarcely left when the flames burst outwards, as if the fire was already contained within it, waiting its chance. The store was not just gutted, but totally destroyed, the marbled walls powdered by the heat. The loss in merchandize alone amounted to $2\frac{1}{2}$ million, but goods worth another $1 million were saved. Leiter's own house and garden in Calumet Avenue served as a temporary dumping ground for the wagon-loads of silks and carpets which managed to cross the smoking ruins, and within a few days the partners organized a sale of what was salvaged. They were well insured, and although some insurance companies failed, the firm's eventual loss was only $500,000, and their assets after the fire amounted to $4\frac{1}{2}$ million. They decided to rebuild, not on the old site which remained derelict for years, but further up State Street, and opened the new store in October 1873, the second anniversary of the fire. This store too was burnt to the ground five years later, and they moved again to the palatial building which remained Marshall Field's until it was rebuilt in 1902.

Levi Leiter was a speculator as well as a dealer in dry-goods. Quietly he had been investing in real-estate long before the fire, keenly watching the trend of the city's growth, investing his share of the profits of the store with acumen and stealth. The fire made or broke millionaires. It made Leiter. He bought up central sites when they were still cluttered with charred timbers and calcinated rubble, and erected on them some of the most substantial buildings in the re-born city, from which he derived a princely revenue in rents alone, like the Grand Pacific Hotel and the eight-floor emporium on State Street now occupied by Sears, Roebuck. Such was the scale of his operations that a post-fire section of the most recent history of the city is titled 'Leiter's Chicago'. His reputation was due not only to the size and number of his buildings and the aggrandizement of his fortune. He did more than any other man to restore the city's credit after the fire, to re-establish its business, to persuade the big insurance companies to re-open their agencies there, and to foster its cultural life by generous aid to the Chicago Art Institute (of which he was President), the Historical Society, the public library and the Chicago Club. He never stood for public office, but his influence and achievement were at one time greater than the Mayor's.

He was a solitary man. He endured society for the sake of his family, but his square-cut face, rendered squarer by his spade-beard, was seldom animated except by indignation in business or tenderness at home. Mary adored him. 'My life here', she once wrote from India, 'is lived with you ever before me as an example', an example of conscientiousness, integrity, firmness and reserve. These are qualities which some found chilling, and Mary had others which were wanting in her father, humour, for instance, and great charm, but he gave her a moral and intellectual base. Seldom can a father's influence on a daughter have remained more evident than his on her.

Chicago was a masculine world to which women were decorative appendages, advertisements of their husbands' success in business, and they were not expected to contribute to it any advice or even consolation, for they were never consulted on such matters. The first rule of the Chicago Club, the élite centre of the commercial world, was that no admission be granted to 'dogs, women, Democrats or reporters'. The women's function was to spend money on their houses, their carriages, their children and themselves in the manner most likely to attract the admiration of the few able to rival them. It was a plutocracy, snobbish beyond any aristocracy because they had no fellow-feeling with the poor. Mrs Leiter could wish for nothing better. The *Bon-Ton Directory* for 1879, 'Giving the names in alphabetical order, addresses and hours of reception of the Most Prominent and Fashionable Ladies residing in Chicago and its suburbs' announced that Mrs L. Z. Leiter 'receives friends any day'. She had an indoor staff of six, and a house which was eclipsed in grandeur only by Mrs Marshall Field's and Mrs Potter Palmer's. The financial ruin of some of her neighbours enhanced the social standing of the survivors, and the frenzy with which the city was rebuilt prolonged the excitement of the fire. Two years later a nationwide economic depression again decimated the millionaires. Samuel J. Walker, for example, a real-estate tycoon, who was said to be worth $15 million in 1873, had lost everything by 1877. But Levi Leiter was immune to disaster. In addition to his town-house, he built in 1879 for $500,000 a mansion on Lake Geneva, Wisconsin, which he named Linden Lodge, siting a fake Dutch windmill on the hill behind, an observatory in the roof, and a trout-pond at the foot of the extensive garden. On the lakeside he moored his magnificent steam-yacht *Daisy*.

It was in luxury that Mary Leiter grew up, and in luxury that she spent all her life. Her earliest schooling was in Chicago itself, and she attended the Academy run by Mr and Mrs A. E. Bournique for instruction in dancing, physical culture and deportment. Music was her earliest interest, and it lasted lifelong. She also began tentatively to write. In the archives of the Chicago Historical Society there is a draft of a play pencil-scribbled in January 1882, when she was eleven, which shows that even at that age she was reaching out towards Europe for romance richer than Chicago's cotillions could provide. The setting of the play is some seventeenth-century Ruritania, and its characters have names like Captain von Valcour and Franz von Dorsigny, handsome young officers whose main occupations were love and duelling. 'No signature?', muses Valcour, sniffing a scented note. 'Hmm! Hmm! a curious adventure. It is perhaps a beautiful woman who will give me a rendez-vous. That would be charming.'

It would be charming, thought Mary, to be a man to whom unexpected things happened, instead of a small girl whose days were arranged for her weeks ahead. She assumed that the comforts by which she was surrounded were provided without effort, and while she was aware of a larger world beyond the nursery, it was a world where men were stern and bearded, and women spent hours together in a boudoir. She knew of the fire, of course, though she could not remember it, and when she was three she was taken to the opening of the new store, and left to play with other children in the kindergarten on the top floor, while speeches were made and toasts drunk in the largest of the gas-lit saloons. It was her first memory. As she grew older, she was sometimes taken to the store by her mother, and was allowed to wander between, and behind, the counters (for she and her sisters were known to all the sales-girls), and she began to learn from her father where all the different stuffs and dresses and bibelots came from, a geography lesson in a glittering bazaar.

These expeditions were rare treats, and she began to sense vaguely the importance of her father in a magnificent world. Young men were frightened of him, and she wondered why. At home he was calm and affectionate, and liked being teased by her, different from her mother, who was often cross, and whose manner would suddenly change when people called. Then she became all sweetness, showing the children off before shooing them gently upstairs. The house was a sandwich, the nursery floor and the kitchens where she was always welcome containing the drawing-room and library which she invaded at her peril.

Mary made friends, not easily, because she was shy, and they were chosen for her from among the Fields, Palmers, Armours and Walkers, who lived either in Calumet Avenue or (which was even grander) Prairie Avenue a block away, and all attended the same school, to which, however short the distance, they were driven in competing family broughams. They met again at children's parties, feeling awkward while mothers' eyes were on them and they were dressed for show, and at dancing classes where small hands were raised and crooked in imitation of young Mr Bournique. Days were spent on Lake Michigan, and longer holidays at Linden Lodge, which the children loved, the change of scene and the change of clothes, of occupation and neighbours, compensating for the absence of favourite possessions.

Mary, in the fuddled way that children think, was waiting for something more to happen. There could be too many pleasures. Everything was available, so nothing was a treat. The prospect of another party with the same children, the same amusements, ceased to be exciting, and minor irritants, such as a scolding or a lost buckle, a recitation imperfectly learnt, clouded day after day. There were quarrels between the siblings: Joseph was rough, Nannie petulant, Daisy too demanding (and why was the boat called *Daisy* when Mary was the eldest of the girls?). She settled for an imaginary world, read vastly, and wrote plays and stories in childish plagiarism of what she read, living a dream-life in which virtue was always rewarded, and if innocence was sometimes abused, it was always, sooner or later, vindicated. She had inherited her parents' strict moral code and went regularly to church, and applied their teaching in mock-motherhood in the nursery. She could be slightly priggish, the calmest of the children, yet capable of sudden indignation, of flashes of jealousy or reprimand, sometimes imperious because that was the example her mother set, but also generous and contemplative like her father. Her mood oscillated between high spirits and impenetrable aloofness. The servants thought her strange.

In 1881 Levi Leiter split with Marshall Field. The cause of their separation was deep-rooted in their different temperaments and past quarrels, but they managed to keep secret the details of the actual breach. What appears to have happened is this. Their dispute about wholesale and retail trading had never been resolved. After the two fires Leiter was even more determined that the sale of luxury goods involved too great a risk and brought too small a return. Field had housed the wholesale side in a separate building, and his pride and joy was the retail store on State Street. He thought it was what every merchant should aspire to, and before long every great city in the United States would have at least one such store, and Field & Leiter would be its model. Relations between the two partners were further strained by legal disputes about the boundaries between certain of their real-estate holdings in the city. It was evident that a crisis was approaching. Since 1869 they had been financially equal partners, each keeping one third of the profits, but this did not reflect the true power-structure of the firm. The remaining third of the profits was distributed among staff-members who had risen to high executive positions. This was another source of disagreement. Field wished to make these men junior partners; Leiter saw no reason why the original two partners should not retain full control and reap the reward of their early enterprise. This was the weakness of Leiter's position. He antagonized these men by his irascibility, distrust and now (as they saw it) his selfishness. Field was their champion, and they his. When it came to crisis-point they were on Field's side, and though they had no voting shares, they could threaten resignation if Field went and Leiter stayed, thus robbing the firm of its top management.

Field told Leiter that he did not wish to renew their partnership agreement when it expired in January 1881. He offered to sell his share to Leiter for the absurdly low figure of $2,500,000, or to buy Leiter's share for the same sum. Let him choose. In fact he had no choice. With all the senior executives pledged to support Field against him, he would have found it impossible to carry on. Unable to buy, he was forced to sell, and on 26 January 1881 the sixteen-year-old firm of Field & Leiter was transformed into Marshall Field & Co., which it remains till this day.

Leiter left with his cash payment and many millions more invested in stocks, mines and real-estate. In a statement to the *Chicago Tribune* he said only: 'For two or three years I have been desirous to retire from business. I have made enough to live on, and the time has come when I should take a rest [he was only forty-six]. I have a good many outside interests that will occupy as much time as I care to devote to work. Some of my leisure-time I will devote to trout-fishing.' A report that Leiter had yielded to the pleas of his wife, who felt that her husband's business connections hampered her social aspirations, was denounced by the *Chicago Times* as 'the senseless vagaries of the gossiping world'. Few people considered that Leiter had been badly treated. In public estimation he had always been the junior and less brilliant partner of the two. The popular verdict, based on the only standards that then counted in Chicago, was that he had made a mistake in refusing to compromise with Field, because the firm's profit continued to double and re-double. Later, the public's qualified contempt changed to envy. Leiter was able to devote his remaining twenty-three years to travel and the acquisition of works of art, while Field was chained to Chicago by his exacting business. Nor did his retirement mean the slow erosion of Leiter's fortune. He managed his affairs wisely, made many new investments, and as property and stock values mounted, so did his wealth. At his death he was worth $30 million, at least four times his estimated fortune when the partnership broke up. Field left over $100 million. Both had started with nothing at all.

Later in 1881 the Leiters moved to Washington. This did not mean a complete break with Chicago. Leiter sold the house on Calumet Avenue, but kept Linden Lodge, and his association with cultural and philanthropic causes in the city dates mainly from after his retirement. He was even asked to run for Mayor in 1882, but refused. The move from Chicago to Washington was not due to any sense of rejection or disenchantment on Leiter's part, nor to ambition for political office, but to Mrs Leiter's hope to create for herself and her family a brilliant social position in a more cosmopolitan scene.

First, she must equip the elder children for their new role by taking them to Europe. She and her husband, with Joseph and Mary and a tutor called Madden, sailed from New York to

Liverpool in September 1881. For all of them except Levi Leiter it was their first visit abroad.

Mary's diary of this journey survives. It is written in careful copperplate, evidently as a holiday-task for her mother's scrutiny. Thus:

22 Sept. 1881. Palace Hotel, London. We went to the tower of London and the armouries and the Queen's jewels there. We went into a room where a man said there were one hundred thousand guns and the railings around the Galleries are made of swords. The armouries are very fine and we saw the beheading block. We came to the hotel and took lunch there. Then we drove to the park and saw the building that Prince Albert laid the cornerstone to and caught cold and died.

In London they followed an itinerary which has changed little since: the British Museum, Madame Tussauds, Westminster Abbey. Mrs Leiter was determined to leave no sight unseen. All that was lacking was society. They met nobody, and lunch was eaten every day in the Palace Hotel. After five days in London they went to Paris. Things were much the same there. Fontaine-bleau, the Gobelin factory, the tomb of Héloise and Abelard ('where the disappointed lovers hang wreaths'), the Bois, Versailles; but the only incident which aroused Mary to more than dutiful reporting, with historical information credited to Baedeker, was the arrival on the dinner-table one evening of a roast pheasant complete with head, tail-feathers and wings re-attached by wires.

Christmas was spent in Paris, rather dismally, at the Hotel Meurice, and in early January the party continued in a private railway-car to Nice. 'A tiresome journey', wrote Mary, echoing her mother, but the Grand Hotel satisfied everyone's expectations. From there they went on expeditions, to Villefranche, to Monaco, and to a Roman amphitheatre, where Mary 'mused', or was expected to muse, 'upon the combats between the Gladiators and wild beasts, which occurred many centuries ago'. At eleven her solemnity was touching. She is 'confined to the hotel with a cold'; she watches gamblers leaving the Casino and thinks them 'sad, troubled and pale'. There were some happier moments too – the Nice carnival, donkey-rides on the beach, the visit of the French fleet to Villefranche. But no moment of ecstasy, no new friends, not even an encounter with fellow tourists. They returned through Paris and London, and arrived back in New York on 8 May 1882 to find 'Aunt Louise on the quay jumping up and down with flowers'. Home was at least more welcoming than abroad. The journey had not been a success.

TWO

WASHINGTON

Home was now Washington. It is not known where the Leiters lived at first, but as Mrs Leiter's death-certificate records that she had been a resident in the capital since 1881, they must have taken temporary lodgings before they moved, in 1883, into one of the grandest houses in the newest district. It stood on Dupont Circle, at the corner of Massachusetts Avenue, an island house which had been built in 1881–2 for Senator James Gillespie Blaine, Secretary of State under President Garfield and Republican candidate for the Presidency in 1884. The Blaines soon found the house too expensive to run and maintain, and let it to the Leiters at a rent of $11,500, at that time the highest ever charged in Washington for a private house. It stands today, little altered externally, and although the interior has now been trivialized by conversion into offices and doctors' surgeries, contemporary descriptions record its appearance when the Leiters first moved in.

In style the Blaine house is a mixture of Romanesque, Gothic and Renaissance. Built of brick, with rubbed or moulded brick courses to emphasize the levels and corbels, it mounts to towers and dormers fifty-four feet above the ground. If it can be granted a 'brooding strength', as the Commission of Fine Arts claims in its careful survey of the building, it is disfigured by its mutton-red brickwork, huge plate-glass windows, and the lack of any pleasing proportion. Inside, it was richly finished in oak and mahogany for the main rooms, and in poplar and pine for the bedrooms. The fireplaces, one to every room, increased in magnificence as you descended. The hall, occupying the whole centre of the house, was baronial in scale with polished columns, and from it mounted the staircase, massively carved in oak. This monstrous castle was to be Mary's home for the next ten years, and the setting for her mother's intended social triumph.

One of her first guests, in 1883, was the most surprising: Matthew Arnold. Then on a lecture tour of the United States, he accepted the Leiters' hospitality to save hotel bills, and Henry Adams warned him that his host, whom Arnold had never met, was 'an ungrammatical self-made man'. The description was unjust in its first epithet, for Levi Leiter had a profound love of books and collected a library of early American history and literature which was to become one of the most famous in the country. But Adams's comment indicates the difficulties that Mrs Leiter faced. If her ultimate object was to find husbands for her three daughters, she seemed to have settled in the wrong place. Washington was unimpressed by money, and Leiter was indifferent to politics. It was an actual disadvantage for a rising young Congressman to marry a fortune, for it destroyed his reputation for 'simplicity', then a political qualification of the utmost importance. Moreover, politics in America was so uncertain a profession that the bride of a high-flyer might find him two years later with both wings broken, a possibility which Mrs Leiter was not prepared to face, even if her daughters were. In a society more masculine even than Chicago's, a rich and unknown woman would find it very difficult to make her way. The young and attractive were flirted with, but they and their mothers were seldom spoken to as equals, and Mrs Leiter had no qualifications whatever to claim exemption from the rule. Her position, like any other woman's, depended upon her husband's, and Levi could give her little help. He never became a figure in Washington, never coveted the most humble office there, for his heart was still in Chicago. He wished to please her, and rented the most expensive house he could find, but the great rooms remained for many years sparsely occupied by guests. It was her daughter, Mary, who eventually filled them. The triumph which was planned for the girls by their mother was eventually achieved for the mother by her eldest girl.

Mary's education was continued mainly by governesses in the Blaine house, and she also attended the fashionable local school run by Madame Cléophile Burr and her daughter. She was accounted a clever girl, though no prodigy, but was soon distinguished by other qualities. A contemporary at Madame Burr's, Virginia Peacock, wrote later of 'her fascination, to which both her teachers and companions were susceptible. Her beauty of face, her poise and carriage, together with a sweet girlish modesty under all circumstances, and a graciousness that was simple and unaffected, rendered her at all times most attractive ... She had cultivated her powers of observation and developed a breadth of mental vision that at an unusually early period not only removed the crudities of youth but gave her poise and finish ... She was serious and earnest rather than scintillating, with a reserve and dignity of manner tempered by a sweetness that admitted no suggestion of austerity. Studious and ambitious, she knew little of frivolity or idleness.'*

Mrs Leiter's upbringing of her daughters was strict, as her own had been. In her diary of 1886 she wrote of 'our quiet house and studious lives', and reiterated her rule that the girls should go nowhere unaccompanied, in contrast to other parents 'who do not attach any importance to this, permitting their daughters to go and come quite alone when it suits their convenience, thinking it beneficial to their independence and strength of character'. Early in the next year her diary recorded her shock on first reading *Anna Karenina*, 'to my fancy a book only to be read by a person well on in years. The depth of depravity in the *haute-monde* is too terrible for the innocent youth of our country. The book is ennobling but caters to a diseased appetite.' Mary accepted without question her mother's moral values. At no period of her life did she react against them. She was not indifferent to admiration, but remained as chaste as ice, and would have thought any aberration from the Leiter code a crime of disloyalty in execrable

* *Famous American Belles of the Nineteenth Century*, Virginia Peacock, Philadelphia, 1901.

taste. In other young girls such modesty might have been thought priggish, and no doubt many so considered Mary. But it was also evidence early in her life of an enviable strength of character, which, allied to calm and grace, set her apart from her contemporaries even before she left school.

Her life, however, was not too rigidly confined. Her mother sent her in the winter of 1886–7 to New York, where she stayed in a rented apartment with a French governess, Mlle Moevier, who taught her to speak both French and German excellently. She also had daily lessons in chemistry, arithmetic and history from a young tutor at Columbia College, Thomas Ewing. In the intervals she studied singing and art. There were summer holidays with her father at Linden Lodge, jaunts with her brother Joseph, now at Harvard, and a first visit to Newport, Rhode Island, with her friend Mary Edgar, whose coming-out ball in September 1886 was the first smart party that Mary (aged sixteen) was allowed to attend.

In June 1887 she went for the second time to Europe, with both parents and both sisters, a French nurse for Nancy and a German maid for Mrs Leiter. Mary's diary for this journey reveals a growing sophistication. She now noticed things, like Mr Gladstone in an opera box more intent on following the libretto than listening to the music, and the English landscape which reminded her of Corot. In Paris the women 'were tearing around streets bareheaded and so untidy', and the Italian music-master from whom she took singing lessons, 'thrust my hand down his neck that I might feel the action of his throat, and kept continually grasping my hand, pressing it not to his heart but to his chest, while he took long breaths. He is old and bald-headed.'

Her beauty was already beginning to attract attention. There was a young Englishman in Paris ('Lord Edward' she calls him, but from her mother's diary he seems to have been plain Edward Morrell) whom she had met at Newport the year before. 'He is an extremely good-looking, broad-shouldered man, with white gaiters and an eyeglass', wrote Mary, 'and he seemed very glad to see me and renew the acquaintance.' He took her, chaperoned by his sister Julia, to the circus, where Mary 'laughed until I almost died', a schoolgirl expression to which she always reverted in later life. They went driving together in the Bois, and Mary sang for him, but when she complained of homesickness for America, he accused her of indifference and they quarrelled. Next day she received from him a bouquet of pink roses, and she kept the card in her diary: 'Forgive, that in heaven ye may be forgiven.' Clearly she did, and was, for we next hear of Mr Morrell established so firmly in the confidence of her parents that 'he planted himself down beside me and one by one the members of our respective families disappeared until we were left alone in a dimly lighted court [at the Hotel Meurice]. We adjourned after two hours tête-à-tête to our sitting-room. We parted rather late.' As a leaving present he gave her a silver *edelweiss*, but Edward Morrell, the first of her admirers, is never mentioned again.

The Leiters returned to London where they were met by Mary Edgar and Joseph, and sailed from Hull to Bergen to join a steamer-trip up the coast of Norway as far as the North Cape. Mary's diary is what one might expect from any young girl seeing for the first time the curiously glaucous interior of Trondheim cathedral, fjords sliding serpentine through mountains, Lapp villages, and islands with holes cut clean through them by the waves. It is full of wonder, and splashed with exclamation marks. The most dramatic passage, dated 29 July 1887, gives an idea of her attitude and style:

Midnight had passed and still the [North] Cape stood before us looking melancholy and weird, draped in a cloud of mist. At one o'clock, the weather was the least bit better and the captain gave us permission to go ashore, provided that no one would attempt to go to the top. Of course everyone agreed, for standing on the rocks was better than standing on the deck. Mr Turner, Joe, Nannie and myself went. Mumma and Papa stopped on board. Directly we landed, Joe led off at a breakneck speed. Nannie shuffled along with Arnold Jr in support. Mr Turner and I paired off and clambered up among the rocks. I never shall forget the scene, as I was standing among the flowers, looking down upon the swarms of tourists, picking up stones and looking amazed. Way up the path Joe was struggling, and in the bay lay our boat, the most discordant thing of all. We up here at

Lands End; there a blast of music aboard a mailship steaming in the bay. The discord echoed among the melancholy rocks and had a most melancholy effect on Mr Turner and me. We gathered a most beautiful bouquet, and after one hours climb, we gathered together. It was quite like a flock of sheep prowling about, and the Shepherd in the shape of the Second Mate, blowing his whistle, to which we all responded. Many of the men were quite out of sight. It was then about two. Fancy standing in broad daylight in the small hours of the morning, picking flowers at Lands End.

The journey back was more adventurous than the steamer-trip. The Leiters hired ponies and a horse-drawn carriage and rode and drove for several days through the valleys to Lille-hammer, sleeping in mountain huts, and thence took the train to Stockholm, where the round of museums and Mary's education were resumed. By this time she was bored of Baedeker: 'There is nothing that I like better than looking at beautiful things, but as a *mere tourist*. . . . .' Her diary for that year ends with those five dots, but her mother's completes the story. They returned to Paris, where Mrs Leiter had her portrait painted by Alexandre Cabanel and Mary took riding lessons. They sailed from Liverpool on 3 December 1887, and were back in Washington for Christmas after an absence of six months.

Next year Mary came out. Her mother had by now formed a circle of acquaintances, mainly through her membership of the Ladies' Mount Vernon Association, and she was able to take her daughter to call on the wives of members of the Cabinet and Supreme Court, and invite them to return the visit to Dupont Circle, which some did. She was also on calling terms in the diplomatic world, particularly with the British Legation, where Victoria Sackville-West, who in 1881 had arrived in Washington aged nineteen straight from Paris and London convents to act as her father's hostess, was one of the first to befriend Mary, and her patronage was considered to be of much importance among the young people of the city. These stylized preliminaries to a début could have led to little more than a few invitations to balls and dinners, followed by a bleak recession. In fact, Mary Leiter became the star of her season, and when it was over, the most adulated girl in Washington, one of the few to penetrate beyond the social world to make intimate friends of older men and women in politics and the arts. She achieved this position entirely by her own wits, character and beauty, and the most remarkable aspect of her success, as it seemed to other girls, was that she did not seem to notice it.

Washington in 1888 was already quite unlike any other city in the United States. 'It is a living curiosity', wrote a contemporary journalist, 'made up of the strangest and most incongruous elements. There is a fairy-tale sense of instability about it. . . . The city looks as if it had sprung up in a morning, or rather as if a whirlwind had picked up some great town, mixed the big houses up with the little ones, then cast the whole together in one miscellaneous mass, keeping intact only the city streets.'* It was also very beautiful, a symbol of the American dream, spacious, monumental and romantic. Sixty thousand newly planted trees lined miles of newly paved streets. Libraries and art galleries abounded. There were few commercial offices, and no factories. The bulk of the residents were transient, coming from every state in the Union, a high proportion of them single males in government service, and most lived in boarding-houses alongside a parallel population of demi-mondaines and 60,000 negroes. There was a democratic tolerance about the place which created perpetual social effervescence. Shanties stood alongside mansions, horse-drawn street-cars were crammed with senators and judges sitting side by side with caitiffs and pick-pockets, and the marble floors of the Capitol were brown with tobacco stains left by inaccurate spitters in circles round the ubiquitous cuspidors.

Washington could also boast a social and intellectual adventurousness unknown elsewhere. There were thirty foreign legations whose young attachés were regarded as menaces by mothers, as paragons by daughters, and immense extravagance in dress and party-giving. The older women competed with the younger, wrote Carp, 'cutting their dresses an inch lower at the bust for every ten years of their advancing age', and displaying increasing areas of powdered back. There were crazes for guessing-games,

* *Carp's Washington*, Frank G. Carpenter, New York, 1960.

for parties at which everyone was required to dress in a selected colour, and wild expeditions in phaetons. There was, besides, a cleverer, élitist world, where literature, art, learning and inspired table-talk reproduced something of London's contemporary cosmopolitanism, an atmosphere deliberately cultivated by men like the widowed Henry Adams in his house at Lafayette Square only a stone's throw from the White House. It was into this extraordinary medley of opportunism and snobbishness, culture and ambition, self-assertiveness and restraint, that Mary now glided with a grace and vitality that made her the envy of the town.

As she was so much fêted, regarded indeed as a phenomenon whom all American girls should emulate, her début was a favourite topic for the Press both at the time and retrospectively after she became internationally famous. The many accounts of her invariably begin with a reference to her father's fortune, and continue with a description of her appearance. As a young woman she was superb. She was 5′8″ tall, her figure marvellously slender with a sinuous grace. Her hands and feet were small, her hair richly brown, arranged in loose waves and drawn back into a love-knot at the nape of the neck. Her eyes were large and grey, her expression alert but unchallenging, her face a perfect oval with high cheekbones, entirely feminine. She was not pretty in the way that Jenny Churchill or Irene Gibson were pretty, for an oval face demands study; but she was beautiful in a way that repaid it. What people noted above all was her poise and carriage. It has been said of many women that they never entered a room without attracting the gaze of all present, but Mary achieved it by 'floating'. The word occurs in three separate accounts of her, and others described her walk as 'undulating', 'swanlike'. Curzon told Cecil Spring Rice that it was her walk which enchanted him when he first set eyes on her in a London ballroom. It signalled a youthful assurance, a confidence in her beauty, an intention to enjoy herself, but also a subtle air of refinement, enhanced by her undefinable gift for wearing lovely clothes.

She trod the fine middle-ground between animation and prudence, 'gay with the lively', wrote the *New York Times*, 'and sympathetic with those who were not always at their ease'. The writer quoted an instance:

> At a dance one evening Miss Leiter was as usual overwhelmed with flowers and cotillion favours. Near her in a corner sat a girl who rarely went to balls and knew very few people: besides, nature had not been too prodigal with gifts in her regard. Noting her absent look, she tried to make the next man who came up to her aware by signs that she would like him to take out the neglected one instead. But either he misunderstood her or did not choose to surrender that dance. Seeing how the land lay, Miss Leiter rose with the archest look on her beautiful face, and taking her own partner's arm, sailed off into the dance. She was evidently explaining what this meant, for when they reached the spot where the lady of the house was distributing favours, Miss Leiter's partner left her side, secured a fine bouquet, and posted across the room to the forlorn damsel in the corner.

Of course the gesture could have had the opposite effect from that intended: the girl could have been mortified by so public a demonstration of her loneliness, and burst into tears. Mary's motive was no doubt sympathetic, but she also knew that she must in some way reduce the pressure of envy and homage that was building up around her. She was no angel of pity. Always courteous, she was not invariably considerate. A star, she would not twinkle to order. It was said that she dropped friends, that she was cold, that she formed few intimacies, that she alarmed people, that she made them aware of the social category in which she placed them. One who knew her well as a girl, Margaret Terry Chanler, wrote that 'she could be tiresome when she "unpacked her library" and tried to talk books and ideas', and Margaret herself was no mouse, having recently defied her family by embracing Roman Catholicism and marrying at the age of eighteen. Her stricture could mean no more than that Mary's intelligence was a standing reproach to the scatter-brained, which was no discredit to Mary; or it could mean that she did not greatly care if she made small people feel smaller, because they bored her. She was not a conceited girl, nor was she vain, but within limits she was proud. She expected attention because she knew that she was worth it. To a stronger will she yielded, and from a stronger mind she was avid for instruction. She judged her contemporaries by adult standards. She sprang straight from the schoolroom to the drawing-room and library. She was not a natural débutante, though a highly successful one. The sweetness of her childhood had been replaced by something stronger and more ambitious, and many of her former school-fellows found the sudden change forbidding.

The culmination of her first season at Washington was the dance which her parents gave for her on 13 February at the Blaine House. She wore white tulle over silk, garlanded with trailing yellow and pink rosebuds, and made her entry, said the *Washington Evening Star*, 'with a mailbag over her shoulder', presumably to contain the 'favours', an odd assortment of ribbons with bells attached to them, smoking-caps, sachets, match-boxes and thermometers. Among the guests were the William Whitneys (Secretary of the Navy), Judge John Davis, W. C. Endicott (Minister of War) and his daughter Mary who in the next year married Joseph Chamberlain, the British Minister and his daughter Victoria, and Margaret Terry Chanler of the critical tongue and eye.

The *Star* mentioned Mary as a guest at every important social occasion that winter, but one item was different from the others: '20 January 1888. Miss Mary Leiter assisted Mrs Cleveland at a luncheon for 20.' How could this girl, not yet eighteen, from a family which had barely won acceptance in Washington, act as co-hostess for the President's wife? But it was true. They were already firm friends. Frances Cleveland was only twenty-three, the youngest First Lady in American history. She had married in 1886 straight from college, when Grover Cleveland was forty-nine, and brought into his bachelor life a freshness and gaiety which transformed him from a recluse into a gallant, and the White House from a morgue into the centre of lively society. It was said that she produced '5,000 smiles at receptions, no two alike', and with her beauty, elegance, tact and vivacity was the first person ever to find, and make, State dinners fun. While the White House was used by the President as an office and for grander social occasions, the Clevelands lived more modestly in a suburb on the heights above Georgetown, and there Mary became Mrs Cleveland's constant companion, dining at least once a week, spending weekends there, riding with her in the surrounding plains, and assisting her at all the smaller functions. It was through this connection that Mary first met eminent men and women like Henry Adams, the John Hays, the Whitneys, the Camerons, the Theodore Roosevelts, the novelist Frances Hodgson Burnett, all of whom her mother was delighted to welcome to Dupont Circle, and they came because of Mary.

Her fame spread to New York. The Leiters went there as soon as the Washington season ended, and she immediately attracted the attention of two men whose approval was regarded as the imprimatur on a rising social career. One was Ward McAllister, who had in his gift the entrée to 'the 400', an élite which he had more or less invented with the connivance of Mrs J. J. Astor, its doyenne, to whom he was distantly related and acted as a sort of Chamberlain. Such an arbiter of social acceptability could have existed in no other place, at no other time, than in New York in the late nineteenth century. The 400 (when McAllister eventually published his list, there were found to be only 300 worthy of inclusion) were a substitute for aristocracy, as Mrs Astor was for a Queen, by which title she was popularly referred to. Admission to the 400 was regulated by a code which all comprehended but none dared analyze, and none challenge. Birth into one of the established families counted for much but was not an automatic qualification; political power but slightly; wealth only to the extent that you could not belong if you were poor; wit and charm and beauty, greatly. Divorce, or an appearance on the stage, instantly excluded. McAllister's object, wrote Elizabeth Eliot in her sketch of him,* 'was to give society the solidity needed to resist the invasion of the flashiest of the profiteers, which he achieved by a skilful mixture of those whom he named "nobs", old crustacean families that had position without fashion, and "swells", those who had to entertain and be smart in order to win their way'.

The basis of his organization was a group known as the

* *Heiresses and Coronets*, New York, 1959.

Patriarchs, of whom there were twenty-nine, all men, who acted as joint hosts at a series of winter balls, to which each was entitled to bring four ladies and five gentlemen, including himself and his family. 'The object we had in view', wrote McAllister in his auto-biography, 'was to make these balls thoroughly representative' – the phrase is laughable – 'to embrace the old colonial New Yorkers, our adopted citizens, and men whose ability and integrity had won the esteem of the community. We wanted the money-power, but not in any way to be controlled by it. Patriarchs were chosen solely for fitness, on each of them promising to invite to each ball only such people as would do credit to the balls.' His success was due to the difficulty of securing invitations to these functions, and the corresponding desirability of them. Inclusion was dignified by brutal exclusion. Levi Leiter was not a natural Patriarch. The clique had been formed with the social isolation of parvenus as one of its main purposes. Mary was the key to the door. When McAllister first met her, he took an immediate liking to her, and his 'unqualified admiration' obtained for her and her family an invitation to the next Patriarch ball. She had arrived.

The second man to enlarge her reputation was Dana Gibson. Many years later, when Mary was being sketched for an official portrait in Calcutta, the artist remarked that she reminded him of the Gibson Girls. 'That's not surprising', she replied, 'because I was one of his first models.' As a young man in New York, Gibson soon became society's leading commentator and analyst. His drawings, exquisitely flattering to the young and deferential to the elderly, are the most vivid of all the records of the world in which Mary now found herself a *nova* star. From them one can recapture, far better than from photogaphs, the looks, dress and deportment that were most admired, and the nuances of snob- · bishness and small social dilemmas which could disturb an equanimity even as firm as Mary's. The captions record precisely the tone, jargon and manner of their speech. The underlying cynicism of Gibson's cartoons was either not noticed or excused for their charm and wit, and his early victims and critics were soon persuaded to become his sitters. Later he took as his chief model Irene Langhorne, Nancy Astor's sister, whom he married in 1895, a belle whose looks upstaged every Virginia belle there had ever been, but he began by inviting to his studio young friends, men and girls, among them Mary Leiter, to pose for him. It was considered a high accolade. They were depicted *incognito* (in any case, all Gibson's girls looked more or less alike, sharing his idealized conception of American prettiness), but sometimes the initials of a favourite would appear, very small, on her handbag, while others, not so honoured, would leave *Life* magazine lying around their boudoirs open at the page, hoping to be recognized. None of Gibson's drawings of Mary is now identifiable. She could have been the girl in 'When Doctors Disagree', the doctors being the old family physician at the head of her couch and Cupid at its foot, for Gibson was a romantic. Mary must have enjoyed sitting for him. A Gibson session was a combination of charade and *tableau vivant* under the direction of a particularly gifted and charming man.

In May 1888 her father took her again to Europe, Mrs Leiter remaining in Washington. It is difficult to understand the purpose of these repeated journeys, for all Mary's friends were in America, and in London where she spent four days, in Paris ten, she made no new ones. 'I hate travelling and loathe sight-seeing, and worse than all dislike doing the tourist act', she wrote to her mother from Lucerne, after crossing an Alpine pass in a blistering snow-storm. In Venice she was so bored that one night she played truant, concealing the escapade from her father, but confessing it, surprisingly, by letter to her mother. She discovered that her hotel was linked to a neighbouring palazzo where Desdemona was reputed to have slept. She arranged with the proprietor of the hotel, who also owned the palazzo, to spend the night there with her maid Charlotte:

At half-past ten we bid Papa goodnight, and retired to our own rooms as usual. But not to sleep. I sent down to the Proprietor to say that we were ready, and the solemn procession moved off. Desdemona's room is at the top of the palace, which is joined to the hotel by a tiny passageway. We walked through a perfect labyrinth of passages and climbed no end of stairs, the proprietor lighting the way by candle. Charlotte was bringing up the rear with a bundle of clothes. We finally reached a narrow hall at the end of which are three steps with a low door at the top. We walked up them through the door and into a large square room. Alas!! not as Desdemona had left it but furnished in the 19th century style. The room was so extremely out of the way and so lonely, that for safety's and propriety's sake I had Charlotte sleep in the adjoining room. The huge bed, I am afraid not Desdemona's, stood near the middle of the room, draped in draperies to keep out gnats. Early the next morning we descended long before breakfast to our more gorgeous but less romantic apartment, and only the remembrance of sleeping where Desdemona had slept remained.

As a diversion it was innocent enough, but that Mary should think this the most exciting experience of her first visit to Venice cautions us against seeing her as a culture-hungry paragon. She was well-educated, particularly in languages, but never learned, and her knowledge of the arts, except possibly of music, remained that of a dilettante whose appetite for information could quite soon be sated. 'She had the kind of intelligence', wrote *The Times* of London in its obituary of her, 'which education develops but never overloads.' That was not an obituarist's circumlocution for something more disobliging. It was quite true. Mary's was not an incisive nor eagerly inquiring mind, but it was very receptive. She preferred to be told things more than to discover them for herself.

The Desdemona incident also disposes of the suspicion that she was a blue-stocking. 'Serious', 'reserved', were epithets often applied to her, not only by the envious, but one never hears her called solemn. She had a sense of fun, especially of the ludicrous, more than a sense of humour. One finds her repeating jokes more often than making one. Her greatest pleasure was to be entertained by people whose minds she respected, *savants* in their mellow moods, statesmen who enjoyed delighting her, and she rewarded them by quick appreciation and the charm of youthful deference. With younger men she was neither a flatterer nor a flirt, but she knew how to please. She was like Pamela Plowden in

England, a girl whom all men instinctively adored, but because convention forbade any reference to her sexual attractiveness, she became for them a goddess, a role which gradually wore her down.

From Newport, Rhode Island, where the Leiters took the Travers house on Narragansett Avenue for the summer of 1889, she wrote to her father (in Chicago): 'It is sometimes hard to steer one's boat clear of all reefs, but your approval so long as I live shall be the thing I shall always aim for, and I am afraid the man will never come along whom I can look up to and love as I do you.' Inevitably she was the toast of Newport. 'Last Sunday', reported the *Boston Herald*, 'the chief sensation was the appearance of Miss Mary Leiter, the Washington belle whose beauty is by this time celebrated, even the buds of last winter dwindling into insignificance before her. . . . Miss Leiter represents exactly the sort of American girl whom we should send over to England with pardonable pride', but apparently for display only, not for marriage. It was an Englishman, however, who first proposed to her, Cecil Spring Rice, a second secretary at the British Legation in Washington. He had no great respect for his Minister, Lionel Sackville-West, who had 'a taste for whiskey, poker and business', he wrote to a friend, 'and a hatred for female society', but became deeply attached to his daughter Victoria, who refused him. 'Springy' was soon as much in love with Mary as he had been with Victoria, who left Washington in the year of Mary's début, and until Mary's marriage to his friend George Curzon he never gave up hope that she might accept him. How strongly she was tempted, if at all, we do not know, because no letters from her to him survive from the Washington period, and in the two volumes of his published correspondence, there are none from him to her. He was a popular and able man, witty and knowledgeable, a gossip, a flirt, and very untidy, which made women act maternally towards him. Curzon described him as 'the best, cheeriest, most unselfish, most amusing of travelling companions'. For a young man in a very junior position he made a great impression on Washington, where he was one day to return as Ambassador. He was a friend of all Mary's older friends, an habitué at the

Clevelands' house. 'What fun it would be if we could all meet again in Washington', Mary wrote to him from India in 1903. 'Think of the President, and John Hay and Henry Adams and Sir Mungo [Sir Michael Herbert, British Ambassador] and Belle [Lady Herbert] and you and I, all gathered together again at Mr Adam's's breakfast table!' This may have been the extent of her feeling for Springy. He was not, in the opinion of many people, and probably in hers, a reliable, marriageable man. His gossiping could turn to malice and intrigue, from which Mary was herself to suffer when her engagement to Curzon was announced. Meanwhile it was good to have him around as a companion, and a rival for other too attentive suitors.

In Washington, Mary's room was on the top floor of the Blaine house, decorated by her own choice in blue, and sitting there she could forget the monstrosity of the remainder. Hers were lovely rooms. She had a view down both the avenues that met in Dupont Circle, bordered by light young trees and wide enough for carriages to pass two abreast in each direction. Let us suppose that she watched them for a moment, and then turned to the invitations that had come that morning, dealing out the cards side by side and arranging them in three sets.

They represented what she had become, perhaps what she had hoped to be. There in front of her were her three lives – her mother's friends, her own, and the largest group, people whom she scarcely knew but who wished desperately to know her. The latter she could refuse, but she was worried by the choice between the others, for the dates often clashed. Did she, at nineteen, owe to her mother the priority she would instinctively have given her a year ago? Was duty the stipulated response to affection? Her mother was easily hurt. Her pride in Mary was only a step away from jealousy, and Mary was well aware of it. She had let drop hints that she was going out too much, that her father saw too little of her (she meant too little of herself), and while Mrs Cleveland could of course not be refused, was it really necessary for Mary to spend all those evenings, breakfasts even, in Lafayette Square? But if she stayed more at home, and asked her friends to meet her there, it would not be a success. Her mother was too demonstrative in her welcome, and either subjected the guest to tedious interrogation or twisted the conversation to topics which gave her a chance to shine, usually some anecdote of her travels. Her father was little help: he sat there, gravely approving. Joe was boisterous, the girls eager. It had been a failure before; it would be a failure again.

There was another problem. Her mother was over-anxious for her to marry. Why she was, Mary could not make out. Marriage would remove her from home permanently. But it was fitting, her mother said, right, natural and proper (she used these terms cumulatively, as if each meant something different and amounted to an unanswerable argument) that a young girl who had been so great a success should put an end to speculation and gossip, to these abominable 'fancy free' paragraphs in the newspapers, and choose her beau – the word made Mary shudder – from the many who pursued her. Mary protested that she had no wish to marry yet, perhaps ever. She found the beaux quite amusing, and they were easily discouraged. She was quite determined that when she made her choice, her mother would have no say in it, would not in fact be told till everything had been settled.

Next year, 1890, she met George Curzon.

The fourth journey which the Leiters made to Europe turned out very differently from the first three. Like Zuleika Dobson on her way to Cambridge, Mary set out from New York to conquer London. If this sounds more calculating than she truly was, one must acknowledge that she had enjoyed her success and wanted to repeat it, that she had had for the moment enough of culture, that she was only twenty, that as one of the brightest and loveliest of the young American heiresses she knew that she would be welcomed if only she could make a start, and that in moderation she was already an Anglophile. All she had seen so far of English society was a glimpse through its windows, but that glimpse, combined with what she had read and heard, made her long to go inside. Mary was enough of a snob, if offered the choice between a dull duke and, say, a brilliant entomologist, as a dinner partner,

1 Levi Z. Leiter, Mary's father, when he was Marshall Field's partner in Chicago

2 Mary Theresa Leiter, Mary's mother, painted in Paris by Alexandre Cabanel in 1887

3 The ruins of Chicago after the great fire of 1871

4 The 'new' store of Field, Leiter & Co., in State Street, Chicago. This replaced their first store, which was destroyed in the great fire, and was itself burnt to the ground in 1877.

5 Mary Leiter during her early Washington period, about 1886

6 Mary (left) and her sister Nancy

7 Mary Leiter as a Washington belle, at the time of her début in 1888

to choose the dull duke. To her the fashionable world was the most desirable world, and the grander the party, the more exalted the titles, the more expensive the arrangements, the keener was her anticipation and enjoyment of it. After all, at twenty it is more thrilling to dance with the Prince of Wales than with a man who has danced with a girl who once danced with him. Apart from titles, there was a difference between the Patriarch balls and Devonshire House. Though admission to both was guarded, London's society was much more open to talent than New York's. Political-power and money-power and intellectual-power were more easily wedded, and didn't need a marriage-broker like Ward McAllister. There was less constraint, and competition was more discreet. 'It delighted me', Mary wrote later that summer, 'to find that in England the higher the rank, the simpler and the more unaffected the person is.' When she complained to her father after a few days in Paris at the start of the 1890 tour that she disliked young Frenchmen 'because they are all such snobs', she may have been generalizing from a single rebuff, or she may have been making a valid distinction between snobbishness which is xenophobe and plutophobe and culturephobe, and her own form of snobbishness which was overtly élitist. In Paris the men were 'self-centred', she said, from which one suspects that they paid her too little attention, or too much, and in her letters to her father she did not distinguish one from the other by so much as a name. 'For most of them', she wrote, 'I have an anti-pathy which is sometimes difficult to conceal. I have met a great many men in Paris, but don't like any of them. They could never make anybody happy.'

In England it was very different. She and her mother, with Nancy in tow (what was her role in all this?), crossed to London in mid-June, the height of the season, and stayed at Claridges. At first they were lonely. 'I think London wonderfully delightful, although I know so little of its people. Everything is in full swing, and we read long accounts of balls we don't go to!' Then some-thing happened: an ignition key was found: it sparked the engine. Mary had a letter of introduction to Sir Lyon Playfair, a Member of Parliament of middle-eminence who had married a Boston girl, and it was he, and not, as has been often stated, the American Minister, who launched her upon London, taking her to a huge luncheon given by the Board of Admiralty at Greenwich on 10 July. The guests of honour were the Prince and Princess of Wales, who distributed prizes to the cadets, and afterwards Mary was presented to them by the Duchess of St Albans who had heard of her from an American friend. That very evening the Duchess took her to the House of Commons, where she met Gladstone and Austen Chamberlain. Next day she returned there as the guest of the Speaker's daughter, and heard Balfour and Parnell speak. Then came a smart wedding; then a visit to Oxford with Sir William and Lady Harcourt; and then, on 17 July, the Duchess of Westminster's ball.

It was at this ball that George Curzon first saw her. Mary did not mention his name in the ecstatic account of the evening which she wrote to her father, and it is possible that they were not introduced, but later he told Spring Rice that he 'had never loved Mary Leiter more than at the moment he first saw her walk into that great assembly'. She opened the ball by dancing the first quadrille with the Prince of Wales himself. It was becoming a Cinderella story, if you can accept that Cinderella's father was worth at least $20 million, and substitute Claridges for a cottage and a stout, bearded and middle-aged Prince for an Adonis. It requires some explanation, for the company that night included the most beautiful women in London, and Mary and her mother were the only foreigners and both almost unknown. She had some advantages in being an American. American girls were fashionable in London. They had a freedom of manner and expression which the British found bracing; they had (and still have) the gift of teasing without impertinence, of pleasing without flattery, a cool assumption that they are welcome for themselves and their nationality, which could lead to disaster were it not accompanied by looks and charm and good manners. Mary had all three. The melody of her voice, it was said, was exquisite to hear, and she had a way of looking up which warned the roués and entranced the cynical and shy. Her self-assurance was no less effective in London than it had been in Washington. She was making a second début, with the experience of two triumphant seasons behind her, and here she was a novelty, her obscure origins and her father's wealth thought unimportant or at most assumed. The Prince did more than notice and recognize her. He went up to her as soon as she entered the ballroom, and one can legitimately imagine that heads turned to each other: 'Who is this girl?'

Ten days earlier Mary had written that the Leiters 'did not know a soul in London'. Now they were invited everywhere. Lunch with the Harcourts, where Austen Chamberlain was her neighbour on one side, the Duke of Devonshire on the other; tea with Balfour in the House; dinner with Joseph Chamberlain and his young American wife; dinners with Ferdinand Rothschild, with Sir Charles Hall, with the Ribblesdales, the Elchos, the de Greys. Harry White, the first secretary at the American Legation, said that in the seven years he had lived in England, no American had created so deep an impression in so short a time. Her letters sounded a note of unashamed pride in her catalogue of conquests, but she was discriminating. To her the British aristocracy was not a parade of mannequins. They were people whom she was beginning to sort out, and the most efficient sieve was the country-house party, an institution unknown in the United States, where young people could spend longer together, alone together, and the civilities of the dinner-table were replaced by the banter of the stables and the tennis court.

A few days after the Westminster ball Mary was invited by Lady Brownlow to Ashridge, her house in the Chilterns. There was a big party, the Pembrokes, the Carmarthens, Alma Tadema, Lord Hamilton, Harry Cust, Thomas Sanderson and a dozen others, including George Curzon. It was the first large English country-house that Mary had seen. She was dazzled:

Acres of park with thousands of deer, and the house is a superb palace, built over a convent where Queen Elizabeth once lived. We were about 30 in the house, which is gorgeous beyond description, the face of white carved stone 60 feet square, four storeys high, and black iron, brass and stone stairways, the ballroom Italian marble and Van Dycks and Rubens, the dining-room panelled in gorgeous oak and brocade. Lady Brownlow is one of the most noble women. I can only compare her position in England with Mrs J. J. Astor's in New York. She has the beauty of an Empress. I returned this morning, and my visit will be one of the pleasantest memories.

The bathos of the last sentence concealed a momentous event. She had fallen in love with George Curzon, and he was greatly attracted by her. Years later he confessed to her that when she took him into the rose-garden, 'I had a strong inclination to kiss you, with difficulty restrained.' During the ten days that remained before she left England, they wrote to each other daily letters which grew rapidly in intimacy, exchanged presents and photographs, and met on every possible occasion. Her first letter to him, written on the day after returning from Ashridge, is the only one to address him as 'Dear Mr Curzon', but it is signed M.V.L. The others have no beginning at all, as if what was already assumed between them could not yet be stated. But there were other ways:

Mary to Curzon: 30 July 1890, midnight. 'A tiny little moonbeam showed me my treasure [an amulet which he had given her] while driving home. I shall put it to the test of the Garuda stone, and my first wish will be that you rest, and leave all that tires you. If every wish comes true, I shall be happy. M.V.L.'

Curzon to Mary: 31 July. 'I got your letter this morning. Thank you for it, dear, and for the words. It is a pleasure for me to have met and known you here. I shall think of you while you are away; and beg you both to come back and not wholly expel me from your memory in the interval. I wish you a happy season in Washington, and American males whose charm will just fall short of making you forget that Englishmen can also be charming. God bless you, Mary Victoria. G.'

To this she replied by sending him a pearl from her necklace, 'and had it set for you as emblematic of the tear I shed at leaving London. You, I mean'. He wore it as a tiepin that night, and promised always to wear it 'in memory of the dearest girl I have met for long. That girl is Mary Victoria.' Her infatuation was too intense to conceal it entirely from her father, and she adopted the familiar device of belittling it, knowing that her mother would be sending home more highly-coloured accounts:

The most interesting man I have seen is George Curzon, son of Lord Scarsdale, Member of Parliament, very clever *and* rising. A great traveller, and author of many books on the East. He is considered one of the cleverest young men of the day and one of the hopes of the Conservative Party. I wish I might fall a little in love with him. You would like him, as he is a hard worker. But the unfortunate fact is that I only think him nice, and he only thinks me nice, so I can't make up any romance to interest and excite you, but I'll try again!

Mary's summary of Curzon's career and character needs some expansion. He was thirty-one, the eldest son of Lord Scarsdale. His mother had died when he was sixteen. He was descended from a family which had come to England from Normandy in the eleventh century and had held for more than 800 years the Kedleston estate outside Derby. At Eton he had been a pheno- menon, at Oxford a paragon. He had carried off almost every prize at both. In 1883 he was elected a Fellow of All Souls, the highest academic honour open to a young man. Three years later he became Conservative Member of Parliament for Southport, and in 1887 went round the world (visiting, incidentally, Chicago, which he thought 'huge and smokey and absorbed in the worship of Mammon in a grim and melancholy way'), and returned through India, which he then saw for the first time. 'When I come back here', he said, 'it will be as Viceroy.' Next year he made his second great journey, to Samarkand, and wrote on his return *Russia in Central Asia* (it was his first serious book so far, and Mary was anticipating others in speaking of his many books on the East). 1889 was the year of his third journey, on horse-back through Persia. He returned to England in February 1890, exhausted, and took a Mediterranean holiday before re- suming his parliamentary duties and starting the great book he planned on his Persian travels. It was on coming home from Greece that he met Mary for the first time.

It was an unusual beginning for a great political career. Curzon had made no great effort to establish himself in the House of Commons. In fact he disliked it, being by nature more a great administrator than a politician. He had spoken but seldom in the House and not very successfully, for his style was considered too rotund for a young man, and he had little interest in the minutiae of domestic politics in which a backbencher was expected to make his first mark. He preferred to travel, in order to enlarge his knowledge of Asiatic art and history in which he had already reached a scholar's standard, and because he wished to make himself the leading expert on the politics of the East, seeing it as his eventual speciality and role. He had calculated wisely. His journeys, and the books that arose from them, set him apart from his contemporaries. He was the only Member of Parliament to have studied deeply, on the spot, the politics of a part of the world where the Cabinet were faced with decisions of immense importance. At first regarded as eccentric, his journeys were soon acknowledged as feats of amazing perseverance and his books as monuments of diligence and research.

If it had been generally known that he was in constant pain, his achievement would have been seen as even more remarkable. He suffered from an incurable curvature of the spine, and throughout his life was obliged to wear a steel corset padded with leather, and if he stood or rode for long, he would be forced to take to his bed afterwards, writhing in pain sometimes for days on end. That was not his only disadvantage as a traveller. He had little money of his own. He financed his journeys from savings and by writing articles for *The Times*. His books made him very little more. A parliamentary salary did not then exist. An allowance from his father, his All Souls Fellowship, journalism and two small directorships raised his income to about £1,500 a year, a negligible sum for a man of aristocratic tastes, dependent upon servants, and aiming to cut a considerable figure not only in politics but in society.

His complex personality will emerge as this narrative progresses. What concerns us now is the first impression he made on Mary. He was good-looking, but not in a conventional way. His face was described as cherubic, and his glance severe. It could flatten to a mask. His manner of speaking both in public and in conversation was literary: he enjoyed the balance of words, would never leave a sentence crippled, and was fond of making well-turned pronouncements as if rehearsed or rehearsing, which often intimidated people. But there was another side of his character of which he would have been careful to make the most that summer's afternoon at Ashridge (for he calculated his effects), and that was his boyishness, his high spirits, which could sometimes rise to buffoonery. Margot Asquith wrote of him: 'No one could turn with more elasticity from work to play'. He could be riotously gay, compose comic poems, act charades, and those who knew him best thought him the most delightfully warmhearted of companions. Particularly women. He had often been in love, and once was deeply hurt, when Sibell Grosvenor turned him down to marry his friend George Wyndham. 'His nature craved the stimulus of feminine companionship and the warmth of feminine affection', wrote his biographer Kenneth Rose. 'He rarely lacked either. He could demonstrate every facet of manly attention, from brotherly chaff to consuming possession; he could excite every womanly emotion, from maternal sympathy to melting infatuation, from roguishness to passion.' He used these talents to captivate Mary, finding her delicious and responsive. To each of them the other seemed to have everything: she – beauty, money, style, alertness; he – vigour, cleverness, humour and a patrician air of serene confidence, as of a man who had inherited much, done much, and was determined to do more.

In early August Mary went with her mother and sister to Cowes, where she was introduced by the Prince of Wales to the Kaiser, and stood with them to watch the fireworks. Then to France again, to Dieppe. It was a sudden let-down. 'Oh how different is France from England! We left England yachting and shooting, and we found France playing croquet on the green.' She had been invited to shoot in Scotland with the Earl of Wemyss, to stay with Margot Tennant at the Glen, to cruise with the Pembrokes in the Western Isles, 'but all these tempting things had to be left for a horrid old continental tour'. They passed through Paris by the Oriental Express to Munich, thence to Innsbruck, Oberammergau and Salzburg. Mary wrote dutiful

[43]

letters to her father, homesick letters to Curzon (homesick not for
America now, but England), and her spirits only revived when
they reached Zurich, because the hotel was more comfortable
than those in Austria, and she was promised a brief return to
England. From London in September they went to Edinburgh,
saw the Forth Bridge which had been finished the year before,
and stayed for two days with Sir Charles Tennant at the Glen.
Mary thought Margot Tennant 'a great girl, clever as she can
be, and rides like a dream'. It was almost her first introduction to
the Souls, the group of young people, of whom Curzon was a
central member, which represented the intellectual avant-garde
of the aristocracy, but in a manner more bantering than self-
satisfied, more witty than erudite, games-playing, flirtatious,
parodists, daring in their personal lives and challenging to their
elders. It was not quite Mary's style. For the first time in her life
she may have found herself uncertain how to respond. Margot's
recollection of the visit (in her autobiography) was not quite so
enthusiastic. 'As she was not interested in flowers, my mother was
indifferent to her, and when she sang snatches of French songs in
a piping soprano along the Glen passages, my father shouted,
"Stop that!", and got up from the writing-table to slam the
door.'

She met Curzon only once again that year, for a few hours.
Ignoring her protests, he shut himself up in lodgings at Norwood
near the Crystal Palace, to write his Persian book: 'Here I grind,
grind, grind, morning, noon and night. I love it. I was never in
better health or spirits. I think of living here permanently in total
isolation from the world', hardly the sentiments a young girl
hopes to hear from the man she loves. Another planned rendez-
vous was cancelled by a three-day visit to his constituency. Duty
had priority over dalliance, as she was soon to learn. On the day
before the Leiters sailed for America, they eventually met in a
London hotel. Mary sang for him. He gave her reports of three
speeches he had made in Southport, and a new photograph of
himself to replace one which she had begged from him earlier, 'so
that I might not be depicted as such a monster in whatever part of
your palatial house my likeness is permitted to figure'. The Souls

were given to undergraduate humour of this kind. It was slightly disconcerting.

It is important to make their relationship clear. Love had not been mentioned between them, and there was no hint of an engagement. There can be no doubt that Mary was in love with him: she had never previously met a young man who could so monopolize her thoughts, for whom she felt so unqualified an admiration. But he was an unpredictable man, even to those who knew him best. His background and ambitions were still unfamiliar to her, and she was uncertain of the current values in England of certain terms which he had used in talking and writing to her, and whether she had done right in his eyes to respond to his flirtatiousness and give him tokens of her barely concealable affection. To Curzon it was not the first of such experiences, as it was for her. He was eleven years older. He had a reputation for charming women, even for waylaying society girls in corridors, woods and trains. Was Mary different? In retrospect he would say that he loved her at first sight, but his conduct in the months that followed does not suggest much more than a sudden attraction, intoxicating for the few weeks while she was around, but transient when she was gone, as if he did not wish to be too deeply involved, having more important things to think about, and not wishing to hurt her. In contrast, Lord Randolph Churchill had proposed to another American girl, Jennie Jerome, within three days of first meeting her, and had been accepted.

After Mary's return to the United States, their correspondence became intermittent. She matched her pace against his, feeling her way, while he gradually lowered the temperature of the London letters by facetiousness, teasing her about his 'rivals' in America, but in such a way as to suggest that rivals would not be wholly unwelcome to him. Perhaps in this he showed his generosity of spirit. Mary was much sought-after, and his affection for her, and hers for him, must not be allowed to gather strength to the point where it became accidentally a commitment, excluding others who might love and suit her more. Soon their letters were spaced a month apart, then two, but she was now calling him 'George dear', the inversion a cautious step nearer to him, and he advised her on the manner in which she should do her hair, complaining that her present style spoiled the outline of her head: 'It makes you stern, contemplative, severe. A woman should be tender, yielding, gentle.' Each had little news that they thought would interest the other. She had been riding and reading and helping with the coming-out of her sister Nancy, while he was busy with *Persia and the Persian Question*, and when he had completed the first volume he was ordered to St Moritz for his health.

There was one incident which reanimated his concern for her. While he was eating a solitary dinner at Norwood, he spotted a short report in *The Times* that Levi Leiter's house in Washington had caught fire on New Year's Day, and the entire upper part destroyed. A maid was said to have been trapped by the fire, and much valuable property lost. Curzon immediately cabled to Mary. In fact she had been in New York that day, and came at once to Washington to find the wreck of the upper storey still smoking. The fire had started in a linen-cupboard at eleven in the morning, and soon thirty-foot-high flames tore through the roof. Within half an hour of the first fire-engine arriving, it was under control. Nobody was hurt, and most of the valuables were saved, the damage being done more by water than by flame. Her father was quite calm, her mother and Joe competent, and only Nancy was in tears because she had lost all her Paris dresses. Mary clambered up the back stairs to salvage armfuls of charred and saturated books. 'Any remaining embers', she told Curzon, 'must have been put out by my tears.'

The house was fully restored within four months, but the Leiters, whether because of the fire or because they had already planned it, decided to leave the Blaine house and build one of their own on the far side of Dupont Circle at the corner of New Hampshire Avenue. The site alone cost $83,000, the building $125,000, and the furnishing was valued at $300,000. It was demolished in 1947 to make way for the present Dupont Plaza Hotel, but many photographs of the exterior remain. The house was enormous. It had to be, to accommodate Levi Leiter's growing collection of books and furniture and the lavish parties which Mrs Leiter planned. Unlike the Blaine house, it had a shape. Its clean rectangular lines were relieved by a series of bays and recesses extending from the raised basement to the roof, and on the entrance side stood a colossal portico of four Ionic columns rising almost the whole height of the house to a classical pediment. Inside, there was first a marble hall, and beyond it the main hall which was said to be more imposing than the east room of the White House. The library was furnished in carved oak with a mantelpiece of pink marble. There was a ballroom and an Empire drawing-room, and a vast dining-room hung with tapestries on crimson walls. For large parties a suite of supper rooms in an oriental style was thrown open in the basement. It was the finest, or at least the most expensive, house in the city. The Commission of Fine Arts had little good to say for it as architecture. They dubbed it 'Venetian-accented Roman revival', and its external appearance as 'a great stratified dinosaur'. That seems hard. It had a certain grace of line and proportion, not unlike an English Palladian house of more than a century before, and while it was certainly an imposing building, its great white façade was shielded by trees, and for a house in the smartest district of the nation's capital, it was much less unneighbourly than the Blaine house across the way.

Curzon resumed his courtship of Mary, if it was that, when she returned to London with her mother at the end of April 1891. They had not written to each other since mid-February, but he gave a small dinner-party for her on the night of her arrival, and for the first two weeks of May, until she went to Paris, he saw her almost daily. Her letters to her father, supplemented by her diary and her mother's (both little more than annotated engagement-books), give a detailed account of her activities if not of her emotions. To London she was no longer a novelty, and her delight in English society was not reciprocated at quite the same pitch as the year before, but now it had a new dimension, the Souls:

May 2. Lunched with the Tennants. Margot, Charty [Lady Ribblesdale], Lord Ribblesdale, Harry Cust. Ava Astor and G.C. called.
May 5. Ride in Rotten Row with Margot. Saw many of my friends, Alfred Lyttelton, Lord Cork and Mr Grenfell [later Lord Desborough]. G.C. dines at Claridges.

May 6. Ride early again. Saw Lord and Lady Brownlow, Lady Katy Thynne and Harry Cust.

May 7. Rode with Katy Thynne and Cust. Tea with Mrs Peel [the Speaker's wife]. G.C. there. Dine in House. G.C., Brodrick, Asquith, George Wyndham.

May 11. Lady Rothschild's ball. Prince and Princess of Wales.

May 13. Mamma and I presented at drawing-room. The Princess Royal takes the Queen's place.

May 15. Ride with Cust. Meet Henry James at dinner with John Hay.

Mrs Leiter was feeling rather out of it. She noted in her diary that at the Rothschild ball the Princess of Wales talked to Mary but not to her, and it was the same when they attended the Drawing Room at Buckingham Palace. The flowers and notes which arrived constantly at Claridges were always for Mary, never for her. However, she thought everyone delightful. She recorded the name of every guest at every function, but only down to Hon. level, sucking the titles like lollipops: 'Lady Brodrick, daughter of Lord Wemyss', 'the Duke and Duchess of Northumberland', and even Curzon still appears as 'George Curzon, son of Lord Scarsdale' a year after she first met him. At the end of each list she always added humbly, 'and Mrs and Miss Leiter'. She was a woman of genuine good nature, but Mary's friends needed to draw on all their social gifts to simulate pleasure in her company. Mary noticed it, and despaired of the English convention that girls must everywhere be chaperoned. She wrote to her brother Joe: 'It is the understood thing that mother and daughter go together, and a girl is never asked alone save in the most informal manner.'

For a few days in mid-season they went to Paris. It is not clear why they did so, for by this time Mrs Leiter was as enamoured of England as her daughter, and like her thought the French foppish, but it was probably to buy clothes and to expose Mary to the admiration of another aristocracy. The lists acquired a new accent: la Princesse de Broglie, la Duchesse de Gramont, la Comtesse de Pourtalès, la Princesse de Wagram, Madame et Mlle Leiter. The Princesse de Wagram, a sister of Lady Rothschild and a friend of Curzon, took Mary in hand. She invited her to come alone to 7 Avenue de l'Alma and received her in her boudoir, where the following conversation took place (recorded by Mary to her father):

'My dear child, I have to talk very seriously to you. You have made a great impression on all my friends and they think you such a charming creature, and I wonder if you would like to marry over here, for should you like it, a most charming marriage could be arranged.' I said, 'My dear Princess, I do not know Paris or Parisians well enough to say.' It will be very hard for you to appreciate the drollness and yet the solemnity of the interview. She was all earnestness. She went on: 'There is a very charming man, Prince. . . . [Mary had forgotten the name] who is very good-looking, will be rich and of great position, and all in my own head I have planned this match, for I am so fond of you. I want you to remain in Paris.' Well, of course I got out of that by explaining that I would not marry anyone I was not fond of, as I had lived on fondness and affection at home, and was quite happy in my home life. She was very sweet, and said with a smile, 'I shall bring you together, for you would like Louis de. . . . and I know he will like you.'

Mary refused to stay in Paris for the assignation, which was arranged for a few days later at a grand costume ball, pleading that the clothes would be too expensive. The Princess was much vexed.

They arrived back in London in time for Mary's twenty-first birthday on 27 May, when Curzon was a guest at a small party at Claridges, and gave her a little enamelled box from Canton, inlaid with silver.

She had told her father that the idea of a French husband appalled her, but now began gently to prepare him for the possibility that she might marry Curzon. Leiter cannot have overlooked her hints. He was deeply fond of her, as she of him, and a very rich man knows how to protect his investments, of which a marriageable daughter is an important part. She told him of two incidents. She was having tea on the terrace of the House of Commons with Lord Rowton, Disraeli's former private secretary, and talking to him about commonsense in men and women, and how quickly it develops in each. They agreed that a woman matured sooner than a man. At that moment Curzon came up, and overhearing the last words said, 'Of course a woman gains sense sooner than a man. Why here is an example, Miss Leiter being the most sensible woman of twenty-one I have ever met. I should call her a phenomenon.' Lord Rowton laughed, and said, 'If that's the tone of conversation you're going to adopt with Miss Leiter, it's time for me to go.' Mary added: 'Englishmen are very different from Americans, and I have yet to understand them fully, but fathers are always consulted and referred to more than in America, where everything seems managed in boy-and-girl fashion.'

The second incident was the visit which she paid to Curzon at Norwood, a hide-out to which he rarely invited any of his friends. He and Mary rowed together for an hour on the Crystal Palace lake under her mother's eye from the bank, and then the three of them dined together. 'He is very nice to me, and I see him often. Wherever I am, he always comes; whether in the House of Commons or after dinner, he always talks to me and does all he can to be charming.' A week later she wrote after a second visit to Norwood: 'I am very happy here, as I quite love cleverness, and here are such wonderfully brilliant people, and they are all very kind and charming, and I am very fond of them. I see George Curzon very often. I know how much you would like him, and he you.'

Mary was swept away from him by parties and weekends. She and her mother stayed with the Salisburys at Hatfield, with the Pembrokes at Wilton, with the Wemysses at Gosford, at Ashridge again, and were only prevented from going to Knole by the illness of her old Washington friend, Victoria Sackville-West. Dressed in white by Worth, Mary went to a state ball at Buckingham Palace, where her mother was so overwhelmed by the gorgeousness of everything that she mistook a Guards colonel for a footman. They went to Ascot, in the Royal Enclosure; to plays, operas and lectures. Sir Redvers Buller gave them tickets for a military review in honour of the Kaiser, and Mary helped Jenny Churchill arrange a tableau for the Londonderry ball. Always in the background, as companions for less splendid occasions, were the Souls.

On 23 July Levi Leiter joined them from Washington. It seems from the absence of any mention of it in Mary's diary that he did not meet Curzon then, and firmly rejecting the social pleasures they offered him, took his family to stay in the Hotel Metropole at Brighton. Mary at last had the leisure, and in her father a confidant, to reflect on what had happened. Curzon had made no further advance to her, unless his renewed concern for her was to be interpreted as such. His manner had not changed since 1890, but his interest in her was now clearly more than a passing fancy. He had been very kind, but he could be strangely distant. For instance, when he gave her the Chinese box for her birthday, his accompanying note said simply, 'In my judgement before attaining your majority you have reached the measure of complete and (what is far less usual) sensible womanhood.' Was that all she meant to him?

The Brighton visit was not a great success. It rained a lot, and the Metropole was full of holidaymakers who had nothing better to do than run races with their children along the corridors. Mrs Leiter bored her husband by anecdotes of the London season which he had already heard from Mary, much better told in her letters, and the string of names which she dangled before him meant nothing to him. He could not see that these people were any more interesting than his friends of the Chicago Club or the Cosmos Club in Washington, in fact less so, because none of them seemed to do any work. He was more interested in Mary.

Mary was rather silent. It could be that she was tired, or had the sense to let her mother prattle on, roused to protest only when Mrs Leiter exaggerated beyond endurance the successes which she, Mary, had enjoyed. Or it might be that she was in love. If she was, it could only be with one person, George Curzon. Whenever his name was mentioned, Leiter said later, his wife would give a sidelong glance at her daughter, and Mary looked away. Her father did not probe, but one evening when they were alone, she talked to him about it.

She said that George (she used his first name without explanation) fascinated her. He had every gift: he was very ambitious: his manners and wit were delightful. She did not say she loved him, or he her. In fact, she said, he could sometimes turn cold. But from her attitude, the way she stumbled over her words and fiddled with her bracelet, Leiter could see that she was troubled, and it would take only a gentle question from him to make her cry. He said that she must be careful. She was very young, very lovely, had had a fairy-story success, and it was widely known that one day she would be very rich. It was natural that men should pay attention to her. She must be on her guard. He reminded her that she had written to him in June, 'I dislike anything masculine in a woman, and try to avoid anything conducive to notoriety.' Well, if she meant that, she should not see too much of any unmarried man, George Curzon for instance. From what she had said about him, he sounded admirable and charming. But how well did she know him? If he was genuinely fond of her, why these bouts of coldness? Unless she was careful, people would see her as the pursuer and him as the pursued. She must not let that happen. He was not saying that she must stop meeting Curzon or writing to him, but let him see sometimes that she too could be cold, and judge from his reaction whether he wanted from her anything more than the companionship that any young man hoped for from any pretty girl.

In this way he avoided asking her directly whether she loved Curzon, and she thanked him for it with her eyes. His advice fitted very well what she had been thinking herself. There were three men in Washington, and at least one in Paris, who had told her that they adored her. She would let Curzon know that they existed. She would not make the mistake which she made last year, of pressing him for a meeting before they went home. She would try to forget him for hours on end, but in Brighton this was difficult. Her mother kept bringing up his name. 'If you're writing to dear George', she said one day after breakfast, 'say goodbye to him from me, and tell him that I shall always watch his career with interest and think of him with affection.' It was a familiar situation, the mother enjoying her daughter's romance more than the daughter, and so spoiling it for her.

They sailed from Liverpool on 7 September 1891, and Mary found on board a letter from Curzon, whom she had not seen

again, thanking her for a copy of Horace's *Odes* which she had
sent him, and her mother for her 'fond message'. He continued:
'And now back to old Persia, with its panorama of mingled
splendour and squalor, the superb oriental medley of dignity
and decay. God bless you always, dear Mary.'

When he was on the point of finishing the second volume of his
book, he was invited by the Prime Minister, Lord Salisbury, to
become Parliamentary Under Secretary of State for India, his
first ministerial post. He had hoped for the Under Secretaryship
at the Foreign Office, but was well content with India. In telling
Mary about his new job, he said that he was amazed by the
respect accorded to him at the India Office by civil servants who
were swells before he was born. He responded to their courtesy
'with ingenuous deference and an almost virginal modesty', a
modesty which also prevented him from explaining to Mary that
the Office had never known a new Minister to be so well informed.
Then he added: 'I infer from what you say, that you or the Nan-
let [Nancy] are contemplating matrimony: your obscurity as to
which it is, suggests the possibility of both. That would be
disastrous.' His subsequent silence (he did not write to her again
for six months) left her in doubt why he thought it would be
disastrous, and how much he minded. When he eventually
wrote again, in March 1892, he apologized for the long, long
time her own letter had remained unanswered, and pleaded
pressure of work: 'Now at last I have sat me down to three hours
of writing, to work off a lot of arrears.' So her letters were arrears!
He ended on a slightly warmer note, telling her that her photograph stood on the mantelpiece of his new rooms in St Ermine's
Mansions, Westminster, where it would be seen by Arthur Balfour, George Wyndham, Wyndham's wife Sibell Grosvenor, and
St John Brodrick, the friends whom he most regularly entertained. But why, if in this way he could publicly acknowledge her
to be his girl, was his girl not given more of his attention?

Persia and the Persian Question was published in May 1892, after
three years of labour. The two volumes amounted to 1,300 pages
and together weighed seven pounds. It was immediately recognized as a masterpiece, but more people pretended to have read

it than read it, and although it continued to sell slowly, thirty years later it had made for Curzon in royalties no more than £405. He sent a copy to Mary, warning her that 'its perusal is little removed from penal servitude' (which is not true: it is a brilliant book). She took it on a trip to the Grand Canyon, and 'guided' influential reviewers in the American literary press to notice it favourably. It was the first time that she had been able to be of practical help to him.

In August 1892 he left London for a second tour round the world, having lost his Under Secretaryship after only nine months in office when Lord Salisbury's Government was defeated in the General Election of July. His companion on the first part of the journey was Harry White of the American Legation in London, Mary's friend. Curzon's main purpose was to visit the Far East, but they travelled west, on a German ship to New York. His dislike of the German passengers was equalled only by his distaste for the middle-class Americans on board, whom he described in his diary, and perhaps to Harry White, as 'the least attractive species of the human genus. . . . Conceive the aesthetic distress of being surrounded by 200–300 *persons* not one of whom is otherwise than positively hideous and of whom the women are a grim nightmare.' New York was little better, 'the men busy, sallow, straw-hatted, perspiring . . . a city whose entire existence appeared to be the apotheosis of business, with but the smallest concessions to sentiment, aesthetics or romance'. But in Washington there would at least be Mary.

Or would there be? Astonishingly they seem to have made no arrangements to meet. The records of Mary's movements at this period are very incomplete, as she kept no diary and corresponded with Curzon hardly at all. In Curzon's own diary of his world-tour there is no mention of her. Unexpectedly he found himself with three extra days in the United States before continuing to Canada, and he invited himself to spend them at the house of a Mrs Rives, whose daughter Amélie he had met in England. They lived in Virginia, and Curzon went by train to Washington for a single night on his way south. He stayed at the Arlington Hotel, and toured the city next morning. 'Grandeur

alternates with magnificence, public buildings emerge from surroundings that are altogether tenth-rate.' He saw the Dupont
Circle house ('red brick of a peculiarly aggressive hue'), but did
not go inside. In the afternoon he pressed on to the Rives house.
Apart from one other man, he was the only guest. 'Upon me
Amy shone with the undivided insistence of her starlike eyes', he
wrote in his diary. 'Oh God, the nights on the still lawn under the
soft sky with my sweetheart!'

He returned through New York on his way to Canada: no
letter to Mary. He crossed the Pacific from Vancouver: no letter.
Eventually a very short note reached her in October, written
from Kyoto in Japan, but its main purpose was to enclose a letter
of introduction to Mrs Leiter for the benefit of a Frenchman who
was visiting Washington. He told Mary that he was about to
start with Cecil Spring Rice, then on leave, for an arduous
journey through Korea, which he descibed, without ever having
seen it, as 'one of the dirtiest and most repulsive countries in
the world'. He wrote to her only one more note in 1892, and
Mary, having few addresses for him and presumably discouraged
by his apparent indifference, replied but once, to Rangoon. In
her letter she slyly reminded him that other men still found her
attractive:

There has been very much of a princeling who came with equerries
and a suite to study American institutions, and I had the misfortune
to be the only institution he wished to adopt, and I have had difficulty
in convincing His Supreme Highness that I was the only one which
was impossible, to which he will still not agree.

She was on the eve of another trans-Atlantic journey. At the
end of November, with both parents and Nancy, she travelled
direct to Italy, and spent Christmas in Rome. There she was
courted ardently by the Marchese Rudini, and tried to play him
off against a rival, the Count of Turin. 'There is an absolute assurance about an Italian that one rarely finds elsewhere', she told
Curzon in her first letter of the new year. 'There is no competition
and no jealousy. None of them dreams that his importance is
questioned.' The Leiters escaped to Naples, and in early January

[55]

1893 continued to Cairo, from where they visited Luxor. She
and Curzon, having missed each other in Washington, now
missed again in Egypt. He was on his way home from China
and Siam:

Feb. 26 1893. *S.S. Australia* in the Mediterranean. I have just found
out that yesterday I was less than 100 miles from you: a fact which
beneficent Providence seemed as usual to take a magnificent delight
in concealing from both of us. This is how I learnt it. Among the
people who came aboard at Port Said was J. M. Cook, head of the
Cook concern. He showed me the list of his Nile steamers, and among
the names of those who had hired them, I saw the magic name Leiter.
Enquiries elicited that you had left Adolphus [his name for Levi
Leiter] and Co. up the river, and had come down to Cairo again to
plunge into gaiety.

It was quite true. She had hurried back from Luxor to attend
Lord Kitchener's ball on the very day that Curzon's ship was
passing through the Suez Canal.

Five days later they were engaged.

They met in Paris on 3 March. Mary and her mother had
travelled back from Egypt in a ship that followed in the wake of
Curzon's, and somehow discovering his presence in Paris, arranged that he would dine with them at the Hotel Vendôme. It
was eighteen months since he and Mary had last met. After dinner her mother left them alone. He proposed to her. She accepted
him.

Years later, after Mary's death, Curzon wrote a description of
the scene to be kept with her letters:

I had entered the hotel without the slightest anticipation that this
would be the issue. She told me her story. How she had waited for
nearly three years since the time when we first met, rejecting countless
suitors and always waiting for me. I told her that while I felt from the
beginning that we were destined for each other, I had not dared to
speak, and had even run the risk of losing her because there was
certain work in my scheme of Asiatic travel which I had resolved to
do, and which I could not ask any married woman to allow her husband to carry out. Some of it, notably the journey to the Pamirs and
Afghanistan, still remained undone: and even now when we became

[56]

secretly engaged, it was on the understanding that I should be at liberty to complete my task before we took the final step.

It was a moment of deep emotion. Mary assured him that if he should die in the Pamirs, she would never marry another man, but retire to a convent. He assured her that she could trust him absolutely. Neither would breathe their secret to a soul, not even to their families, until he returned from his final and most dangerous journey, and then he would marry her.

The drama had every ingredient: the sudden discovery of mutual, but hitherto undeclared, love; its secrecy; the prospect of danger for one of them, and two years of silent anguish for the other. It is a pity to spoil it. But Curzon was an emotional man. He wrote his retrospective account as he turned over his dead wife's letters, recollecting the unsullied happiness of their married life. Surely it must have begun, as it ended, in absolute love? On her side, it is indisputable. She told him later how in Rome she had knelt on the staircase of the Scala Santa, praying that as a Christmas present God would induce George to propose to her. Her love for him had survived long separations, the competition of many suitors, the pull of her family and her country, and Curzon's periodic affectation of indifference.

But had it been an affectation? It was strange, looking back, that if his thoughts were continuously of her, he could have left them unexpressed for months on end, when he must have known that she awaited his lightest word. Yes, he had an immense amount of work to do in politics and on his books, and his travelling impeded correspondence. But half-a-dozen letters during a separation of eighteen months is an incredible preliminary to a declaration of long-concealed but undying love. He had even forgotten her age: 'You must now be 23 or 24', he had written from China, when she was only twenty-two. He had known that he would be in Washington: he had known that she would be in Egypt. Where were the desperate attempts that any lover would make to arrange a meeting? How can one explain away his three days with Miss Rives in Virginia? Then there was that odd phrase at the beginning of his note: 'I had entered the hotel without the slightest anticipation that this would be the issue.' This could mean that he had it in mind to make a declaration to her one day, but intended to postpone it once again, risking the possibility that she might not be free when he was free, a calculation that does not presume infatuation. Or it could mean that he suddenly lost his self-control. Imagine the scene. He was returning from the East after seven months absence. He had endured great hardships. He was on the last lap of his way home, but had not reached home. In Paris he suddenly rediscovered comfort, welcome, civilization, French food and wine, and his beautiful American girl whose eyes showed that she adored him. He was left alone with her. He was overwhelmed by affection, and perhaps felt some remorse. He asked her to marry him. She consented. From that moment he never retreated, and never wished to retreat. It was a commitment of honour, which turned gradually into a commitment of love. That is a biographer's interpretation of what might have happened, based upon a crude understanding of the way the human heart behaves. How angrily would Curzon have disputed it!

There are two other aspects of their engagement which must be explored. The first is the question whether Curzon married Mary for her money, and the answer is a slightly qualified No. In fact she had no money of her own, apart from a few jewels, since everything was provided for her by her father, and for pin-money he gave her an annual allowance. But she had handsome expectations, not only when he died, but when she married. It was the universal American and English custom for a rich father to endow the bride. How could Curzon avoid the reflection that to marry an heiress would solve his financial problems? It would open to him opportunities, such as Viceroy of India, which in his present state he would be obliged to refuse. His father owned 10,000 acres with an annual rent-roll of £18,000, and on his death would leave a gross estate of over £450,000. But Lord Scarsdale was only sixty-two: he might live for years, and in fact did not die till 1916, ten years after Mary. Curzon was in a hurry, not only for expensive offices of state, but for an establishment. He was living in bachelor chambers. He wanted a house in London and a house in the country, where he could entertain, which he could fill with works-of-art, with servants, with children. He could never make that sort of money by politics and books. But he might acquire it by marriage.

Why then do I believe that his decision to marry Mary Leiter had little to do with her money? Because, in the first place, he was a proud man. He was well aware that if he married Mary, cynics would be quick to attribute his choice to one motive alone, her father's wealth, which would be insulting to himself and his wife. It was almost a reason for not marrying her. If her money was so important to him, why had he delayed so long, and made so little effort to win her? He sensed that she would have accepted him within a month of their first meeting, and their marriage could have taken place in the autumn of 1890. Instead, he waited five years, the very years when he needed money most. And why pick an American, unless this American had a great deal more to offer him than financial security? There were English heiresses available too, bearing historic family names which would presumably have created a more favourable *prima facie* impression on Curzon than a name like Levi Z. Leiter. Curzon disliked Americans. He was heavily prejudiced against them. In his two visits to the United States he had found nothing, and nobody, to commend them. Levi Leiter, with his Jewish-sounding origins and, in Curzon's eyes, a lack of any element of distinction, represented everything that he most abominated there. Now he would be linked to him for life and be beholden to him for money. He imagined Mrs Leiter as a frequent self-invited guest at Kedleston, perhaps sleeping in his dead mother's bed, patronizing his father's tenants, and the prospect did not attract him. Although Curzon saw in Mary's dowry a prize which would go a long way to compensate him for his future mother-in-law, it was a contributory motive only, not the main one. His main motive was that of all the many girls he had known, Mary Leiter pleased him most. She was in every way equipped to share his life, and by her fidelity to him before he had given her any reason to trust his own, she had already proved it.

He now told her, in fact insisted, that they could not marry for two years, that their engagement must remain totally secret for all that time, and that their wedding might never take place at all because he might be killed in the Pamirs. She accepted these three conditions meekly. The first was just endurable, the second unkind, the third agonizing. For two years she would have no defence except sullenness against her importunate suitors, even against such a likeable man as Cecil Spring Rice who was one of Curzon's closest friends and would think both of them treacherous and heartless when he was eventually told. She could say nothing to her father, who was the only person to whom she went habitually for comfort and advice. The first of a long series of deceptions which she was now committed to practise on him was her letter describing her evening at the Hotel Vendôme. She wrote simply: 'George Curzon came to dine last night. He told us much about his journey which was wonderfully interesting.' If Mary was to endure all this anxiety, what was there to prevent her sharing it at least with him?

She accepted the necessity for Curzon's journey. He knew the whole East, except for one of its most important parts, Afghanistan and the frontier regions between India and Russia. That blank spot on the map was the blank spot in the pattern which he had devised five years earlier for the first major stage of his career. He told her that he had not declared his love sooner because he did not think it fair to marry when he had so much hard travelling ahead of him. If it was unfair to a wife, was it not equally unfair to a fiancée? If he had considered his earlier and less ambitious journeys barriers to the expression of his love, why was not this one too? Perhaps because it was the last. Still, his conduct showed much selfishness. 'I am spared all the anxiety of a great courtship', he told her with scant gallantry, 'and I have merely, when the hour strikes, to enter into possession of my own.' This journey would be a great strain on him, the more tolerable because he had willed it. It was an even greater strain on her, for she had not. He made it quite clear from the start that in the big decisions he expected her to bend to his wishes. 'Give me a girl who knows a woman's place and does not yearn for trousers. Give me in fact Mary.' She immediately agreed: 'I well know, dear, that now as always you must do as you will.' That was an important surrender.

On the day after their secret engagement, when Curzon was about to leave for London while Mary remained in Paris, he wrote to her:

You were very sweet last night, Mary, and I do not think I deserved such consideration. While I ask you, and while you consent, to wait, you must trust me, Mary, wholly, even as I would trust you, and all will be right in the end. I will not breathe a word to a human soul, and since that is the line we take, it will be well that I should not write too frequently for fear of exciting suspicions. You need not fear that I shall not think of you, and rely upon your fidelity as upon a rock. You will let me hear how you are going on, Mary, won't you, and some-times if you are down in your luck, you will remember that my kiss of love has rested upon your lips. God bless you, my darling child.

In Paris the Princess's Prince still pursued her passionately, but she managed to shake him off, and returned to London on 24 April. For much of the time she was ill in bed at Claridges with influenza, and saw little of Curzon (only half-an-hour a week, she complained), and on 16 May returned to the United States on the *Teutonic*, sending him a lock of her hair before she sailed. They would not meet again for a whole year.

She went direct from New York to Washington, to sleep for the first time in their new house; then to Linden Lodge; and then to Newport in August. Mrs Leiter was in mourning for the death of her brother, and Mary's social life was muted. But Newport that year was full of Indian Rajahs and European princelings, and she was much in demand for banquets. One of her new admirers was the Grand Duke Alexander, first cousin of the Czar, and she pumped him for his views on Russia's southern border, repeating to Curzon everything he told her, information which he acknow-ledged as extremely valuable, confirming all his suspicions of Russian strategy. He was writing *Problems of the Far East* about his experiences in Japan, Korea and China, renouncing all pleasures but the pleasure of composition. At the same time he was planning his great journey. He told Mary that it would be his 'last wild cry of freedom', a phrase no doubt designed to arouse in her his own romantic conception of what lay ahead, but which might have been expressed by a lover to his betrothed with greater tact.

So deeply absorbed was he in his book and plans that he gave little time to society or parliament, and took but one short holiday, with the Tennants at the Glen, where he strongly urged Margot, the first of his girls, to marry Asquith, which she did next May. He wrote to Mary more frequently than he had promised, but with a bantering affection more than a lover's whimsy. For instance, he returned to the subject of her hair, as precise as he always was in his instructions. She was to arrange it 'low down on your neck, in big coils or knobs, and not brushed up from your ears, but waving along longitudinally in deep rich undulations'. She obeyed, and sent him a photograph of the result. Then he scolded her for her spelling: she had written 'wierd' for 'weird', and 'accompaneist' for 'accompanyist'. She replied that this was the way they wrote those words in America. It was no good: 'You must learn how to think and spell as an Englishwoman, my child.' He was pleased when she told him that the President and Mrs Cleveland continually invited her to help them with the entertainment of visiting swells, because it gave her an experience which she would soon find useful, 'perhaps on a larger scale'. He added:

Some people are born to stand up and shine before the world; others are:

Violets by a mossy stone
Half hidden from the eyes.

The violets are good in their way and place. So are the tall arum lilies in theirs. In public life one wants the latter.

But when she uttered a cry of despair about 'people who propose to me: I have no idea if other women have as much difficulty in that line as I have', he paid no attention, even when she told him of the rumour that she was to marry the recently widowed William Whitney, then considered a possible Presidential candidate, and the newspapermen were clamouring at her door for confirmation or denial. Spring Rice had temporarily given up the contest for Mary's hand, perhaps because he guessed the truth, for Mary said he was 'always going on about' her and Curzon, but she told him nothing. Curzon too was being pestered, not by would-be brides, but by their mothers: 'I am continually being asked about whom I am going to marry, and I surprise myself with my air of conviction as I dispel their surmises.'

March 3rd 1894 was the anniversary of their engagement, which both marked by reaffirmations of their love. Curzon was now devoted to her, and during the thirteen years of their engagement and marriage, there is no hint that he ever betrayed her loyalty. If it appears from this narrative that he was sometimes neglectful of her and even on occasions inconsiderate, the overwhelming fact remains that Mary herself never thought so, and she was a woman with her own pride, quick to resent any slight, and with standards of probity as high as Curzon's own. Never once did she reproach him, nor feel reason for reproach, and her submissiveness to him can be explained only by a respect, admiration and love which she never felt for any other man.

In their correspondence Curzon found it more difficult than she did to express his tenderest feelings. He could seldom strike the right note. In anticipating their reunion in London in June, he was capable of writing this extraordinary sentence:

Wide open and eager with delight will be the lover's arms into which (given a reasonable seclusion) you will spring, and already in anticipation are being formed the kisses that lips will leave on lips.

It was not the style of the period: nobody else wrote love letters like that. Deeply sincere though his feeling for Mary was, he saw himself acting a role, and the role of lover demanded an eighteenth century courtesy, a sweep of the plumed hat, one foot advanced slightly before the other. Emotion must be extravagantly, but decorously, expressed; humour kept for more fitting occasions; lust (he probably never used the word in all his life, but he knew what it meant) never allowed to sully the delicacy of his prose. Language mattered enormously to him. It was the test of a man's quality. Sometimes he allowed a fine phrase to fashion a thought – an idea splendidly expressed must be true – or discarded the only appropriate adverb because it violated the laws of sound. His style derived from a classical education and the tradition of parliamentary oratory. If he had not been so thorough a scholar, he might have agreed with Livy and Lytton Strachey that an historian must be prepared to make Pompey instead of Julius Caesar win the battle of Pharsalus if the turn of the sentence required it. Curzon had a rich and eloquent style. It would be totally unjust to dismiss his books and speeches as concoctions of verbal confectionery. He expressed himself with vigour and clarity, and often with great beauty. But the style was apt to get in the way of the sentiment, and what was magnificent in a speech or set-piece passage of prose became absurd and inhuman when writing to his girl.

Always he considered the effect of his words on a person's behaviour. That parenthesis ('given a reasonable seclusion') was typical of him. He did not want to find Mary throwing herself into his arms at the quayside. The idea would never have entered her head, but it was as well to remind her of the need for discretion. He was a man of the world; she was an inexperienced and emotional girl. 'You are a young child, though a stately woman, and you are on the threshold of life.' So he set the scene for her, in tone and circumstance.

In June 1894 they met, not on the quayside, but in London. Their reunion was a great success, but it lasted only two days, because she was committed to go with her family to France. It had one important outcome. She won his consent to tell their secret to her parents. Her mother was enthusiastic for the match, but her father, although he said little, seemed more sad at the prospect of losing her than happy for her happiness.

The date of Curzon's departure for India was drawing near. Mary wrote to him from France:

Those three little words in your Paris letter 'If I die' made me miserable enough putting the acknowledgement of the possibility, even the probability, of such a calamity. So in case all these forebodings of trouble happen, I thought I should like to tell you what I shall do if I do not follow the wise example of my Aunt who died within a short time of her love. This is a gloomy beginning to a letter and I shall never refer to it again and we are not likely to talk about anything painful if we have a day together in Paris. You know I shall not marry if you do not come back. Do not smile incredulously for I am not likely to change my mind. You know I have not in four years (which are probably the most impressionable of a girl's life) in spite of immense pressure to do so. The worldly marriages have not the slightest attraction for me.

So what I want to do is be of as much help as I can to an organisation of educated women who do a work very much like the one Mr Talbot is doing in the East End of London. They are religious for that is what holds them together, but not in the sense of prayers but in teaching and extending their wonderfully good work over an immense field. . . . I have thought a great deal about it after you decided to go and after Springy startled me one day by telling me that the dangers of the journey were almost unmentionable. I should renounce my large share of my father's estate and only ask him for a sixth of what I needed in the work. And that is what is difficult for me to write you, for I fear you may not understand it. I should love to do for your Kedleston what you and I planned to do together and release it from its debt, which is not likely to be done (is it George?) by your bothers. It could be done so that no one but your father and brothers would ever know. It is the only thing I should love doing in case you did not come back. . . . Tear this up as soon as you have read it.'

Curzon was much moved, but he replied that neither he nor his father could ever acquiesce in such a scheme, and forebade her to mention it again. To her protestation that she could never marry anybody but him, he begged her not to consider it a vow, 'since the bitterness of loss would be enhanced, not lessened, by the feeling that I had not merely shattered your youth, but crushed a lifetime'. Curzon, who was not a religious man, seemed to be so carried away by his emotion that he was visualizing himself dead (his exact location remained undefined), looking down on Mary in her convent, and suffering eternal torments of remorse for what he had done to her. The idea that Mary would simultaneously be looking up, her eyes filled with reproach tempered by charity, did not at that moment occur to him.

They had a few hours' farewell in Paris on 3 August. Then he

left for India. She sent him this wonderfully apposite quotation
from a poem by Ibsen that Grieg had set to music:

> *Tu me reviendras, o mon doux fiancé,*
> *Pour ne plus me quitter.*
> *Je t'ai donné mon coeur; il attend résigné*
> *Et ne pourra changer.*
> *Que Dieu veuille dans sa grande bonté te protéger*
> *Au pays lointain que te tient exilé,*
> *Loin du foyer.*

They did not meet again until the eve of their wedding. During
the two years of their engagement they were together for just two
days and a few snatched hours.

Curzon went by train to Venice, and thence by sea to Port
Said. Mary was taken by her parents to Baden Baden, where she
was dreadfully bored and worried. She met an Austrian with
thirty-five quarterings who had been in love with her, and although now engaged to another girl, immediately switched his
attentions back to her, and she had great difficulty in repelling
him. In Egypt Curzon met another of her old admirers, a certain
Bax Ironside, who was ludicrously proud of his pedigree. Some
of his brother officers obtained an ancient stone and carved on it
in hieroglyphics BACS IRUNSETTE, then buried it beside the
Nile in a place where Ironside was tricked into discovering it. He
was completely taken in, boasting that he had now traced his
ancestry back to the Eighteenth Dynasty. 'Lord', wrote Curzon,
'what you have escaped!'

He had set out without having obtained permission to visit
either the Pamirs or Afghanistan. In fact both the Government
at home and the Viceroy (Lord Elgin) had expressly forbidden it,
and his letter to Abdur Rahman, the Amir of Afghanistan, had
remained without an answer. On his arrival at Bombay, he was
handed a message from the Viceroy which repeated the veto in
even stronger terms. His journey to both countries was highly
undesirable from many points of view – political complications,
rivers flooded, no supplies, tribes rebellious. Curzon relied on his
powers of persuasion face to face, and in this he succeeded, con-
fronting Lord Elgin at Simla with unanswerable arguments why

he should be allowed to proceed. In Kashmir, to his overflowing delight, he received the Amir's telegram. He would be welcome in Kabul. Mary saw it with different eyes: 'I implore you not to go to Kabul. If the Amir dies, the danger will be terrible, and it would be quite inhuman of you to run such a risk: a kind of out-and-out desertion of M.V.L.' He did not receive this letter, written on 12 August, till 20 October. It was put into his hands as he rode back on the last stage of his journey through the Pamirs. He paid no attention to her pleas. Let her enjoy her tour of the Loire châteaux. He was after remoter and bigger things.

He did not write to her between his arrival in India in mid-August and his return to Chitral on 12 October, while at every opportunity he was sending back articles to *The Times*, in which she followed his progress, agonizingly. She did not reproach him for his neglect, since she knew that in the wild country beyond the Karakorams where all the winds of Asia meet to howl a common dirge, there were few inhabitants and no method of communication except by runner. On his return to Chitral he consoled her:

If you could see me riding on and on day after day and look into my mind and see what I am thinking about, and looking forward to and gloating over, I do not think that you would have much cause to be dissatisfied. Perhaps I don't express my concern for you very much or very often. But I am so hard-worked and exhausted that I can collect no thoughts for letters, and am inclined to leave out the things that seem to be obvious. So don't punch into me any more, or have any more doubts or misgivings. The time of waiting is drawing to a close and you will find me loving enough when we meet.

He told Mary nothing about what he had endured in the Pamirs, simply describing Chitral itself, which represented for him a return to humankind if not to civilization, for it was 'a remote mountain state composed principally of murderers, patricides, fratricides and criminals of the deepest dye'. He had ridden from Kashmir over the passes to Gilgit, and then through one of the most striking physical features of the universe, the Hunza valley, which is bordered by eight crests each over 24,000 feet high from which descend glaciers over thirty miles long. Today the journey as far as Baltit, the Hunza capital, can be made by

Land-Rover. For Curzon it meant riding a narrow track cut in the face of a precipitous gorge. At Baltit he called on the Mir or Thum of Hunza in his crumbling palace. (There, two years ago, in one of the smallest of the rooms, I saw pinned to the grotesque wall-carvings a single photograph torn from an illustrated magazine of 1900. It was a photograph of Curzon.) Hunza was only the beginning. He pressed on with his troupe of porters and one European companion, Henry Lennard, a soldier whom he had known at Eton, to the plateau of the Pamirs at an elevation of 14,000 feet, where lay the headwaters of the Oxus which no previous traveller had seen. The danger was now extreme. There were glaciers and torrents which he was forced to ride across in constant risk of slipping to perdition. His pony died of exhaustion. He was often obliged to swim through glacier-cold rivers, and to climb without equipment rock-faces which would challenge an expert today.

One must remember that Curzon was not a fit man. He had had no time while in England to prepare himself physically for his ordeal. The curvature of his spine made riding agony, and at the start he had badly wrenched his ankle. He made this journey because he felt he had to make it. Politically it was scarcely necessary, except to visit Chitral, which he could have approached more easily from the south. There was no information to be gained in so desolate a region as the Pamirs. There can be no politics without people. But there can be geography. His purpose was to do something which no man had ever done before, to be the first to see the sources of the Oxus and cross the roof of the world, and to prove to himself that while he was still young, there was nothing beyond his powers. On his return to England he lectured on his journey to the Royal Geographical Society, and was awarded its highest honour, the Gold Medal.

From Gilgit on 21 October 1894 he sent a cable to Mary announcing his safe return, and she received it next day in New York harbour, on board the *Majestic* which was waiting in quarantine after the Atlantic crossing. She wrote in ectasy:

I can't speak for thankfulness. You are safe! You are safe! Safe for my love, and oh dear, I cannot write for joy. I have never had a moment of such transcendent thankfulness in all my life.

Now he was off to Kabul. The danger there was not the terrain, for the route through the Khyber Pass was easy compared to the Pamirs, but the hostility of the Afghan tribes. A British expedition, six weeks before, had lost eleven of their men despite an escort of 2,000 soldiers and the safe-conduct of the Amir. Curzon had an escort of no more than twelve, and no European companion. The Government of India refused to send an officer with him, not even an interpreter, because his journey was being undertaken as a private citizen and entirely at his own risk. But he made it. The Amir sent 150 of his household cavalry to meet him outside the capital, and he entered Kabul in state, magnificently dressed in a uniform emblazoned with medals which he had hired, quite without entitlement, from a theatrical costumier in London, and was installed in a large suite of rooms in the Amir's palace. He was allotted horses, guards, and a large sum of money for his expenses. The rumour spread that he was the Queen's special representative, and crowds gathered to watch him pass. He wrote to Mary on 20 November from Kabul: 'I assure you there is no more risk for me here than in Piccadilly, and I am doing perhaps some public service. How long I stay, or which way I go out, I do not know. I am dealing with an Oriental potentate, and I have to feel my way, and show no particular desire or inclination.'

He spent two weeks in Kabul, honoured by the ruler with a daily audience, at which jokes and mutual flattery were soon succeeded by political discussion, mainly concerning the Russian threat to the northern borders, but once about the Amir's most cherished wish, never realized, to pay a state visit to London. Curzon's own account of that interview in his *Tales of Travel* well illustrates the characters of the two men and his gift for recreating a comic scene:

AMIR: When I come to England and to London and am received by the Queen, shall I tell you what I will do?

CURZON: Yes, Your Highness, I shall be glad to hear.

AMIR: I understand that there is in London a great Hall that is known as Westminster Hall. Is that not so?

CURZON: It is.

[69]

AMIR: There are also in London two *Mejilises* [Houses of Parliament].

CURZON: It is so.

AMIR: When I come to London I shall be received in Westminster Hall. The Queen will be seated on her throne at the end of the Hall, and the Royal Family will be around her; and on either side of the Hall will be placed the two *Mejilises* – the House of Lords on the right, and the House of Commons on the left. Is that not the case?

CURZON: It is not our usual plan; but will Your Highness proceed?

AMIR: I shall enter the Hall, and the Lords will rise on the right, and the Commons will rise on the left to greet me, and I shall advance between them up the Hall to the dais, where will be seated the Queen upon her throne. And she will rise and will say to me, 'What has Your Majesty come from Kabul to say?' And how then shall I reply?

CURZON: I am sure I do not know.

AMIR: I shall reply: 'I will say nothing' – and the Queen will then ask me why I refuse to say anything; and I shall answer: 'Send for [Lord] Roberts. I decline to speak until Roberts comes.' And then they will send for Roberts, and there will be a pause until Roberts comes, and when Roberts has come and is standing before the Queen and the two *Mejilises*, then will I speak.

CURZON: And what will Your Highness say?

AMIR: I shall tell them how Roberts paid thousands of rupees to obtain false witness at Kabul and that he slew thousands of my innocent people, and I shall ask that Roberts be punished, and when Roberts has been punished, then will I speak.

On leaving Kabul, Curzon was given by the Amir a special decoration, a gold star inlaid with diamonds and rubies. He had indeed performed 'some public service'. He had acquired a vast amount of information which he transmitted to the Viceroy, and established between Afghanistan and his own country a relationship which would be of great value when Curzon found himself four years later Abdur Rahman's equal as Viceroy of India. On the personal level he had made a new friend. He and the Amir

continued to correspond, and on his marriage Curzon sent him
Mary's photograph. The Amir replied, 'From my knowledge
of phrenology she is very wise and a well-wisher of yours and
better than 1,000 men. ... If she should at any time thrash
you, I am certain that you will have done something to deserve
it.'

Curzon rode back towards India through Kandahar. On the
road a galloping horseman drew up to hand him Mary's letter
written on the *Majestic* seven weeks before. She received his
second 'Safe' telegram from Quetta on the first day of the new
year, 1895. He was back in England by the end of January. He
had survived, and no obstacle to his marriage now remained.

Mary had returned to Washington determined to study German
and singing, and to renounce the social life. People, she said,
thought her either mad or engaged, and she settled for the former.
The confession did not, however, deter a new suitor, Prince
Borghese, who was rather badly off, from making elaborate
efforts to capture her hand, begging all her friends, including
Springy, to tell her that he was a most brilliant creature, and that
their life together would be one unending pageant. Springy
passed on the message, himself again in despair for love of her.
She now took his proposals, and he her refusals, almost as a matter of course. He said that he would attend her wedding in one
capacity only, and needled her, though she was fond of him, by
asking why she never mentioned George's name. 'I never do', she
told Curzon, 'because you are so much in my thoughts that I fear
my voice will give away too much tenderness.' She continued
with a strength of emotion that is unmistakeable:

It is not a question of whom you could live with, but of whom you
could not live without; and who in every condition of life, great or
small, is the one to whom every fibre of your body and mind responds
with devotion and love.

There was one problem which was becoming urgent. Curzon
must tell his father. Mary was already familiar enough with the

ignorance and prejudices of the English upper class on any subject concerning America, to fear an outburst. Lord Scarsdale might think her, if not actually a Jewess, little better than an Indian squaw. To help Curzon with his explanations, she innocently revived for him the legend of Governor Carver of Plymouth who had come over with the *Mayflower*, adding that later Carvers were Chancellors of New York State. The Leiters, she said, were originally Calvinist parsons in Holland with a 'von' before their name, a claim quite without foundation, though she did not know it. In fact Lord Scarsdale took the news well. Curzon had no need to make use of Mary's dubious genealogies. His father said, 'So long as you love her and she loves you, that is all that matters. You are not likely at your age to make a mistake, and she is old enough to know her mind.' Curiously, Curzon did not feel able to tell his father the whole story, letting him understand that only now was he about to propose, and that 'I thought a favourable answer was not improbable'. He showed him Mary's photograph. Nothing more was needed to convince the old man, and he wrote her a kind letter of welcome.

Curzon himself wrote to Levi Leiter. They had not corresponded before, and although Leiter had known the situation for about six months, he had hardly mentioned it, even to Mary. Now he and Curzon exchanged letters of mutual respect. Leiter's began: 'Dear Curzon, I am at this moment in receipt of your favour of 29th ult', and ended, 'Believe me yours, L.Z. Leiter'. Cordiality was lacking on his side, obsequiousness on Curzon's, but money was mentioned. Leiter would settle on his daughter £140,000, and give her in addition an annual income of £6,000. Curzon had hoped for £9,000, which with his allowance of £1,000 from his father ('a paltry sum, I fear, but my family is poor'), would make their joint incomes £10,000 a year, 'but I have no doubt that we can get on perfectly well with less'. When her father died, Mary told him in confidence, their income would be £30,000, and if meanwhile they were ever in need of something special, there was nothing that her father would not do for her.

They began to make wedding plans. There was no dispute between them about where and when they should be married.

London was out of the question; Linden Lodge was too far and too cheerless. The wedding must take place in Washington at Easter, during the Parliamentary recess. Curzon said that he wished for a quiet wedding. So did Mary. She wanted to invite no more than thirty or forty 'dear friends', and hold no grand party afterwards. When Curzon asked her who the dear friends would be, she began to enumerate them: Well, the President, of course, and Mrs Cleveland, the Chief Justice, the Secretary of State, the Attorney General, the Theodore Roosevelts, the Cabot Lodges, Henry Adams, the Camerons, the British Minister. . . . It soon became clear that the quiet wedding would be one of the social events of the season, and neither of them found it difficult to become reconciled to the idea. For a short honeymoon friends would lend them a house outside Washington, and then they would return together to England. Trousseau? From Paris. Bridesmaids? Mary's two sisters. Who would marry them? Bishop Talbot of Wyoming, an old family friend. The best man posed a problem. Springy? Perhaps not. Relations? There would be a few Leiters there (Mary thought her father had a brother living in Leitersburg), but there would be Carvers. From the Curzon side, only his brother Frank.

They decided that they must announce the engagement on 4 March 1895, six weeks before the wedding, simultaneously in Washington and London. This would give Curzon time to clear off arrears of work before the expected flood of congratulatory letters reached him, and leave a short, but not too short, interval between the announcement and the wedding. Very close friends could be told on March 2nd. They agreed to say that they had known each other for several years, and had become engaged (presumably by correspondence) after his return from Afghanistan. The truth would sound too strange, and involve endless explanations.

Springy was the first outside their immediate families to be told, and he behaved atrociously. At first he pretended to be delighted. He looked forward to Curzon's arrival in Washington to dispel the suitors, like Odysseus's in Ithaca, and wrote him a letter of sincere friendship and congratulation, saying that he had had 'a terrible suspicion that she was going to be lost to us by marrying an American'. Then he began to circulate rumours which soon reached London, betraying Curzon's confidences about his relations with other women, particularly a Miss Morton, whom Curzon had met only twice in his life; and he told Mary that the Curzon sisters would much dislike his marriage, not because she was an American but because she was prettier than they were. He also warned her that in England wives do not count much with husbands: 'A man chiefly has a home to stay out of it.' Springy had 'a hard, revengeful side' to his nature, she explained. He had never wholly forgiven Curzon for winning a Fellowship at All Souls, when Springy didn't. 'His one pleasure is to give pain. He is very eccentric and wayward. But he has never spoken to me against you.' The rumours were quashed, and Springy was forgiven, though there could now be no question of inviting him to be best man: he would be an usher only. Mary continued to see him occasionally and corresponded with him throughout her life, but his letters are disappointing. He adopted the more pompous of Curzon's literary mannerisms without their wit. The strangest fact to emerge from them is that he never called her Mary. She was always Miss Leiter; then Mrs and Lady Curzon.

When the news became public, their friends wrote to each of them letters of fulsome hyperbole. The interest of them today lies mainly in the aspects of Mary's character which the writers chose to emphasize. The cliché about her was 'lovely of face and mind'. Margot Asquith called her 'a lovely sunny companion'. Mr Gladstone wrote portentously: 'I have heard some accounts of the bride as enable me to give a further emphasis to the feeling with which I now wish you my blessing upon the coming union.' G. W. Smalley, the Washington journalist and writer, put it more charmingly: 'I think over my friendship with you and with him and collect my memories and put them side by side. They all seem to fall naturally into place together, as if the two lives were made to be lived together, and as if each had found the twin soul which halved their own.' The funniest was Lord Pembroke's letter to Curzon: 'It was very clever of you and extremely

[74]

characteristic to get engaged to Miss Leiter at Washington on top of the Pamirs. You must tell me how it was done.'

Curzon cabled to Mary that in London there was 'universal delight'. He either did not realize, or was concealing from her, that some comment was less enthusiastic. Shane Leslie wrote later: 'Curzon had kept his associations hitherto so high that it was a surprise when he married beneath a Curzon.' In the United States there were other reservations. The press, on the whole, was kind. A typical editorial comment was that 'the lady whom the country is proud to call her fairest daughter is marrying a man of splendid ability'. But there was inevitable disappointment that this fairest daughter was following the example of so many others by marrying a foreigner. The President, Mary said, 'just grunted' when told the news. Henry Adams cabled from New Orleans, 'We wish you every happiness that our brotherly affection can imagine, but we are broken-hearted.' Springy (but his evidence, although a diplomatist's, is unreliable) wrote to Francis Villiers that the United States was consumed with jealousy for Britain, and 'that a beautiful and wealthy girl like Miss Leiter should go abroad to marry' was the last straw. Mary became aware that this aspect of her engagement was being widely discussed. She described the feeling as 'very bitter', not against her personally, but against the practice: 'Why do not American girls marry Americans, and devote their talents and money to their own country?' Curzon, of course, was not a foolish, impoverished, predatory young nobleman. His name was well-known in the United States among those who set the tone, and a brilliant career was foreseen for him and therefore for his wife. Mary was not marrying Curzon for a title (he did not even yet possess one), but for love and a worthwhile role in life. But although not wasted, she was about to be removed, and that hurt.

Curzon left England on 10 April, arrived in New York on the 17th, and was in Washington a day later. He brought with him Lord Lamington as best man, his brother Frank, and the Kedleston diamonds for Mary to wear on her wedding day. He stayed in the great new house on Dupont Circle, for Americans had not adopted the English custom of keeping bride and bride-groom apart in separate houses on the wedding eve. Two whole days were spent with Leiter's lawyers, drawing up the legal settle-ments. Then, on 22 April 1895, they were married.

Mary had insisted, the evening before, on being left alone for an hour in her own room at the top of the house. She wanted to discover what she felt. The waiting years had at last come to this fulfilment. They had not been wasted years, for she believed that the test had strengthened her, and George too, and that they approached their marriage with a confidence in each other which no normal engagement would have brought about. Still it was odd, that they who had been engaged for longer than any two people she had ever heard of, should have seen each other less. Thank goodness, she reflected, that she had not married at the time when she still enjoyed adulation and social success, and might be regretting that she had to give it all up so soon. Now it was the other way round. She was infinitely relieved by the thought that never again would another man court her. She had begun to feel like a rabbit cornered by dogs, with no hole to bolt to, and it had reached the point when she almost hated men, which God knows she didn't want to. She had felt herself becom-ing a recluse, and she must fight against it. She had health and vigour, and the blessed gift of calm. As a married woman in England she would be discreet but not dull. That was it. Discreet but not dull.

She had been nervous of meeting Curzon again. He was a year older, with thousands of miles of travel behind him, and he had come, as he said, to claim her as his own for ever. The possessive-ness, the permanence of it, was alarming, although that was what she wanted too. And of course sex (Mary was a virgin): the darkness behind the closed door.

There were things in him which might put off other women. His almost feminine fussiness, for example, his time-table mind, his perfectionism and occasional irritability, his addiction to detail. How different he was from Springy! If you asked Springy to come at half-past-three, he would turn up at five, and apolo-gize for being early. George was an organizer, of himself and other people. Well, she would not quarrel with him about that. She was quite prepared to be a submissive wife, which her friends thought strange, because she had been so independent as a girl, so proud, some thought. But none of them understood how fed up she was with being the person on whom the whole household relied for every sort of arrangement (this wedding, for example), and as the natural recipient of everyone's confidences. All of them – her brother, sisters, mother, servants – came to her with their problems, and there had been nobody to whom she could go with hers. Now she would be the protected, no longer the protector. Curzon was a strong man. She had had enough of weakness. She hoped passionately for his success. Their life together would be a series of expeditions; there would always be another peak.

She must have asked herself how much she minded leaving America. It was the parting from her father that she dreaded most. He had grown old quite suddenly. She had found him wandering round the house these last few days as if lost in some-one else's. Twice he had seemed about to speak to her, and then moved away. She sensed that he did not like Curzon very much – his politics, his aristocratic manner, his never having made money, his Englishness, and of course taking her away from him – all this would account for much of his recent gloom. She must find an opportunity to talk to him alone tonight. And her mother? Mary never thought much about her mother, except with guilt. Mrs Leiter was so determined to please and be pleased that there seemed no room left in her for any genuine emotion. And Nannie and Daisy and Joe – they would all miss her. Would any of her friends? Was there anyone in the whole of Washington who would notice a month later that she was gone? Springy? Oh yes, Springy. And old Mr Adams, and Frances Cleveland, and a few others. But heavens, she was not going into exile! They would all come to Europe, and she would return to the States.

She would return. But stopping being an American, trying to become British, leaving her country – what did she really feel about that? She found she minded more than she had expected. All those associations, right back to and up from Chicago, all those places and people, they were all American places, American people. Her trips to Europe had been just trips, with the certainty of returning after a few months to the place where she belonged. Now she would never return except as a tripper in reverse, and never again would she quite belong, anywhere. By the law of the times, she must surrender her American nationality. For the rest of her life she would be acting a role, the role of a pseudo-Englishwoman. It would all be very different when she returned to London as Mrs Curzon instead of Mary Leiter. She was not Margot Asquith; she was not Lady Ribblesdale; and by God she was not – did the names suddenly flash into her mind? – Sibell Grosvenor or Miss Morton. Would Curzon wish she was?

The President did not, after all, attend the wedding. He was prevented by protocol from doing so. But Mrs Cleveland did, and so did all the other expected guests. It took place at 11.30 in the morning, at St John's Church on the far side of Lafayette Square opposite the White House, where Joseph Chamberlain had married Mary Endicott six years before. It is a lovely white church, built by Benjamin Latrobe in 1815, a building which Wren might have designed, but which Washington people called quaint, crisp outside and crisper within, with a half-hoop gallery supported on slim white columns. Mary arrived in an open carriage between solid banks of spectators, dressed in white satin trimmed with old lace, and a full train – 'simplicity itself', said the *Chicago Tribune*, which meant that Worth's couturiers had worked on it for weeks. From the coronet of Scarsdale diamonds on her dark hair fell a shimmering veil. Other diamonds were fashioned into a necklace, with pendants dripping to the corsage. She wore no gloves, which excited comment, and carried no bouquet, but the reporters noted with satisfaction that she looked pale. Curzon, according to the Washington *World*, 'was a very pleasing prospect, when people found time to look at him. . . . The top of his head is well developed, extraordinarily well, in fact – which shows that he has imagination, a very desirable quality.' What they could not know was that his back was giving him intense pain.

Afterwards there was a reception in the Leiter house. Mary

[78]

and her husband stood to receive the guests before an immense onyx fireplace in the Empire drawing-room beneath her lifesize portrait by Alexandre Cabanel. A banquet followed in the ball-room. They left, chased by thrown rice, to stay for five days at Beauvoir, Virginia, a house lent to them by John R. Maclean. There they gave a few small dinner-parties to introduce Curzon more intimately to Mary's friends. On 27 April they went by special train to New York, and sailed to England on the *Etruria*. Mary never saw the United States again.

THREE

LONDON

THE *Etruria* was a foul ship, and the Curzons had a miserable journey, though they were given the best of the accommodation. The food was bad, the cabin dirty, the berths too short, and the bar ran out of champagne. On the last two days they drove into a fearful storm, which hurled a roast chicken into a corner under their bunk from which nobody could extricate it. Curzon was still in pain, and irritable with everyone except Mary, but by the time they docked at Liverpool he had prepared a voluminous Committee report and written two lectures.

They went straight to Kedleston. At Liverpool the Chairman of the Cunard Line came on board personally to greet them, and a special train awaited them for the journey to Derby, consisting of an engine and a single coach. At Derby the welcome was more extravagant. Lord Scarsdale was on the platform with his daughter Geraldine, and Mary was now meeting both of them for the first time. She passed on his arm through a privileged group of city fathers to two great barouches which were drawn up in the station yard. She and Curzon drove off alone in the first of them, his family following in the other, and they progressed slowly through the crowded streets, which were decorated as if for a Coronation. The bells of all the churches rang out in welcome, and at intervals the carriages halted for a child to present a bouquet or the Mayor a speech. A crowd of 35,000 lined the 2½ mile route, and cheered them all the way to the gates of Kedleston, where forty mounted tenants waited to escort them to the house.

Even for a tourist the first sight of Kedleston is one never to be forgotten. In the manner dear to eighteenth-century English landscape designers, the visitor discovers the house by serpentine approach through trees, which part suddenly to reveal a lake crossed at its narrowest point by a bridge of aristocratic but not disproportionate magnificence. On the slope of the far bank, set in a park of verdant trimness and a garden of great lawns and trees, lies the house. In any other country it would be called a palace. Two wings curve outwards to terminate in symmetrical buildings, each by itself a residence fit for a country gentleman of expensive and refined tastes. The whole composition has as its centre-piece a vast raised porch composed of six columns of honeyed stone, to which you mount from the gravelled drive by flanking staircases. On the garden front Robert Adam had added his masterpiece, a triumphal arch that swells into a dome. It is not Roman, but it borrows Roman ideas and transforms them. It is sturdy but decorative, firm but graceful. Kedleston cannot be called simple, but it is undeniably serene. A classical building of monumental size, it blends with the surrounding countryside to create a scene of Theocritean beauty, a symbol of patrician permanence and calm.

Mary scarcely had time to take all this in before she stepped from the carriage to be welcomed by five further sisters and three brothers, all of whom kissed her. She was led to the great podium between the columns, and turned to face 550 tenants assembled to greet her. Their spokesman delivered an address, first in speech and then on illuminated parchment, and presented her with their wedding present, a huge silver tray. A band played. Photographs were taken. The family then went inside to have tea. Mary had never seen such a room as that which she first entered. Twenty huge fluted monoliths of Nottingham alabaster were ranged each side of a long empty hall, and beyond it she glimpsed through the open doors a circular saloon that rose sixty feet to Adam's dome. These rooms were not for use, but an eighteenth-century adaptation of the Roman *atrium* and *vestibulum*, halls through which you pass to the more intimate rooms beyond, which Adam had designed down to the very stoves and door-handles, quickly varying his style from the grand to the domestic, the elaborate to the pretty, and illustrating his enjoyment by turning from one material to another – alabaster, marble, bronze, iron, wood, stucco, plaster, paint – from which he contrived his exquisite designs in turn.

Mary was anxious to find everything perfect. The house was 'quite magnificent, and not too large' (by Dupont standards). George was wonderful, displaying an entirely unsuspected facet of his character as he joked with the keepers' wives. The sisters, though plain, were sweet to her. Lord Scarsdale, 'a quaint old man, tall, thin and very distinguished, was charming to me beyond words'. The favourable impressions of her first visit to Kedleston were not to survive her second and third, but for the moment she felt that no bride had ever had a more wonderful homecoming.

When the Curzons reached London, they found that their house, the first fruit of Levi Leiter's generosity, was already prepared for them. It was at 5 Carlton House Terrace, overlooking St James's Park, one of the most splendid town-houses in England. It belonged to the Earl of Caledon, but as he lived almost all the year in Ireland and had four young sons (one of whom was to become Field Marshal Earl Alexander of Tunis) and no daughters, he had little use for the house and let it to the Curzons.

Curzon had seen to all the decoration and furnishing of the house before he left for Washington, and had engaged all the servants. Mary found herself in the familiar role of housekeeper, but it was all very different from Dupont Circle. When she had previously been a guest in English houses, she had found little to complain of, but now that she had to manage everything herself, she thought it hell. Nothing worked. The WCs stank, the only bathroom was in a cupboard, goods were never delivered on time, and the servants were tyrannical. They would do as much work as they thought they were paid to do, and not a stroke more. When she complained that the grocery bills were too high, the cook gave notice. She was served so little food to eat herself, that she had to send her plate back to the kitchen 'three or four times' for a refill. Then the footman ran off with the parlour-maid, and the best of the housemaids broke her leg. It was intolerable. Mary, having expected to live like a princess, or at least in the manner to which a daughter of L. Z. Leiter was accustomed, found herself haggling over the price of tomatoes in Covent Garden market and queuing up at the Army & Navy Stores, because the servants, knowing that otherwise complaints of the cost would follow, insisted that she accompany them. Of course Curzon helped her. He enjoyed domestic budgeting. 'Would you like to know how much meat we consumed last month per week per head?', he asked her once. She said she would. He gave her the figure to the exact ounce, its cost to the last farthing. On coal, on hay, on wine, on cigars? She was all attention. He would even dust, finding specks of grime invisible to anyone else, and insisted that he alone should touch his oriental treasures. Although he was working sixteen hours a day on his official business, she found him touchingly considerate when she spoke to him of her troubles. Years of bachelorhood seemed not to have affected him. 'I fear he spoils me as much as you have always done', she told her father. 'His disposition is unique.'

Their first grand party was a disaster. It was a dinner in honour of Shahzada Nazrullah Khan, the younger son of the Amir of Afghanistan, and the company included the Prince of Wales, the Duke and Duchess of St Albans, the Marquesses of Dufferin, Breadalbane, Zetland and Montrose, and Joe Leiter who was on a visit to London. At the last moment three of the most dazzling ladies, Lady Dudley, Lady Londonderry and the Duchess of Sutherland, chucked. Mary's *placement* was in total disarray. Then Nazrullah brought with him uninvited aides, and sent ahead his own chef, who created such confusion in the kitchen by demanding oriental spices which even Fortnum & Mason's could not supply, that the food, western and eastern, was pronounced by the departing guests to have been extraordinarily nasty.

All this Mary retailed with humour to her parents, but reading between the lines they must have guessed that she was unhappy. She was no longer fêted in London. People were annoyed with George for marrying an American, and with her for being one. 'My path is strewn with roses, and the only thorns are the unforgiving women.' She began to notice their mean stratagems to

upstage their social rivals, including herself. 'London life is a con-
tinuous, striving, striving, striving to keep going, the little people
praying to be noticed by the great, and the great seldom lowering
their eyelids to look at the small.' She was homesick. 'George is
devotion itself to me, but England can *never, never* take the place of
home to me. . . . There is nothing in the world I care for but my
own family and George. As yet I am not attached to my new
country.' The Souls had once accepted her because she was a
novelty. Now she rarely saw them, and one reason was that people
were amazed that she could allow her personality to be so eclipsed
by her husband's. Consuelo Vanderbilt, who married the Duke
of Marlborough in November of this year, considered that her
deference to him exceeded what anyone could have imagined
possible in an American girl of her intelligence and spirit. Her
devotion was thought by the older generation highly meritorious
in a young wife, but to the younger she seemed no longer the
Mary of her girlhood. It was a passing phase. She was to recover
her gaiety and vigour. But it took time. While it lasted, she was
thought disappointing, beautiful but a bit dull. Her American
journalist friend G. W. Smalley went to the root of the matter:
'You are an American *au bout des ongles*', he wrote to her, 'and you
can never be anything else, with your American brilliancy, your
American beauty and American intelligence. . . . You have had
perhaps too much homage; it might do you good to be neglected
a little.'

In June 1895 Curzon was appointed Under Secretary of State
at the Foreign Office by Lord Salisbury, now again Prime
Minister, who retained in his own hands the office of Foreign
Secretary and needed Curzon's help in speaking for the Government in the House of Commons. Curzon showed his disappointment: he had hoped for a Cabinet post. In compensation he was
made a Privy Councillor, the youngest man (at thirty-six) to hold
the honour within living memory.

A General Election followed in July, and he took Mary to
Southport for her first exposure to the brutal reality of British
politics at its basic level. While his constituents were delighted by
her, she was horrified by them. They thought her the most beauti-

ful creature they had ever seen, and liked to imagine that she and
Curzon were still on their honeymoon. The Liberal candidate
sneered at this unfair advantage, and a hostile newspaper commented after the poll that Curzon owed his re-election 'far more
to the winning smiles and irresistible graces of his American wife
than he did to his own speeches'. Together they drove round
Southport canvassing, blue rosettes attached to the horses' ears
and ribbons to their tails, Mary looking pleased, shaking hands,
listening attentively to Curzon's many speeches though she understood little of their content, adoring him, he adoring her, and
giving an impression of such untarnished pleasure and excitement that even her husband was taken in. He wrote to Levi
Leiter (who was paying the entire cost of his campaign), 'She says
she has never been so happy in her life.' What must Leiter have
thought when by the same mail he received Mary's own account
of the election? And what would the goggling citizens of Southport have thought had they known how much bitterness her
smiles concealed?

I think I must pour out my heart to you, and tell you how I *loathe*
this place. The people are an ungrateful lot of vulgar cockneys,
provincial to a degree and very stupid, and they do not half appreciate George. . . . This miserable 3rd-class seaside resort, a 4th-rate
Brighton, is full of idle loafers. My only regret if he is elected here is
that we shall have to spend part of every year among these people,
frowsy women and horrid men.

A few days later she wrote:

I loathe this place more than any other I have *ever* been to, but this I
can only say to you. The people are an idle ignorant impossible lot of
ruffians. I smile at them and look sweet because it would be the end of
us if they knew all that I thought.

The ruffians re-elected Curzon with an increased majority,
and he and Mary went to Kedleston for a few days to recover.
There she experienced her second disillusionment. She now
found her father-in-law disagreeable and his house decrepit. The
glamour of her first arrival had entirely dissipated. 'Lord S.', she
reported to her mother, 'is the most tyrannical old man I have

[85]

ever seen, besides being the most eccentric.' She felt sorry for his spinster daughters, nice girls whom he scolded from morning to night for not being married, when he never allowed a single young man to enter the house. Not one of Curzon's friends had ever been invited to stay there, and if they had been, they would have been utterly miserable. Everything was subordinated to the caprices of the host. 'He is an old despot of the 13th century.' He would not endure a minute's unpunctuality. You could scarcely lift a spoon without his permission. His eccentricities might have been tolerable had they been more endearing:

He is very fond of examining his tongue in a mirror. When he sits reading or writing he makes the most fiendish grimaces. He sleeps with his feet 2 ft. higher than his head with no blanket over him in the midst of winter. He has 18 thermometers in his sitting-room, and the tables are covered with magazines and railway guides and almanacks of 1839, all covered with dust. He does not like to have his name repeated, and if anyone Lord Scarsdales him, he begins to make faces and turns away. He wished me to call him Papa, but I have never brought my lips to it, for anyone less like my own beloved Papa I cannot imagine.

The worst part of it, according to Mary, was his refusal to tolerate any alterations to the house. Structurally Kedleston was in good repair, but within it, no changes had been made for a hundred years. The fabrics were decaying, the furniture falling to pieces, the plumbing was unspeakable, the guest-bedrooms scarcely habitable because they had not been occupied for half a century. 'He looks at the dilapidated rooms', wrote Mary, 'with grim satisfaction.' If ever Curzon risked a suggestion for modernizing the house, his father ignored him completely, unwilling to admit that one day it would belong to him. Once he asked whether his father would allow him, at his own expense, to repaper and furnish the old nurseries, and instal a bathroom next door. It would make a charming suite for any of the married children when they came to stay. 'His only answer was to get up and go out of the room, and in the door to remark, "I have no answer to make to such a proposal, and I should never consider it for a moment".'

[86]

Mary's revised opinion of her father-in-law should not be regarded as her final one, nor as more than approximately just. She was in a black mood. She had hated the Southport election, and she was feeling ill: she was expecting a child. If one turns to more balanced accounts of Lord Scarsdale's character, like Kenneth Rose's, one discovers that more, but not a great deal more, could be said in his favour. The first surprise is that he was a clergyman. He was the Reverend Lord Scarsdale, Rector of Kedleston and the neighbouring parish of Mickleover, an inherited incumbency. Although he did not officiate at the services, leaving them to a curate, he took his parochial duties quite seriously, visiting the sick and poor. He also played a conscientious though modest part in local affairs, as Governor of a school and member of the water-board. But his main achievement in life was the management of his estate. He left it in first-rate condition. He would rather spend money on a labourer's cottage, it was said, than on his own splendid house. But in suggesting that Kedleston had been allowed to run to seed, Mary was exaggerating. It is true that it was cold and gloomy, but the superb Adam interiors and much of the original furnishing survive in perfect condition to this day, and Lord Scarsdale had been one of the first owners of a great house to instal a fixed bath with running water, and electricity reached Kedleston ten years ahead of Knole. Nor was he quite the misanthrope that she depicted. He had a few old friends whom he would entertain regularly and well, even after his wife's death in 1875. What is true is that he was a man of almost painful reserve, and found it difficult to establish an intimacy with any of his eleven children. Of George he was fond and proud, but could seldom bring himself to the point of telling him so. As for Mary, he had shown her great consideration on her engagement, writing her one of the most charming letters she received, and from time to time in future years she reciprocated his feeling for her, once speaking of him as a man 'as tender and affectionate as my own father', the highest praise that she could bestow.

[87]

The next three years of Mary's life were the only ones on which she looked back with sadness, and which seemed in retrospect, apart from the birth of two of her three children, wasted. It was as if a spark had died in her, only to be blown to life again when she became Vicereine at the end of 1898. Her life dipped: so, it seems, did her character. She became querulous, bored. We know everything that she was doing and thinking, because throughout this period she wrote heart-broken letters to her family, and they kept them all. Indeed, we know too much. The fullness of her letters only emphasizes the emptiness of her life. What she did was unrewarding; what she felt was bleak. The main interest of these years is to discover what had happened to her, and why.

The basic troubles were that she had no intimate friend in England, and that Curzon was always working. For hours on end she was left alone. She read little, and even music had ceased to be a consolation. The Curzons seldom entertained, and if they were invited out, he would usually make his work an excuse for refusing, and she could not go alone. She, to whom the White House had been a second home, never set foot in Downing Street, and they were seen in society so little that people soon forgot them. After all, she was only Mrs Curzon, the wife of a young Under Secretary. Shortly before her marriage she had begun to dislike society; now she missed it. She missed even its insincerity. When the Curzons did attend a grand party, it was no longer the same. There was a chilling difference between, 'Mary, I have never seen you looking lovelier', and 'Mrs Curzon, how delightful that you and your husband were able to come.' Is that what happens when one marries? If only she could have deep-frozen some of the surfeit of compliment with which until so recently she had been fed to the point of nausea, and could now take it out to savour in small pieces! She had always excited admiration. All that was over now. Being neglected, she thought the British snobbish, particularly the women. In March 1896, after the birth of her first baby, she wrote to her mother:

You are the only person in the wide world who knows how I have suffered this year. . . . George and baby are the only people who exist for me in England. I am so much more sensitive and reserved than English women, and I never feel any sympathy with them, and I don't feel that they do with me, so that my life centres on my own house.

That does not ring quite true. She had never felt like that about English women before. England contained just as many 'sensitive and reserved' women as America. She knew London's society well and had thought it even more delightful than Washington's, since men paid women more respect for this very quality, their reserve. Perhaps they carried it too far. Once married, women were confined unless they had the strength of will to break out, for they were totally excluded from men's interests and must create their own. Other American brides had assimilated quite happily, but too little social effort had been required of Mary in the past. Success had come to her too easily. Marriage had given her a new prop, but simultaneously it snatched another away. Her popularity was no longer automatic. She needed worship, and now received it only from her husband. In circumstances which were difficult but not impossible, she could have used her charm and talents to make a new circle of congenial friends, instead of relying on the old circle of her husband's, to whom she was no longer so interesting because she had married him. She did not make that effort, and in consequence felt discarded, attributing her isolation to the attitude of English women in general, when it was due to her own failure to adapt.

She said that her life now centred on her house, but even that added to her unhappiness. After only four months in Carlton House Terrace they decided that they could not afford the rent, and leased Arthur Balfour's house, 4 Carlton Gardens. While this was being made ready for them, they lived in a Georgian house in Reigate in Surrey, the Priory, which they rented from Lady Henry Somerset. Both were charming houses, and Mary could have found a happy occupation in furnishing and redecorating them, had not Curzon, ostensibly to save her trouble but because he enjoyed it, taken all this out of her hands. He would not allow her to choose even the curtains or the colours of the walls. He seemed quite unaware that she might have her own preferences in such matters, for which, besides, her father was paying. 'The house [Carlton Gardens] looked charming today', he wrote, 'the drawing-room pretty, the staircase (now quite finished) a little dark but decidedly handsome, the other rooms nice. I am going to have the colour of the outer hall slightly altered. All carpets and curtains to be in by Christmas.'

Mary was left with the running of two houses which reflected another person's taste. It gave her no pleasure. The staff in Carlton Gardens, though the house was much smaller, was on the same scale as it had been in Carlton House Terrace. From scattered references to her various domestics, all of whom periodically gave trouble or notice, usually both, it is possible to reconstruct the roll. There was a housekeeper, a butler, two footmen, a chef, three housemaids, a kitchen-maid, a scullery-maid, a lady's maid, a nanny, a nursery-maid, an odd-man, a coachman and two grooms. This large household had little to do but wait upon each other. The Curzons rarely entertained, and their personal needs were very simple. If all that is ordered from the kitchen day after day is a cutlet for lunch and two cutlets for dinner, the chef grows slack, and when required to make a special effort, is no longer capable of it. The rot spread throughout the staff. When Lord Scarsdale came to spend a night at the Priory, 'It was the signal for everything to go wrong. His fire is forgotten and goes out; no coal in his scuttle; all the meals late; a roast of mutton proves bad; the breakfast so nasty that nobody could eat it.' The chef, after this disaster, demanded a rise in wages from £100 a year to £120. 'English servants', wrote Mary, 'are *fiends*. They seem to plot among themselves. They are malignant and stupid and make life barely worth living.' As must have happened so often at that period, the mistress's time was consumed by interviewing, soothing and scolding the very servants who were engaged to save it, and in getting cross with people who existed primarily to prevent her getting cross.

Then there was the climate. It was either misty, windy, too hot or too cold, and the air of London was so polluted that Mary felt

[90]

herself unable to breathe. She seemed to have forgotten what Chicago could be like, summer and winter. But the English had taken no precautions against either. She alternately sweltered and shivered. She seemed never to have the right clothes. The water-pipes either failed in the drought or burst in the frost. There was an unpleasant business with the cess-pit. The drive of the Priory was so deep in mud, or so clogged with snow, that the phaeton could not leave to meet Curzon at Reigate station. One day Mary was acutely distressed (she always loved animals) to see two ducks trapped by ice in the middle of the lake, squawking for help, but the ice was too thin for anyone to reach them, and of course there was no boat. Next morning the ducks were frozen solid.

Cumulatively these social, domestic and climatic upsets caused Mary intense misery. Her father, and later her mother, came to England to visit her that first year, horrified by the increasingly morose tone of her letters, but their visits only accentuated her homesickness. They sat over the coal-fire exchanging memories of home, and Mary wept at the time, and wept even more when they were gone. 'My dear mother, you made the evening hours so sweet by sitting there with me before dinner. I love the chairs you sat on, and try to see you there, and my eyes fill with tears. I never knew how much I loved you all until I had to be separated from you. After all, one's own blood is the dearest thing in the whole world, and I shall feel my separation more and more as years go on.' Then again: 'I cling like an old ivy-leaf to my beloved family. I positively live for the posts when I sit here alone day in and day out.'

In the middle of all this, in October 1895, occurred the Venezuelan crisis, which threatened war between Britain and the United States. The dispute over the boundary between Venezuela and British Guiana had dragged on for many years. Now President Cleveland sent a message to the Congress stating that any attempt by the British Government to enforce its claims would be regarded by the United States as a *casus belli*. The matter must be ended forthwith, in favour of the Venezuelans. The *New York Journal* asked whether the 'American wives' in influential positions in Britain might not settle the matter. There were at least ten of them, including Lady Randolph Churchill, Mrs Joseph Chamberlain, the Duchess of Marlborough and Mrs Curzon, the wife of the Under Secretary of State for Foreign Affairs. The *Journal* continued: 'If war were thrown upon England, Mr Curzon would lose immediately, through his wife, $15,000,000 in American securities alone. This was Miss Leiter's private fortune when she married Mr Curzon last spring, and at the first note of trouble her stock would drop to $2,000,000, and, at more trouble, to probably nothing at all. This is a solid and substantial reason why Mr Curzon would not favour war, and why Lady Scarsdale, as Mrs Curzon's title will be some day, would work against such a calamity.'

Of course the innuendo was disgraceful, and probably libellous. Mary had no private fortune of her own, and her father's endowment was greatly exaggerated. She was doubly distressed, by the possibility that her two countries might fight each other over so trivial a boundary dispute, and that it could be publicly stated that her husband's views might be influenced by his concern not just for her (as was natural) but for her money. However, she had to consider on whose side she was, and she wrote as follows to her mother:

I am wondering what I should do if England and America followed Cabot Lodge's advice, and went to war about Venezuela. I should wear the American flag under my jacket if I could not wear it on the outside as the wife of an English official. One's country is always one's country. Laws may change one's nationality, but they cannot change the heart, and mine is *and ever will be* American.

The dispute ended in compromise, but it shook Mary so fundamentally at a moment when she was already disillusioned with England, that she never wholly reconciled her two loyalties, though they never came into such acute conflict again. If war had come, she said, 'Nothing could have kept me from bundling home, baby and all. Nothing but dear George could anchor me here.' The two statements were pathetically contradictory. Because of her dislike of England she would have bundled home:

because of her love for one Englishman, she would have remained. That she could even pose the alternatives, shows how
agonizing her dilemma was.

Curzon was everything that she had hoped for, and more.
Among the many tributes which she paid to him in her letters
home, none is more remarkable than her advice to her sister in
1898 when Nancy seemed on the verge of an engagement:

> Take time to make up your mind; for one quickly realises the reali-
> ties of life when married, and those quiet peaceful days in your lovely
> rooms at Dupont will be gone for ever. I always think that the sweet
> test of affection is if you feel that when he comes into a room the band
> is playing the Star Spangled Banner and that the room is glowing
> with pink lights and rills are running up and down your back with
> pure joy. Then it is all right, but don't give your heart away until you
> feel *all* this, which I feel when George appears.

Never in her letters did she say a word in criticism of him, except
of his working habits: 'He sits and sits at those Foreign Offices
boxes until I could scream! I feel he is working himself to death,
but he will do it.' It was his nature, his duty, and she would do
nothing to deter him. 'I hear on all sides', she wrote in another
letter, 'that Margot has hurt Asquith's career by making him so
lax in attending the House, and I don't want anyone to say that
marriage has hurt George.'

All the same, Curzon showed extraordinary obtuseness in
failing to notice that his habits were making his wife extremely
unhappy. There was nothing in his work that he wished to share
with her, as Asquith did with Margot. Before India, he never
talked politics with her, and when his friends came on political
business, he took them to another room. He deplored the intrusion of women into public life. 'The terrace of the House is as
crowded with women as the Royal Enclosure at Ascot', he had
written to Mary in 1893, 'and the encroachment of the sex fills
me with indignation which no blandishments can allay.'
Women's emancipation he described as 'the fashionable tom-
foolery of the day'. His wife was someone to cosset him, and for
him to cherish and amuse, when time allowed. He had a paternal

view of marriage: a wife was like a daughter, presumably busy with her feminine occupations, while he was busy with his. Of course there were occasions when Mary must appear with him publicly, and he was glad to be seen with her, and he knew that she was with him. These occasions were part of his duty, and hers. They were not primarily for fun, and he considered, if he gave the matter any thought at all, that she was probably as glad to avoid them as he was himself. In this he was mistaken.

In a memoir written in 1915 and never previously published, Elinor Glyn, who loved him and whom he loved, had this to say about Curzon's attitude to women:*

He has always been loved by women, but he has never allowed any individual woman to have the slightest influence upon his life – it is only collectively that they influence him. He likes their society for entirely leisure moments – they are of no real importance in his scheme of things. He likes them rather in the spirit in which other men like fine horses or good wine, or beautiful things to embellish a man's leisure, but not as equal souls worthy of being seriously considered or trusted with that scrupulous sense of honour with which he would deal with a man. They are on another planet altogether. . . .

He must be free and unhampered, and his apparent submission to this group of his friends is probably merely from habit, and because they know his ways and do not give him any trouble, and continually flatter him. His attitude to them is benevolent and affectionate; his language is filled with audacious sallies. He delights in startling them and playing upon their moods, but only so long as they do not bore him.

He is a most passionate physical lover, but so fastidious that no woman of the lower class has ever been able to attract him. Since his habit is never to study the real woman, but only to accept the superficial presentment of herself which she wishes him to receive, he is naturally attracted by Americans, who fulfil all that he requires of women: and even if he were to see how they use him for their own ends, it would only lazily entertain him as one more evidence of the nefarious way of this astonishing sex!

He could never love any woman with a supreme love – that love which gives body and soul to the loved one without thought but of

* The original manuscript is owned by Lady Alexandra Metcalfe.

worship. He could never allow any woman to interfere with him or influence his life, or the unconscious desire to express his own personality in doing his duty. The woman in his life would always have to have the place behind his. Thus he would load her with gifts and benefits, and with the most passionate devotion he would give her love, especially physical love, and spend time with the greatest unselfishness in thinking out schemes for her benefit. If she had sense enough never to express her own personality in opposition to his, and greatness enough never to realise his almost divine gifts, she would be happy.

But she would have to understand him, and only to take that broad splendid view of him which concerns itself with vast and noble aims. His pride would never forgive a woman who wounded it. No woman could have a real influence on him, and could only be either a solace, a servant or a slave, never a real Queen. He has probably never paid real homage to a woman in his life; it is women who pay homage to him. He is so physically attractive that he arouses passion even in the many friendships he holds casually, and it would be extremely difficult for any woman to keep her head or her senses unmoved, even in relations of pure friendship. A sensation of sex would be bound to creep in.

He never gives a woman a single command, and yet each one must be perfectly conscious that she must obey his slightest indication. He rules entirely, and when a woman belongs to him, he seems to prefer to give her even the raiment which touches her skin, and in every tangible way shows absolute possession, while in words avoiding all suggestion of ownership, all ties, and all obligations, upon either side. It is extremely curious.

This harsh judgment is all the more remarkable because it was not intended to be harsh. When Elinor Glyn wrote it, she and Curzon were deeply attached to each other. She revered him. Her memoir is titled 'Pen-portrait of a Great Man', and its concluding words are, 'He is Olympian, not Dionysiac. The noblest ruler since August Caesar elevated Rome.' Her assessment of his character was not that of a discarded and embittered lover, but of a constant companion who gloried in his treatment of her. One must read it, however, with certain reservations. It was the assessment of a mistress, not of a wife. Elinor Glyn, red-headed and green-eyed, was a novelist, and was in the habit of cutting her outlines sharp. She had never known Mary, and when she first knew Curzon he was middle-aged and had achieved a position in public life second only to Asquith and Lloyd George. Twenty years earlier he might have been a different man. Perhaps in her reference to American women there was an element of spite, for though Curzon would seldom speak of Mary after her death, his very silence showed how deeply he still felt her loss, and his actions and written record at the time confirm it. Elinor Glyn could have been jealous of that memory.

That apart, the Glyn memoir goes some way to explain Mary's unhappiness during these three years. She did not have the strength, nor the desire, to contest Curzon's will. Like Glyn she accepted her lot as a privilege. She would not admit even to herself that he could be inconsiderate. But between 1895 and 1898, he was. He failed to nourish her intelligence and love of the arts. He failed to notice her loneliness. He failed to help her with her difficult adaptation to English life. He failed to introduce her to new friends, or encourage her to make her own. All his endearments, all that totting-up of grocers' bills, all his concern for her when she was ill, did not compensate for his neglect of her other needs. Until India, where he himself was lonely, he did not discover how much she meant to him. In London he flirted with her, but never talked to her; treasured her, but never understood. He was too busy to take the trouble to find out what sort of person she was.

On Christmas Eve 1895 Mary and Curzon were alone at the Priory, and there was every symptom that her baby was about to be born prematurely, and might not live. The gynaecologist Sir John Williams was summoned from London, and a miscarriage was averted just in time. On the last day of the year Mary was moved to London, lying on a litter constructed inside a landau embowered with white roses, Curzon following in a phaeton behind, and with relays of horses the journey from Reigate was accomplished in 1½ hours. For the first time they occupied the

Balfour house, 4 Carlton Gardens, and it was there, on 20 January 1896, that their first child, a daughter, was born. They named her Irene, for peace.

Mrs Leiter had travelled to London for the event, and remained there six weeks. Mary's attitude to her mother had changed, first due to homesickness, then to the birth of her child, both of which reminded her how much she owed to this affectionate though volatile woman. Curzon too warmed to her, as men often do to their mothers-in-law during the crisis of a first birth, and by proxy to Mary's father too, telling her that he considered him 'the highest type of American – able, broad-minded, free from great prejudices, and the most distinguished type of man'. All was amity. To her sisters Mary wrote: 'George keeps me cheered up. He has a string of the most fantastic nicknames for me [it was then that he began to call her Kinkie, and she to call him Pappy, as they did for the rest of her life]. He is full of wild jokes, and he makes even little baby laugh.' Then she added: 'He wont hear of our entertaining at all this season, so that I shall have none of the strains that that entails. We are getting out of the gay world.' They were invited out so little, that she was able to make a single evening-dress do duty for a whole year.

She no longer minded much. All her attention was on the baby. Eyes as big as plates, her sweetest smile, her funny ways, are endlessly described. Once, in March, they went to Paris, where Curzon was stricken flat by his spinal trouble. In May they stayed with the Salisburys at Hatfield. It was their first week-end away, apart from Kedleston, since their marriage more than a year before. Their fellow-guests included the Prince and Princess of Wales, the Londonderrys, the Lansdownes, and the star of them all, Consuelo Vanderbilt, the newly, but unhappily, married Duchess of Marlborough. Mary knew herself to be outshone by her compatriot:

Everybody raves about Consuelo, and she is very sweet in her great position, and shyly takes her rank directly after royalty. She looks very stately in her marvellous jewels, and she looks pretty and had old lace which makes my mouth water. I never saw pearls the size of nuts. In a grand party like this, George and I have rather to tag along with the rank and file, but we are very happy and dont mind being small fry.

They were asked to Ascot, 'but G's work defeats all form of amusement', and dined once with Jenny Churchill, once with Sibell Grosvenor, and gave a single party themselves. That for Mary was the London season of 1896.

In the autumn they went to Scotland. The plan was that they should rent a lodge from the tiger-laird of Braemar, Farquharson of Invercauld, but when they reached it, they found the lodge poky, surrounded by turnips and beyond them by bleak moors, and moved to Inverlochy Castle, outside Fort William, a neo-Gothic granite house, with towers and turrets of different heights to simulate building over many centuries, and an interior solid and ostentatious, with romantic inglenooks and window embrasures from which they could watch ships passing in and out of the Caledonian Canal. Behind, Ben Nevis swept down to the back door. Lord Scarsdale joined them with his sons Frank and Alfred, and while the men fished, Mary grappled with a new race of servants. For six days Curzon was in bed with a hurt foot, working all the time. As Mary was kept in the house by rain for days on end, with only her in-laws for company, the visit was not a great success. To cheer themselves up, they went to the Highland Games, hired a pony and bicycled the roads, but Mary's spirits rose only with the arrival of her American friend G. W. Smalley, and then of her mother, accompanied by Nancy and Daisy. This was Mrs Leiter's fourth visit to Britain in the twenty months since Mary's marriage. She bustled around like a mother-hen worried about her chick.

She and Mary went later that autumn to Venice and Florence, and returned through Paris for a shopping-spree. 'People in Venice', she wrote to her father, 'dont grow old, for they have no worries or troubles. They drift about in gondolas and live in perpetual peace. I prefer less peace, and a life full of zeal.' What zeal was there in London? She returned to find the house dismal and servants departed without notice. Or at Kedleston, where they went for Christmas? The New Year was a little more fun. They

stayed for a long weekend with the Duke of Devonshire at Chatsworth, 'a kind of Arabian Nights splendour, a setting fit for an
English potentate', but Mary, echoing her husband, thought
such feudal grandeur out of place in modern England, the
Duchess disagreeable and (for some unstated reason) immoral.
Curzon's reaction was even more censorious: 'That fashionable
card-playing, race-going lot are an idle set, and their life is very
empty and vapid. Neither Mary nor I could have stood it for
more than a week.' So there was Chatsworth, and all places like
it, struck off their visiting list.

Kedleston, unfortunately, was not. Mary was summoned back
for another visit in mid-January. Lord Scarsdale had been
flattered to notice at Christmas that his grand-daughter's eyes
never left him. 'Intelligent child', he murmured, 'taken a fancy
to me', when her mother knew very well that Irene was only
staring with horrified fascination at the grimaces which passed in
rapid succession across Lord Scarsdale's face. This time he
decided to interrogate Mary about the United States. 'Do you
have sea-fish in America?' 'I suppose you don't know how to
make mince-pies where you come from?' 'I suppose you don't
know how to serve a good tea in America?' Mary, with some
courage, replied: 'Why don't you ask me if there are any civilized
or white people in America?'

She was not only bored, but unwell. She had recurrent headaches, which were to trouble her for the remainder of her life, and
these, added to Curzon's continuing unsociability, robbed her of
the vitality and pleasure that she craved. Her state of health and
mind at this period can be judged by the letter which she wrote to
her father from Chatsworth:

I hope to get fat some day, though I dont know quite how I am
going to do it, for I get thinner and thinner. I do very little. There are
things I cannot help doing, married as I am, but I do nothing that is
not absolutely necessary. I never rush about London seeing people and
exhibitions and concerts and theatres and charities and the hundred
things the world expects you to do. I wish I had the strength, for no
one would enjoy more than I the vast amount of interest and amusement that London affords. I do nothing outside my own house, and

only see people on a visit like this or if they come to the house. I quite realise that I shall never be able to take my place and be a help to George unless I get strong, for an ailing wife is no help to a politician. She must always be ready to be a kind of smiling hand-shaking machine.

She seldom visited the Southport constituency, and only once, when they went to Berlin in April, did she accompany Curzon on one of his missions abroad. They took the Reigate house again for a few months, and in the autumn went to Scotland, which fully restored her to health. Once more the Leiters came over to see her, but as usual their visit had only one lasting effect: 'When you all sail back, I shall realise that I have anchored my life away from you all.' On Christmas Day, from the Priory, she wrote: 'I have no news, for I am as quiet as a mouse and see no one at all and do nothing, as all my time is swallowed up by taking care of baby.' So that was the end of 1897, another dead year buried. It had been the year of Queen Victoria's Diamond Jubilee, when the whole of London was celebrating.

The next was very different. In 1898 Levi Leiter lost $10,000,000, and Curzon was appointed Viceroy of India.

Leiter's loss was due to the failure of his son Joseph to corner the wheat market in Chicago. Although this disaster may seem remote from Curzon's ambitions, it had a certain effect upon them, and the story, one of the great dramas in the commercial history of the United States, should be summarized as a preliminary to what follows.

Joseph Leiter was a clever, buoyant, likable man, who seemed to embody, more than his father, the intense restlessness of Chicago. Mary had written to Curzon at the time of their engagement: 'You will like Joe – he is the jewel of the family. He calls forth an affection from every sort of living thing.' He was a romantic. At one time he thought of buying up the Great Wall of China to save it from ruin. He was the first man to sail his own yacht round the world without crossing the Equator. He published a cook-book. In religion he was an Episcopalian, and in

8 Mary in 1890, when she first met George Curzon in London

9 Mrs Leiter, and her youngest daughter Daisy, in 1892

10 *Above* Levi Z. Leiter in older age, a
portrait by Alexandre Cabanel

11 *Right* The Blaine house, on Dupont
Circle, Washington, where the Leiters lived
from 1883 to 1893

12 Mary at the time of her marriage to George Curzon in 1895

13 Kedleston Hall, the Curzons' home near Derby

14 Mary and her mother in London in 1896, with her first daughter, Irene

politics, surprisingly, a Democrat. But his major interest was in business. Soon after he left Harvard, he assumed control of his father's Chicago properties, and proved so capable a manager that Leiter gave him $1,000,000 to engage in speculation on his own account, and he soon made a fortune, principally in mining and railway stocks.

In 1897, when he was only twenty-eight, he launched what the *Chicago Tribune* called 'probably the most gigantic and sensational attempted coup in the history of modern commerce'. His object was no less than to buy up all the wheat in America. By April 1897 he had 18 million bushels in store, with the promise of 22 million more. In the autumn he could have sold them at a profit of $4,000,000, but he hung on in the hope that the price would rise still higher. He had not reckoned with the ingenuity of his chief rival, Philip D. Armour, who moved in a further vast quantity of wheat from Canada by using ice-breakers to clear a passage through the great lakes, something never attempted before. Joseph bought that too, at a much higher price than his first consignment. His storage and insurance costs alone were now $4,450 a day. In the spring of 1898 a further 10 million bushels were added to Joseph's granary. In June the Department of Agriculture forecast a bumper crop that year, and the price of wheat immediately slumped. Joseph was left with 50 million bushels which he had bought or promised to buy at an average price of $1.45 a bushel, and could now sell for only 85c. His loss amounted to $9,750,000, which his father paid by selling or mortgaging part of his Chicago real-estate.

Mary followed these events with horror in the English newspapers. The publicity given to them was enormous. Joseph's manoeuvres were now affecting grain markets worldwide, and the effrontery of the young man had captured popular imagination. She was asked at a London party if it was true that her father had lost his entire fortune. She bitterly reproached her brother for his recklessness and the damage he had done to the family. Above all, she was appalled by the possibility that the link between them might harm Curzon's prospects, and that her father, who had promised him generous help, might not now be able to afford it. For it was at the very moment when Joseph's corner collapsed, in mid-June 1898, that Curzon heard that he was likely to be invited by Queen Victoria to go to India as her Viceroy.

It is necessary to return more than a year to explain how this remarkable honour came to be paid to a man aged only thirty-nine, who had occupied no senior office and was not even a peer. The short answer is that he asked for it and deserved it. Curzon had made a great reputation as the exponent of the Government's policy in the House of Commons. He was not universally liked in Parliament because his manner was considered either too terse or too ornate, and he made little attempt to conceal his contempt for the ignorance of his colleagues. One of them, T. P. O'Connor, referred to 'his little tricks of condescension, the almost John-sonian pomposity of his rhetoric . . . than which there is no quality which the House of Commons more seriously resents'. But nobody questioned his knowledge, his industry or his skill. Salisbury had made his task no easier by refusing to tell him the reasons for Cabinet decisions which Curzon had to defend in public, and the Prime Minister had an easy-going approach to foreign policy, once defining its purpose, 'to float lazily down-stream, occasionally putting out a diplomatic boat-hook to avoid collision'. Curzon's inclination was to greater belligerency, but loyally he kept to his brief. Salisbury was more than satisfied with his performance. 'He is a man', he wrote to the Queen, 'in many respects of great ability, as well as of extraordinary industry and knowledge. Lord Salisbury has had an opportunity of observing him already for two years and a half, and is of opinion that his character and powers have developed with official work.'

Curzon wanted the Viceroyalty more than any other office in the gift of the Crown. He felt himself uniquely qualified for it. He had visited India four times, and was on terms of personal friendship with India's powerful neighbour, the Amir of Afghan-istan. He had studied India's problems, internal and external, on the spot, travelled extensively in the region, written at enor-mous length about it, and as Under Secretary had come to know the workings of the India Office at home. If it were objected that he was too young, his reply was that the office was so exacting that it could benefit from a man in the prime of life. If the rejoinder was that his prime was weakened by ill-health, he answered that his energy had always triumphed over his disabilities, and always would. All these arguments he submitted to his chief in April 1897, when it was rumoured that the Marquess of Lorne, husband of Princess Louise, the Queen's fourth daughter, might be appointed to succeed Lord Elgin when his Viceregal term expired at the end of 1898. Lord Salisbury had replied evasively, but not unhopefully, and a year later Curzon renewed his application, claiming, 'I can truly say that my anxiety in the case arises from an honest and not ignoble desire to render some service to a cause which I have passionately at heart.'

His eagerness, added to his proved merit, was impressive. Lord Salisbury recommended his name to the Queen, and the Queen, who knew Curzon quite well, and had met Mary once at Windsor, approved. She had only one reservation. Would Curzon treat the Indians well? 'They must of course *feel* that we are masters', she wrote to Salisbury, 'but it should be done kindly and not offensively which alas! is so often the case. Would Mr Curzon feel and do this? Would Mrs Curzon, who is an American, do to represent a Vice Queen?' On both points Salisbury was able to reassure her.

Curzon told his wife of these negotiations, enjoining her to keep them secret. The first hint in her letters came on 7 June, when she asked her father if the 'von' Leiters had any known armorial bearings, and should she apply to the Consul in Amsterdam? Then towards the end of the month, when Joseph's financial crisis came to a head, she wrote:

George is going to be made Vice Roy of India as soon as the House of Commons rises. It cannot be known before, as G. will at once have to vacate his seat. . . . It takes my breath away, for it is the greatest position in the English world next to the Queen and the Prime Minister, and it will be a satisfaction, I know, to you and Mamma that your daughter Maria [sic] will fill the greatest place ever held by an American abroad. Heaven only knows how I shall do it, but I shall do my best to be a help to George and an honour to you and Mamma, and I shall put my trust in Providence and hope to learn how to be a ready-made Queen.

She added a few details. The appointment was for five years. They would probably leave for India in late November. They would need no servants, because 600 awaited them at Government House in Calcutta and 400 more at Viceregal Lodge in Simla. They would take Irene with them, and the new baby whose birth was expected at the end of August.

To Curzon she ended a letter: 'Goodbye my angel beloved Vice Roy. I feel very humble about my few qualifications to be Vice Reine, but I fear you can't change me now for a kind of Katie Thynne, and I shall have to do my best.' Lady Katherine Thynne, who married Lord Cromer in 1901, was a daughter of the Marquess of Bath, and represented to Mary everything that she found most elegant in English society, and everything that was most intimidating and false. Katie was also a friend of the youthful Virginia Woolf, who shared Mary's reservations about her. It was the only point where their two lives touched, and perhaps the only opinion which they held in common.

The announcement was made on 11 August, and both Curzons found themselves the talk and idols of the town. From that moment until their departure, their preparations were on a scale of an ocean liner fitting out for a maiden voyage. Mary must go to Paris to order from Worth a trousseau worthy of an empress, and a seamstress lodged for two months at the Priory cutting and sewing a bale of simpler cloths. Curzon must have a thorough medical check, from which he emerged clear of all organic disease, and with the hope that his spinal pains might actually ease with time, provided that he did not work too hard. Then there was the Freedom of the City of London, a Court ball at Buckingham Palace, and dinners at Oxford and at Southport. 'We begin to be treated like grandees', wrote Mary. 'Station-masters always meet us, carriages are reserved, and low bows and crowds staring.' It was nothing to what was to come.

All these festivities coincided with the last stages of her pregnancy. The baby was born on 28 August, another girl. They

toyed with Indian names for her – Monyabai, Gyanadai, Chima-
bai – thought any of them too much for the poor child to bear in
later life, and christened her Cynthia Blanche. Curzon of course
engaged the nurse. In a letter extending to nine pages, he
described his interview with one of the applicants:

> She is not the least like her photographs . . . is ladylike, yet not quite
> a lady; neatly dressed, shows acres of gum and files of artificial teeth;
> has a rather curious way of rolling her lips when she speaks and an
> utterance very clear and precise and sometimes almost mincing in its
> accuracy. She is not in the least like a nurse, but exactly like an
> indigent lady placed in charge of children with a scientific and
> practical knowledge in which indigent persons are usually deficient.
> . . . Having put her through half-an-hour's questioning, I then asked
> her if she wanted to ask anything of me. She replied by the following
> rather extraordinary question: might she take out a bicycle with her?
> I said I would enquire, but thought that if the roads permitted it, there
> would be no objection to her taking exercise in that way. . . .

Lying in bed after her confinement, Mary studied the history
and geography of India, while Curzon was received at Balmoral
by the Queen, who requested him to read aloud a telegram just
received from Kitchener. It was the news of Omdurman. She
created Curzon a peer. He was never to hold the name of
Scarsdale, except as a subsidiary title. He was to be Baron (later
Marquess) Curzon of Kedleston, in the Peerage of Ireland, a
constitutional device which would enable him to re-enter the
House of Commons on his return from India if he wished. Mary
was too honest a woman to conceal from her family the pleasure
which her new title gave her: 'Oh the ladyships! I feel like a ship
in full sail on the high seas of dignity.'

In November the Queen invited Lord and Lady Curzon to
Windsor. Mary was distressed and disfigured by an inflammation
of the eye, and found the first dinner an ordeal, for nobody spoke
above a whisper, and all covered their awkwardness by jabbing
unpleasantly at their food. When the Queen sent for her afterwards, she shrank with nervousness. The Queen was kind. 'Let
me have a good look at you', she said, putting on outsize spec-
tacles. 'She asked me about my eye and my troubles with

wetnurses, also spoke about Indian native women, and about Khartoum and the Sirdar. She was very animated, and said, "When you have another child, you must call it after me"', an instruction which Mary, thinking one Victoria enough in the family, firmly disregarded when the time came. Next day she was summoned again. The Queen gave her an Indian order of diamonds, turquoises and pearls, and asked her to write to her from India. When Curzon joined them, she congratulated him: 'Your wife is both beautiful and wise.' Nothing was said about America, and of course nothing about Joe. But the Queen, whose memory had not dimmed with years, must have reflected that this lovely girl with the poor eye was about to occupy the highest position which any American had held in the British Empire. Lord Wellesley, in the early part of the century, had married an American, Mary Caton, widow of Robert Patterson of Baltimore, but the marriage took place twenty years after the expiration of his term as Governor General of India in 1805.

There were financial problems to settle. The Viceroyalty cost its incumbent so much money that nobody had been able to accept it without a private fortune of his own. Curzon had none. His personal resources were no more than the £1,000 which his father allowed him annually, and the income from his marriage settlement which now averaged £3,500 a year. The only money which Mary owned personally was $5,000, of which she received the interest. The Viceregal salary was £25,000, but all of it went on maintaining the huge staffs at Calcutta and Simla. Without further help from Levi Leiter, Curzon could not meet even the initial expenses of his office, and Leiter was himself in financial trouble owing to Joe's miscalculations. Mary's embarrassed appeal could not have come at a worse moment, but help was essential. The Curzons discovered that they were required not only to buy from the outgoing Viceroy all his plate, horses, carriages and the contents of his wine cellar, but to pay their own fares and freight for the voyage out. All this came to £9,717, to which the Government made only a minimal contribution. In addition, Mary's trousseau from Paris had cost well over £1,000, and Curzon must have a variety of uniforms and Mary some jewels. Leiter did his best, but all he could manage at the moment was £3,000, and he gave Mary a tiara. Part of the balance they had to raise immediately on arrival in India by the humiliating expedient of requesting an advance on the Viceregal salary.

In these circumstances it seems extraordinary that Curzon should have saddled himself and his father-in-law with another, and quite unnecessary, burden. He took a twenty-five year lease of 1 Carlton House Terrace at the very moment when he was about to go abroad for at least five years. It cost £25,000, and a further £2,500 to put the house in good repair. He could only raise the money by a bank loan, which Leiter guaranteed and on which he paid the interest, and the loan was slowly reduced by the annual rent of £2,000 which Curzon received from his sub-tenant, a Mr Choate. His motives can only have been to snatch up a bargain, as he thought it, and to provide Mary with a home when she returned to London on holiday, and himself with a splendid setting for the next stage of his career after India.

Their preparations were complete. It only remained to say goodbye. They went to Southport for a huge reception at which Mary had to stand for hours 'wearing my india-rubber smile'. They stayed with the Duke of Portland at Welbeck Abbey for a gala ball, and with Lord Cowper at Panshanger, where Mary's old friends of the Souls surfaced to wish her well – the Ribblesdales, the Brodricks, the Grenfells and Arthur Balfour. Several of them were also guests at the final farewell dinner held at the Hotel Cecil on 9 December, the night she left London. Consuelo Marlborough, Jenny Churchill and a score of Englishwomen joined their husbands to do honour to the young woman whom for three years they had all but ignored.

John Hay, the American Ambassador in London who was about to leave for Washington to take up his appointment as Secretary of State, wrote to her:

No Vicereine has ever gone to India with so full an equipment of knowledge and capacity. No Vicereine with such resources of radiance and charm. Poets are prophets, after all, and the word of Rudyard Kipling at his first sight of you in my house in Washington has come true.

She couldn't remember exactly what Kipling had said, but was the rest of it true? Did she have that knowledge and capacity? A new life, unlike anything she had ever known, now opened before her, a life in which she would be a proxy-Queen, the cynosure not just of a thousand eyes, but of hundreds of millions, eyes even stranger and more observant than the eyes of Southport people, perhaps more hostile. Her youth had in a sense prepared her for this, but not the first years of her marriage. Hitherto she had had almost no position as Curzon's wife, no role. Now suddenly she had the greatest role of any English-woman but one, and she was not even English.

Her father had come to spend a week with her in November. He was in a quiet, gentle, worried mood. They had scarcely mentioned Joe, but she could see that he blamed himself for what had happened. He could have stopped him in time, but wanted him to win his spurs, he said, and after all, Joe had made a success of everything else he had touched.

About her own future, he said that she must learn all she could about India. The only way to survive was to become interested. It was no use acting like a queen when one wasn't by training a queen. People would be waiting for her to trip up, especially the wives of British civil servants and officers, who would be quick to say that any mistakes she made were due to her nationality, when with a young Englishwoman they would attribute it more generously to her inexperience.

If she could reach out and beyond them to touch the hearts of the Indians, she would be setting the British an example they badly needed, helping Curzon in the best way she could, and creating for herself a role greater and certainly more interesting than that of the semi-divine being which she would otherwise appear to be. There was no need for her to change her character or manner. A durbar was nothing more than a bigger party, an elephant a bigger horse, and there would be many people to manage both for her. She would find, he said, that nobody would act quite naturally with her; but she must try to be natural with them, remember their names, get them to talk about the things they knew best, since everyone enjoys being asked questions to which they know the answers. In this way she would simultaneously give pleasure and acquire much needed information.

Mary was convinced that he was right. Afterwards she must have wished that she had talked to him more about being the first American Vicereine. She had no strong views about Empire, but people might assume that as an American she disapproved of it, particularly as a young American. She must never give them cause to think that she was taking sides, but if, as he said, she made an effort to know the Indian people, might that not be interpreted by the British as anti-imperialist? There was not only a whole new code of snobbishness to learn, but an even subtler code of race relations, in her case tripled. The truth was that she still felt more American than British. As soon as she had become fairly used to being Mrs Curzon, she was jumped up into Her Excellency, Lady Curzon of Kedleston, Vicereine, another vast step away from being Miss Leiter. She could not help missing her family more and more, and now they would be 10,000 instead of 3,000 miles away, for five years! Unless she made a great effort, her homesickness would show and the British wives would sneer. She would have no real friend – how could a Vicereine have friends unless she imported them? – and Curzon would work and work and work.

As her mind ran on, she knew with half of it that nothing is so bad or good as you expect. The important people were on her side. Other, not specially talented, women had done this job and survived. It was not as if the Vicereine was expected to govern India. Why, she thought, why had she become so difficult to please? Six months ago she was unhappy because too few people paid any attention to her. Now she was unhappy because too many people did. As a girl the idea of becoming Vicereine of India would have seemed incredible, wonderful. Now that she actually was, she was scared. She reminded herself of her Washington resolution: discreet but not dull. It hadn't exactly worked out in London. But in India it could. It must.

She was on her way. Immediately after the farewell party at the Cecil Hotel, she rushed home to change, and from there went to the station to catch the midnight train to Plymouth. Next morning, 10 December 1898, she embarked on *S.S. Arabia*, to find her babies fast asleep in their bunks. With their nanny, they had come round by sea from the Port of London the day before. Curzon was to catch up with them at Marseilles.

FOUR

CALCUTTA

THE voyage to India took three weeks. Gales in the Bay of Biscay were followed by gales in the Gulf of Lyons, and for Mary life on board the *Arabia* alternated between the courtly concern of the Captain and ADCs, and wails of complaint from her babies and Cynthia's wet-nurse, an immense peasant girl from Normandy who had the face of a Madonna but could neither read nor write. On Christmas Day, when they were steaming through the Red Sea, Mary performed her first Viceregal function, to give each girl on board a doll as a present from the P & O, and a tin soldier to each boy. Next day they landed at Aden, the first outpost of their empire, in a State barge rowed by eight negroes stifled by their red liveries, and lunched with the British Resident. Then followed the long stage across the Indian Ocean to Bombay, which they reached on 30 December 1898.

At Bombay Mary realized for the first time the extraordinary distinction and isolation of the position which she and Curzon were to occupy. 'We might as well be Monarchs', she wrote home. The 'Vice' was forgotten. They went ashore from the *Arabia* to a landing-stage which was carpeted in crimson cloth, and after speeches of welcome, drove seven miles to the Governor's house through packed streets lined by soldiers, while at intervals bands played God Save the Queen. Above their heads was held the Golden Umbrella, one of India's most ancient and venerated symbols of royalty. In the evening there was another State drive through the streets, followed by a dinner for a hundred people and a reception for 1,400 more, at which the Curzons stood on a gold carpet while the guests filed past, bowing but not speaking. All this Mary accepted with serene pleasure. She seemed not to mind being stared at, was never at a loss for the right word or gesture, and knew instinctively when to allow her husband to take precedence and when to advance ahead of him, a matter of complicated protocol any breach of which would have been instantly noted by an entourage who attached enormous importance to it. There are many newspaper accounts of their arrival in Bombay, and all give as much space to the Vicereine as to the Viceroy. She was the object of intense curiosity, equally to the Indians and the British. The description of her in the *Advocate of India* is typical:

A tall stately woman with blue eyes, masses of dark hair, and a face that could only be described as a picture. Her self-possession of manner was as evident as her beauty, and during the half-hour that the proceedings [at the landing-stage] lasted, she was pre-eminently the most self-possessed individual under the white and yellow stripes of the manlap. As she leaned with crossed hands on the twisted silver handle of a parasol that matched her dress one could detect no suggestion of nervousness in a single twitch of her fingers.

The crowds were quick to notice other things: the vitality of the Viceregal pair, their evident pleasure in being married to each other, their readiness to smile, Curzon's splendid choice of words in responding to the addresses of welcome. Their two young faces promised a vigorous and beneficent rule. A happy omen doubled the cheers: two calf-cows broke away from their owner to lead the evening cavalcade. That the Vicereine was an American did not pass unacknowledged – the Stars and Stripes alternated with the Union Jack in the street decorations – and Mary's exhilaration at the sight of it responded to the crowd's. She bowed and waved with unforced delight.

Next day they drove in state to the railway station, and strode red carpets to the Viceregal train, newly painted white. There were guards of honour at all the principal stations en route, and on arriving at Calcutta (the capital of the Indian Empire until it was transferred to Delhi in 1912) the ceremony of welcome exceeded Bombay's. They were escorted to Government House by a squadron of cavalry, a company of infantry, and the Viceroy's Bodyguard, 120 strong, each man carrying a pennanted lance. 100,000 Indians lined the route. The wide central steps of Government House, used only for the arrival and departure of the Viceroy or visitors of great eminence, were swathed in red carpet, and they mounted them between ranks of motionless soldiers to be greeted at the top by Lord and Lady Elgin, three Maharajahs and their suites, and senior British officials dressed in the most splendid uniforms to which their rank entitled them. In the distance the cannon of Fort William boomed a metronomic salute.

For the first few days the Curzons were guests of the Elgins, Curzon concealing his impatience to be rid of them. Elgin had been a barely adequate Viceroy, unambitious and uncertain in his policy, socially ill at ease, shy and silent. When on his return home he resumed his seat on the council of his native Scottish town, it was said that he should never have left it. Curzon arrived full of energy, determined to leave a mark on India which would change it unrecognizably and unalterably. But too hasty a transition would diminish the glory of the office. A Viceroy must not replace his predecessor, but succeed him. The formality of departure must equal the formality of arrival. The Elgins withdrew gradually, from the private rooms to the state rooms, from there to the ceremonial steps, and Curzon drove with them to the ship that took them from Calcutta back to England. Only when they were gone, did Mary dare explore the palace that was her inheritance.

Government House, Calcutta, had been built a century earlier by Viscount Wellesley. By a curious chance, his architect, Captain Charles Wyatt, an officer of the engineers, modelled it on Kedleston, or on drawings of it in architectural books of the period. Although the plan of the two houses was basically the same – a central pile linked by curving wings to symmetrical buildings at the corners, with a dome behind – the Calcutta house made a first impression quite different from Kedleston's. It was larger, and at the same time meaner.

Kedleston was built of stone; Government House of painted brick. Kedleston was grey and horizontal, placid and warm; Government House rose white and cliff-like, its curving wings extending to four buildings instead of two, to three storeys instead of one, and it had too many windows, like a face with too many teeth, resembling a government office more than a private house. Inside, the copy of Kedleston's marble hall was trivialized by too low a ceiling (a ballroom had to be fitted in above), and by columns of stuccoed brick instead of alabaster. It led to a throne-room in place of Kedleston's circular saloon, and no use was made internally of the dome, which was closed by a ceiling and became a storage place for trunks. Nor was there any decoration or furnishing comparable to Adam's exquisite fili-gree. The walls were hung with huge portraits of royalty and viceroyalty, the furniture was heavy and early-Victorian, and, as was natural in a house where the tenants were so transient, no personal ornaments mitigated the severity of the rooms. For large parties desperate attempts were made by the staff to impart an air of informality by setting around them wholly inappropriate objects, like a photograph of the Curzon babies which Mary discovered just in time to snatch it away from under Devis's great portrait of Warren Hastings.

The awkwardness of the house soon became apparent. At Kedleston the Scarsdales occupied the central block only, and the terminal buildings were used for kitchens and servants' quarters. At Calcutta the main rooms were used only for big parties and ceremonial occasions, and while one of the wings contained the Council chamber with its attendant offices and another was allotted to the Viceroy's guests, the other two, separated by the whole width of the staterooms, were the two halves of the Viceroy's personal apartments. Mary's bedroom, she told her parents, 'is so big that you can just see from one end to the other. Half of it is curtained off to make a sitting-room. Dressing in the evening with smoking candles is very difficult ... I never knew a more inconvenient house than this. The dis-tances are perfectly awful between my room in one wing and the children's in another. To get to them I have to go along my corridor through an immense drawing-room, across a ballroom of several acres, through another huge drawing-room, down another corridor, eventually to their day nursery.' The kitchen was not even within the house: it lay 200 yards away from the nearest corner, in a Calcutta back-street, and every dish had to be carried across the garden in wooden boxes. This same garden housed a menagerie of noxious animals. Flying foxes flung themselves from tree to tree, and at night jackals emerged from the drains to howl in the shrubberies, while stinking civet cats would climb to the eaves and sometimes enter bedroom windows. Mary once woke to find one, five foot long, drinking the glass of milk at her bedside.

Of course Curzon made changes. He shot the jackals and the cats. In his first year he installed electric light and fans, and made for Mary a sitting-room, and for the children a nursery, in a single wing. But he did not move the kitchen, and it was not until his last year as Viceroy, 1905, that Government House had a single bathroom with running taps. The enormous staff of servants, and the smooth organization of their work by highly trained majordomos, did something to compensate for the inconveniences. If Mary wanted a bath, one man heated the water, another fetched her tub, a third filled it, a fourth emptied it, each of a caste corresponding to the degree of humiliation the job entailed. At dinner-parties, whether there were six guests or 120, a footman stood behind each chair. When Wellesley was criticized by the East India Company for the extravagance of his building and its establishment, he said to Lord Valentia, 'I wish India to be ruled from a palace, not from a counting house; with the ideas of a Prince, not with those of a retail dealer in indigo.' It was a sentiment that exactly coincided with Curzon's own.

He believed that the Viceroyalty should reflect the dignity and self-assurance which the people expected from their own princes. He wrote in *British Government in India*:

From the days when the East India Company acquired the Government of India and appointed a Governor General, the incumbent

of that high office has always been expected to maintain a considerable degree of state, to follow a very strict ceremonial observance, and
to entertain on a lavish scale. Such a practice was not only in exact
harmony with Indian tradition, which associated sovereignty with
splendour, but it was also demanded by the British population of
Bengal, who expected the head of the Government and the representative of their own Monarch, to deal with the native Rajahs and nobles
and also with themselves on a footing not merely of equality, but of
vantage.

Many Governors General and Viceroys of the past had taken a
different view, some because the Company or the Government
urged them to economize, some because they felt it outrageous
to live like Akhbar when millions of their subjects were starving,
and some because they were by nature simple men or shy. The
occupants of Government House, as of the White House, had
been alternately lavish and modest in their hospitality. To one it
was a court on the scale of Louis xiv's; to the next a place primarily for work. Lord Elgin had been one of the latter. A contemporary press report said that he 'could scarcely disguise the
weariness with which he received on State occasions the formal
marks of homage'. Curzon was not quite the Roi Soleil whom
Lord Hastings, among others, had aped, but he enjoyed ceremony, and insisted that it should be done with a magnificence
that fitted his opportunity, character and role. Ceremonial and
entertainment, at that level, are complementary. A State dinner
was all the more enjoyable just because it was slightly alarming,
just because the presence of one man and one woman so far
removed above the guests exacted from them a traditional
deference that gave every function, at least in part, the character
of a charade.

Curzon was sometimes accused of inflating his own importance
by the scale and drama of his entertainments, and he retorted
that as he had no private fortune of his own, lavishness was not a
charge that could be brought against him, and that his parties
were no grander than those given by many of his predecessors
and successors, but they were better organized. They reflected
his conception of the Imperial role. His account in *British*

Government in India of the reception of a Rajah at Government House shows how splendidly his imagination and language responded to a great occasion, how architecture, robes, sound and silence, the dignity of the principals, the immobility of the acolytes, combined to reaffirm the permanence and nobility of their relationships:

The Viceroy looked down the long vista of the Marble Hall with its gleaming white pillars, absolutely empty save for the Body Guard in their magnificent uniforms, standing like statues on either side. In the distance could be heard the music of the band playing upon the great exterior staircase. An intense silence prevailed, broken at length by the crunch of wheels on the gravel and the horse-hoofs of the Body Guard, as they escorted the carriage containing the Prince to the foot of the steps. At that moment thundered out the guns from the distant Fort, giving the Chief his due salute. . . . Not until the total was completed did the procession attempt to move forward. Then he would be seen to advance along the crimson carpet laid outside and to enter the Marble Hall in all his panoply of brocades and jewels, the Foreign Secretary leading him by the hand. As they approached at a slow pace along the polished floor, not a sound was heard but the clank-clank of the scabbards on the marble. At the stated distances the Prince, who was followed by his retinue, gave the stipulated bows. He then entered the Throne Room, where the Viceroy, according to the rank of the visitor, either descended from the steps of the Throne to greet him or awaited him on the dais.

Only three months of the year, from December till February, were spent by the Viceroy at Calcutta, the remainder at Simla or on tour. But during those three months he was expected to give a State evening party, a garden party, a fortnightly dance, two Levées for men only, a Drawing Room for ladies, official dinners of up to 120 people every Thursday, and smaller lunches and dinners several times a week. Sometimes he and the Vicereine dined out with important dignitaries of church and state. Mary's attendance at all these functions was obligatory, except for the Levées, which she watched from behind a screen. One early experience illustrates the anguish that they often caused her:

Yesterday I had one of my headaches, but in spite of it I went to a party on board the Admiral's ship. George also, and I smiled when I could have sobbed with pain. When I came back I had to be carried upstairs, and the doctor thought I was mad to go out to the Lt. Governor's to dine, but a dinner of 70 had been arranged for us and I could not give out. I nearly fainted twice dressing, and nothing but my will carried me through. I was carried to the carriage and had to drive 3½ miles to the house. I thought at times that I should die, as when I arrived I had to shake hands with 70 people and talk all through dinner, and afterwards I had to talk with each lady. The only thing I ate was a water-biscuit and a teaspoonful of brandy. I collapsed in a heap in the carriage on our way home. Our doctor met me at the door and I was carried up to bed.

Being the centre of attention, she could not relax for an instant, and everyone was terrified of her. Every man was employed by her husband; every woman was the wife or daughter of a member of his staff. They did not know what else to say when they had discussed the weather and asked after her children, and left all the conversational openings to her. Protocol and precedence were so strict that her neighbour at dinner might be the same man night after night. It was tolerable at Drawing Rooms, when the ladies simply filed past and curtseyed, but on all other occasions the ADCs were instructed to bring up suitable people at intervals of three minutes to the Viceroy and Vicereine, who sat in great chairs on a dais; or Mary was required to walk round the room in one direction, while Curzon circulated in the other, and talk to each guest in turn. Curzon described one encounter which must have been typical of many: 'Mrs Cameron was so nervous that her blushes came right through her powder, while she made a series of dips and curtseys and undulations that threatened at any moment to land her on her back.' Friendship was difficult, intimacy out of the question. It had been said of a previous Viceroy, Lord Canning, that after the death of his wife, his only companion in Calcutta was a mouse that played with him on his bedroom floor. There were visitors from abroad, who might have afforded the Viceroy and Vicereine some relief, but rarely did, as most were tourists with whom they had little in common. Quite soon after her arrival Mary began to receive appeals for hospitality from Americans whom she had met perhaps once in her life, at Washington or Chicago, and who considered it would give her the utmost pleasure to talk to someone from 'home'; while English loafers of both sexes treated Government House as a free hotel, helping themselves from the cigar-boxes and even stealing the stationery as mementoes of their unwanted intrusion.

Mary managed to conceal the strain so successfully that few people were aware of what she suffered. Compliments showered on her. *La Vie Parisienne*, an unlikely source of information, described her as 'tall, slim, infinitely gracious and beautiful, dressed with a patrician elegance, superb shoulders, thick hair faintly gilded, and magnificent eyes'. But the young Winston Churchill, staying with them in this same month (February 1899) while he was writing his book *The River War*, saw her differently:

'I have come here for a week and am staying with the Curzons', he wrote to Lady Randolph. 'Everything is very pleasant and I have found him very delightful to talk to. His manner is wonderful. All the aggressiveness which irritated me at home is gone. They have both won everybody's heart. But I fear he works too hard – nearly eleven hours every single day. So his secretary tells me. And you would be shocked to see how Lady C. is changed. She has had a sharp attack of fever and will not, I think, stand the climate which will spoil the whole thing.'

It was not the climate which much worried Mary, except when she was on tour in the intense heat. She often found it more tolerable than London's. Nor did she or Curzon ever succumb to any of the tropical diseases from which one of her predecessors, Lady Canning, had died. They were well protected by the best medical attention, but each had brought to India a weakness which the climate did nothing to assist, Mary the recurrent headaches which had started soon after the birth of her first child, and Curzon the pain in his back and legs which was aggravated by the need to stand upright at functions for hours on end.

The strain on Mary was primarily social, the obligation to appear always at her best. That she succeeded in this was her first achievement as Vicereine. The natural tendency of courtiers and journalists was to flatter her, and many of their tributes might be discounted were it not for their mounting unanimity and enthusiasm. They were expected to say of a Vicereine that she was beautiful, dignified and gracious; but they need not say repeatedly, as they said of Mary, that she was kind, simple and full of fun, unless she gave constant evidence of it. She was regarded as Curzon's perfect partner, more approachable, more tender, fulfilling the public role which a woman can and a man cannot, just as Queen Elizabeth covered up the shyness and softened the asperity of George VI. To give one instance: at a children's party at Government House a small boy found himself in trouble with his collar, and instead of running to his mother, or to any of the other women standing by, he went instinctively to Mary, who fixed it for him with a laugh. Such small incidents were noted and widely recounted, and cumulatively they gained for her a reputation for warm-heartedness which did nothing to diminish the more regal qualities expected of her. No other woman in India considered that she would make a better Vicereine, and Mary aroused little jealousy. She had the rare ability to enter a room without pride or ungainliness when all eyes turned on her, the ability to dispel awkwardness by first approaching the one person who would respond in kind, to give a thousand people simultaneously the feeling that they were personally welcome, the capacity, in short, to charm a crowd, a queenly capacity. It is an art, not the result of training, but innate, not a matter of imitation but of a natural delight in performing a difficult duty well.

Her attitude was nonetheless guarded. It was the universal expectation that a Vicereine should be slightly mysterious, and she was. The *Chicago Tribune* put it well in its obituary of her: 'It was remarked that she had none of the aggressive self-confidence which, rightly or wrongly, is usually attributed to ambitious American girls, but she attracted by reserve and a thoughtful, studious manner and an engaging sympathy.' 'Engaging sympathy' was Mary's central quality as Vicereine. Curzon once wrote to her from Simla: 'You are the most humble, the most unspoiled creature in the world. I have never detected in you a ray of vanity, and it is your sublime unconsciousness of all that is most remarkable in you that is one of your incomparable charms.' She conveyed the feeling that she would rather occupy her elevated position than any other the world could offer, that her pleasure in it was due partly to the fact that it was also her duty, and that she hoped that her example would help other women forget the trials and tedium of their common exile. The compensations were enormous, the opportunities as vast as the responsibilities. She was uncomplaining, adventurous, grand without pomposity, sympathetically dominant, a wife primarily, but a woman who could make her own contribution. When she visited Calcutta schools and hospitals, as she did frequently on her own initiative, she elevated a role into a mission. She dignified a task and made it seem enjoyable. She led the women, and entranced the men. She brought to India a glamour which outsiders assumed had always existed there, but which she did much to create. She drew on a tradition and made it live.

The Viceroy and his wife must have some relief from the heat and constant scrutiny of Calcutta, and they had two places of refuge, Barrackpore and Simla. Barrackpore was a large country house fifteen miles up the Hugli river from Calcutta. The grounds had been laid out by Lord Wellesley in the manner of an English park, with a menagerie in one corner, but the great mansion he planned was never completed. The present house was his 'temporary bungalow' enlarged by Lord Hastings (1813–23) to form the Governor General's summer residence before the court moved regularly to Simla from 1864 onwards. Curzon used it as a weekend retreat 'from the ceaseless persecution of official routine', and Mary was often there for longer periods with her children. It was an imposing house with colonnaded verandahs, though poorly furnished and lacking electricity. The riverside garden was beautiful, containing a Gothic 'ruin', a mock-Georgian church, bamboo pergolas and a golf-course. The Curzons always made the short journey there by steam-launch, 'to land by the glimmering tomb of Lady Canning', Curzon wrote, 'and to walk up the gravelled terrace to the house, the hand-borne lanterns twinkling in the darkness ahead'. They loved Barrackpore. In the cool weather they lunched under the huge banyan tree, a natural tent, and kites swooped down to take their share of the meal as the servants carried the dishes to and fro. Of course the Viceregal state was still considerable. A large part of the staff moved there with them, and when the children drove round the park, it was in a landau with three nurses, two coachmen and two footmen. When the Curzons drove, it was in a barouche escorted by sixteen postillions and outriders dressed in scarlet liveries with the Viceregal monogram stitched on them in gold.

Simla, like Barrackpore, was an entirely British creation. In 1819 there was nothing there but a thatched cottage in the midst of virgin forest, and it was not till 1829 that the Viceroy, Lord Amherst, began to spend a few summers at Simla to escape the heat of the plains. Later Viceroys followed his example, but intermittently, and it was left to Sir John Lawrence, in 1864, to convert what had become an occasional habit into an annual routine, taking with him his staff and Council for the months between March and November. A town grew up among the rising hills, a town which attempted to reproduce the domestic felicities of Surrey under the shadow of the Himalayas, with a Gothic church, assembly halls, a theatre, hotels, a race-course, and villas of architectural pretensions which mounted with the rank of their occupants. The disadvantages were that Simla could only be approached by a difficult sixty-mile drive up steep hills from the railway terminus, and that although the residents escaped great heat, the climate was unpleasant in other ways, cold until April, dusty in May, and then monsoon-drenched until September. Simla society was composed of annual migrants, members of the Secretariat, officers on leave, women who had left their husbands toiling in the plains, and they re-

garded Simla much as Regency London regarded Brighton, as a
place for amusement, flirtation and display, both masculine and
feminine. In *Plain Tales from the Hills* Kipling lampooned a
typical Simlaite, Ahasuerus Jenkins, an unambitious soldier
with a pleasant singing voice:

> *He took two months at Simla when the year was at the spring,*
> *And underneath the deodars eternally did sing.*
> *He warbled like a bul-bul, but particularly at*
> *Cornelia Aggripina, who was musical and fat.*

The centre of this society was Viceregal Lodge. It had been
built by the Dufferins only ten years before the Curzons reached
India, and was a monumental neo-Elizabethan pile encrusted
with towers and cupolas of stone, which reminded one visitor,
Edwin Montagu, of a Scottish hydro, 'with the same sort of
appearance, the same sort of architecture, the same sort of
equipment of tennis-lawns and sticky courts, and so forth.
Inside it is comfortable, with suites of apartments comparable
to those of the Carlton or the Ritz.' When Mary first saw it, in
March 1899, she laughed:

You never saw a quainter spot, [she wrote to Curzon, who was still
in Calcutta], the house slipping off the hills and clinging like barnacles
to the hill-tops – and then our house! I kept trying not to be disappointed. At first you only see the ugly side. Every rich male in America
builds *exactly* such a house. The inside is nothing fine, but nice, and oh!
Lincrusta you will turn us grey! It looks at you with pomegranate
and pineapple eyes from every wall. Dead-beat as I was, I tore round
the ground floor with Irene, and I missed the dining-room but thought
the ballroom was certainly what it intended to be, and the sitting-
room nice. . . . There are plenty of little guest-rooms, tiny bedrooms
with drawing-rooms out, and the plan of the house is in many ways
absurd, and everything suggests cheapness and lack of space and air
but you cant have palaces on mountain-tops, and a Minneapolis
millionaire would revel in this, and we shall love it and make up our
minds not to be fastidious. The fireplaces, corner-cabinets, papers,
curtains and furniture reek of Maples, but a look out of the window
makes up for it all, and I can live on views for five years.

'Bright brown' had been Lady Dufferin's choice for the interior decoration. 'Think of choosing brown for rooms', wailed Mary, 'when the world contains such noble colours as crimson, green or blue.' Of course they gradually made changes. But they could not change Simla's atmosphere of social frivolity and petty scandal. Curzon hated it. 'One of its loathsome features,' he wrote to Mary after three summers there, 'is its sinister novelty, always having to begin again with each year a new set of idlers, gossips and liars. I do not think there is a more pitiable position in the world than that of the Viceroy and his wife set down for 7 months amid that howling gang of jackals.' There were two places where they could find temporary refuge, Mashobra, a charming gabled weekend house with a pretty garden, and Naldera, a tented camp seventeen miles from Simla, where Curzon could eat and work out of doors under the great deodar trees and the children could play. But duty always recalled them to Simla, where they were expected to entertain on a scale only a little less lavish than Calcutta's, and to attend many more outside functions, like polo-matches, races, concerts, amateur theatricals, prize-givings and weddings. As the routine did not vary from year to year, one example can be lifted from a newspaper report of 1902 to illustrate innumerable other such occasions. It was a garden-party at Viceregal Lodge, at which Mary received the guests for a whole hour, each name announced by an ADC:

The Viceroy's band, which had been playing bright music, ceased its performance, and the reception of Lady Curzon came to a sudden end, the people stopped walking and talking, the generous refreshment tents were hurriedly deserted, a curious hush came over the assemblage, and all eyes were turned in one direction. Then the band struck up God Save the King, and up walked Lord Curzon in frock-coat and top-hat, preceded by a single aide-de-camp in uniform. The men bared their heads in the sun and made an avenue, through which the Viceroy, leaning unwontedly on a stout stick, but otherwise looking well and active, walked to a large shamiana and sat down with Lady Rivaz. Then the band returned to its ordinary promenade music, the people resumed their walking and talking, the refreshment tents regained their crowds, cheerful conversation resumed its buzz, and presently Lady Curzon moved out to converse pleasantly with friends. When the sun had sunk low in the clear heavens, the Viceroy and Lady Curzon left the grounds together, and thereafter the festive crowd dispersed.

And so on, day after day. Night was no solace, because Curzon's insomnia was increased by the Simla climate, and the dawn chorus of birds at his favourite retreat, Naldera, woke him soon after sleep had eventually come. No narcotic was of the slightest help.

He was discovering how important Mary had become to him, a discovery he might never have made had they remained in England, where public office and the companionship of old friends would have drawn him further away from her. In India she was his only equal, his family his only distraction. When he was alone in Calcutta, and she in Simla, he missed her dreadfully: 'All my days are the same, work, work, work.' He did not have a single companion there except Bishop Welldon, and found no intellectual stimulus, no new ideas, even on matters of government business, among his staff. His ADCs were young army officers of good family whose conversation was limited to sport and gossip. 'No one is of much help to me in anything. In England one could always turn to one's colleagues, Arthur [Balfour], St John [Brodrick], Goschen, for advice. Here the Viceroy is all alone, and no one else has an opinion on anything outside his own department or profession. Ropper [his Private Secretary, Sir Walter Lawrence], has no independent judgement, no critical faculty. So the strain upon me is very great. I am dogged tired.' Mary tried to restrain him, but knew that it was useless: 'Oh do listen to your poor lonely Kink, and don't do so many things. Your life and your strength are so precious, and it drives me wild to think of the unnecessary sights you go to see in such a temperature. But you listen to no human voice of warning or beseeching.'

He seemed possessed by the idea that he would not have time to complete his task in India, and worked incessantly. Believing that civil servants were incapable of originating a new thought, and could not be trusted even with the routine, he did their work for them; and they, finding the Viceroy resolute, unbelievably well-informed, critical and apparently untiring, became more dependent than ever upon his detailed instructions. There had never been such a Viceroy. His purpose was no less than to overhaul the entire machinery of Government, against the weight of all tradition, precedent and resistance to reform. Only a few months after reaching India he wrote to Pearl Craigie: 'I am prodding up the animal with most vigorous and unexpected digs, and it gambols plaintively under the novel spur. Nothing has hitherto been done under 6 months. When I suggest 6 weeks, the attitude is one of pained surprise; if 6 days, one of pathetic protest; if 6 hours, one of stupified resignation.'

His extraordinary powers of concentration and memory, of analysis and eloquence, made him appear to his staff superhuman, which increased his isolation. He aroused such respect and fear that his human qualities were ignored. To everyone he was the Viceroy: to nobody except Mary, George Curzon. His jokes were not seen to be jokes; his many considerate acts were searched for hidden motives; his lightest sallies regarded as imperial pronouncements. When he once said that no self-respecting woman would allow cold tapioca to be served at luncheon, there was consternation in Simla, each person having a different name for the hostess who had offended him. His impatience could make the average man feel invertebrate, and people were so paralyzed by his authority that they appeared stupider than they were. His noble aspirations were beyond the reach and sometimes beyond the comprehension of lesser men. His love of justice, his hatred of cruelty, his contempt of meanness and snobbishness, his scorn of apathy and sloth, his remarkable gift of language on paper and in speech, aroused admiration, but they were also regarded as further evidence of his unapproachability and lack of sympathy, paradoxically, because they expressed the very opposite. His staff knew that he was often in pain, but because he triumphed over it himself, they assumed that he would make no allowance for the enervating effects of the Indian climate on others. Because his expected standard in everything was excellence, he seemed rarely to thank a subordinate for a job well done. His reprimands for ungentlemanly behaviour could be withering. He told his military secretary not to bite his nails and scratch his legs at dinner; he summoned the young Churchill, his guest, to warn him that 'diarrhoea of talk' was unbecoming at the Viceroy's table. And this example of his unpredictable, though understandable, anger illustrates the terror he aroused in his ADCs:

This morning [he wrote to Mary from Mysore in 1902] we had a coronation service at 9 am. in the park. All the troops were drawn up in a great square. I was under a small gold awning in the middle of one side. The service lasted about 40 minutes. The sun was appalling, and we all streamed with perspiration. My leg ached as if it would drop off, but of course I could not sit down alone in view of the crowd. At the last moment, that great long-shanked idiot of an ADC suddenly without any instruction or warning darted through the crowd and planted in front of my seat the green baize footrest. I could have killed him with rage.

In earlier pages I have quoted from Elinor Glyn's unpublished memoir some passages which analyzed Curzon's attitude to women. Of equal interest is her assessment of his total impact:

His brain is so remarkable that there is no subject – small or great – that he could not master. His whole life is an expression of the noblest purpose and desire for the finest ends. His grasp of things is so complete that he sees in an instant the right thing to be done. If he is doing anything he believes to be right, the more opposition that it arouses, or the greater the unpopularity incurred, the more tenaciously or even obstinately will he stick to it. . . . His will is of iron. His nerve and resource never fail him. The necessity for activity dominates him to such an extent that it has obscured somewhat the line between actual duty and pleasure. . . .

After a first explosion of exasperation (with fools) he unconsciously subsides into a patient, resigned, contemptuous indifference, immeasurably wounding to little natures. He is arrogant, and this is one of his great charms. Because his arrogance is unconscious, it is of the true and real aristocrat, the living expression of that long line of men commanding their inferiors, the unconscious revelation of great pride in noble deeds, great self-control, great ability. . . . He does not antagonise the lower or upper classes, but the middle, who nearly always speak of him with suppressed indignation. The small dishonesties, meannesses and dishonours of servants and trades people exasperate him, their ways are such a contrast to his own lofty scrupulous sense of honour. His own manners are those of the greatest *grand seigneur*, polished, courteous and aloof in a general company, and stern and icy when he is preoccupied. He can withdraw into himself, and then he is unapproachable even by his children. But he has charm, and can convert an enemy into a friend by one of his beautifully expressed sentences and his rare smiles. He has a loveableness, and at times a childishness and playfulness.

Mary would not have disputed a word of this. Her admiration for Curzon was total, but not unanalytical. She expressed it most vividly not in her own words (because she never rose to such eloquence, and would have thought it absurd for a wife to write such an encomium to her husband), but in a quotation she sent him from Macaulay's *Life of Pitt*, saying that it describes 'another great man. I wonder if you will recognize who?':

No person could hear Pitt without perceiving him to be a man of high, intrepid and commanding spirit, proudly conscious of his own rectitude and of his own intellectual superiority, incapable of the low vices of fear and envy, but too proud to feel and show disdain. Pride, indeed, pervaded the whole man, was written in the lines of his face, was marked by the way in which he walked, in which he sat, in which he stood, and above all in which he bowed. . . . His pride, though it made him bitterly disliked by individuals, inspired the great body of his followers with respect and confidence. They took him at his own valuation. They saw that his self-esteem was not that of an upstart who was drunk with good luck and applause. It was that of the magnanimous man so finely described by Aristotle in his Ethics, of the man who thinks himself worthy of great things, being in truth worthy. . . . In the small circle of his intimates he was amiable, affectionate, even playful. They could hardly admit that he who was so kind and gentle with them could be stern and haughty with others.

When alone together he and Mary became Pappy and Kinkie. The tone of their letters, one can assume, was reproduced in their private talk, and much of it was certainly concerned with the triviality and tribulations of their public life, each being the other's only confidant. It is unlikely that Curzon spoke to her much in the early years about the details of his work. What would she know about Land Assessments and the Indian Education Bill? But she could hear him out on the unpleasant mannerisms and unhelpful subservience of his staff, and they could plan what needed to be done together and what they could avoid. When they emerged in public, she was obliged to adopt towards him some of the deference she observed in others. 'The lot of a Viceroy', she wrote half-jokingly to St John Brodrick, 'is one of absolute aloofness and everyone is in mortal fear of the august being. Being a Yankee I can't understand it, but I manage to assume the necessary amount of awful respect for His X when we appear in public.'

Her family, who often visited her in India, found it more difficult. In 1899, when Nancy and Daisy Leiter came to Simla for the first time and stayed seven weeks, there were no complaints about their conduct because they were still slightly awed. When they came again next year, their heads were turned by the attention they received from the young officers and officials. As the Vicereine's sisters they were naturally invited everywhere. As two unmarried, rich and attractive girls (Daisy was the prettier) they were much courted, and they responded with a mounting animation which soon led to indiscretion. Mary had to speak sternly to them. They must not tell their new friends stories about the private life of Viceregal Lodge. They must not call the Viceroy 'George' except when they were alone, and they must give him precedence, as she did herself, when they entered a reception room. The girls were astounded that their sister could address them in such terms, that an American could so humble herself before her husband. At the next big party they approached Curzon with exaggerated obsequiousness, prostrating themselves before him in mock imitation of what they imagined to be the oriental manner. Nobody thought it funny.

They were sent to their rooms. Their high spirits, however, were unquenchable. On another occasion they received an invitation from a Rajah to visit him in his palace in a remote part of the country. They started off secretly, pursued by a telegram from the Viceroy explaining that this particular ruler was not *persona grata* with the Government and ordering them to return at once. They ignored his instruction. Sir Walter Lawrence wrote in his diary: 'Socially the advent of the Leiters has done great harm.... The situation all through the year was very painful and difficult.' The scandal even crept into western newspapers. *Vanity Fair* scoffed at 'the royal rank given to the Vicereine's sisters', and Mary was much distressed.

It was normal in the autumn months for the Viceroy to tour a different part of his dominion, and unless he was visiting a plague or famine area, he was accompanied by his wife. Mary kept a manuscript diary of these tours, and had it typed out afterwards, sending a copy to her parents. The ceremonial of their official visits and entertainment was naturally formal and repetitive, and rather than trace her progresses in detail, her diaries gain in interest from being anthologized. She was a natural and unrestrained writer. Her descriptions of India had not been equalled by a woman since Emily Eden's. There was no self-pity in her accounts of even the most disagreeable occasions. In short retrospect they amused her, and she never allowed exhaustion to spoil her fun or cloud her observation. Nor did her spirits flag as year followed year. Her diaries increase in animation, and improve in descriptive power, as India unfolded one by one its infinite resources.

1899, November. *Bhopal.* 'The way was lined by Imperial Service Cavalry, and when these gave out, the State infantry. Aged veterans with orange beards and orange trousers, holding out rusty muskets before them, stood about 3 feet apart, and behind them the most wonderful crowd of natives, camels, elephants, in every rainbow colour, native bands on the backs of elephants playing God save the Queen, and trumpets shrieking royal salutes. It was impossible not to laugh at the grotesque show, the splendour and the squalor and the picturesqueness of it all.'

1899, December. *Lucknow.* 'At 3 a Rani, who is in strict purdah, came to see me. Her sedan chair was brought to the middle of the room and the carriers withdrew. Out popped the Rani, wearing huge Turkish trousers of bright pink, a white jacket, and at least 60 yards of bright blue gauze wound about and dragging behind her. On her head was a very quaint silver ornament, four arms of a Dutch wind-mill 8 inches across fastened on her forehead, and the windmill kept turning round. Her hair was parted up the back and bunched amidst silver roses at the top of her head. She spoke a little English, and I asked her how long it had taken her to come in her litter, expecting her to say 5 minutes, but she said 20 years!'

1900, December. *Bangalore.* 'I am so glad that our tour is coming to an end. The strain of it is very great and our days are filled with politics, philanthropy and charity, and our evenings with society. ... The fatigue of night after night of dinner-parties, frightful music, worse food, and company with whom you have nothing in common. It is all I can do to fill my part. We are surrounded by plague and cholera, but every precaution is taken for us. George goes through agony with his back, but only I know it.'

1901, December. *Burma.* 'To the untutored eye one place in Burma is the key to the whole. Look well at a dazzling sky, a dense green glorious earth; pop golden cone-shaped pagodas wherever harmony calls out for one; people the earth with pink petticoated beaming Burman men and women; tone down all this vividness with ubiqui-tous monks, solemnly shaved and wrapped in saffron togas; and you have the main lines of every picture in Burma. A Viceregal visit frames the impression in an unnatural setting of gazing crowds, presentation of addresses, tents filled with local officials, and Burmese dances danced by rows of little women. As these dances are in progress under every tree and on every platform at every public arrival, we stopped to look at the first, and then hurried by the rest, as the graceless contor-tions left us unmoved, though a Burman will watch the swaying bodies and twisting wrists all day and night.'

1901, December. *Mandalay.* 'The palace is like a roofed-in forest of

[131]

immense gilded teak-trees. In the chief Hall of Audience, before the lion throne, where the King formerly received Ambassadors, stands an altar, a spreading eagle-desk and a little harmonium. The English church (which creeps into all unexpected corners of British dominion) has intruded itself into these amazing surrounding. ... The great pagoda of Mandalay is only huge, not beautiful. As I walked through one of its doorways, a woman sat surrounded by straw baskets in which were hundreds of little birds. I could not conceive what they were for, knowing well that Buddhists do not eat animals or fowls, so I asked the Commissioner who was with me, and he said the birds were caught and placed in baskets as it was an act of merit to let them loose. An act of merit so easily accomplished was irresistible, so I bought hundreds, and as the woman put them into my hands I let them fly away, and they circled in swarms round my head, to the delight of the little laughing Burmans. So I bought bird-merit cheaply, but the fate of the small birds was pitiful, as hawks swooped down.

'I did many commonplace things in Mandalay, such as open bazaars, go to garden-parties, and attend nightly dinner-parties. I saw all the members of the dethroned Royal Burmese Family, who had escaped Thebaw's slaughter of relations, and quite a dozen princesses came to see me. As they came in, each advanced bending low, and presented me with an enormous cigar. Every creature smokes in Burma after he or she is weaned, and a huge cheroot wrapped in bright paper is as necessary to a baby as to an old man. I accepted all the cigars gladly, but didn't smoke. I presently asked if these ladies had any children. They said, Yes: they were all below in the bullock carriages. I begged to see them. So a little drove came up, of all ages from 3 to 10, and they plumped on all fours as they came in, and advanced crawling into the room *à quatre pattres*.'

1902, March. *Hyderabad*. 'After handshaking and introductions and inspecting the guard of honour, we proceeded to our carriage, which was an immense canary-yellow chariot, with a golden-damask canopy supported on silver poles, and drawn by four white horses, covered with gold and silver harness and trappings, ridden by yellow postillions and led by innumerable runners and grooms. In this barge George and I proceeded through the decorated and densely crowded streets. Behind us came the Nizam in a second royal yellow shandry-dan, and Staff, Ministers and Generals following in vehicles of decreasing splendour, till the tail of the procession showed a dilapi-

15 On arrival in India as Vicereine, with Irene and Cynthia, 1899

16 George Curzon, in Viceregal robes

17 Government House, Calcutta

18 Viceregal Lodge, Simla

19 Curzon and Mary make their
state entry into Delhi for the
Coronation Durbar, 1903

20 Mary in her famous peacock
dress, which she wore at the State
Ball of the Delhi Durbar

dated fiacre in yellow. The streets to the Residency were lined with the Nizam's troops in every variety of costume, from the gorgeous Golconda lancers in yellow and silver to the Arab regiments in Turkish turbans and flowing drapery.

'At 11.30 George received the Nizam in Durbar. He came attended by all his nobles, with his full escort of Golconda lancers, and made a very fine show. He is a very small, shy little man, who seldom speaks, and he is without any of the gorgeous ornaments usually inseparable from Oriental majesty. He wears a black frock-coat and a small yellow turban, and the blue ribbon of the Star of India.

'In the evening Colonel Barr, the British Resident gave a banquet for us. I went into dinner with the Nizam. He sat imperturbable and silent at my side while I went through the alphabet with subjects in my attempt to talk to him: A – Arab horses; B – Colonel Barr; C – Calcutta and curries; D – diamonds; E – elephants; F – foreign princes, who infest India at present; G – Golconda (the old diamond mines that are in Hyderabad); H – Habibullah, the Amir of Afghanistan. You would have thought that this magnificent variety would have lasted through dinner, but each topic died at its birth and only produced a gentle "Yes" or "Exactly" from His Highness. George witnessed my efforts with amusement, and eventually leaned over the narrow table and asked him about the Delhi Durbar next January, but even this inspiring subject produced only a flutter of the eyelid.'

1902, March. *Hyderabad*. 'The Nizam sent us on a tiger-shoot which lasted four days. On the fourth day we walked two miles in a temperature of 100°, and my shoes were scorched. Of course I had on black glasses, a huge helmet and a back pad, and a thick wadded curtain over my head, and a thick umbrella, and ice in my mouth. . . . As the beat got near, a big angry tiger dashed out, but was too hidden in the rocks to aim at, so he only bounded about roaring and then returned to his cave. Then a furious tomtoming and shooting by beaters began, and fuses were thrown among the rocks to dislodge him, and we advanced on our elephant to get a nearer shot, the shikari thinking the tiger was sulking. Still nothing happened, and several shikaris boldly descended from the elephants to direct the beat, and the line of guns closed up. Captain Wigram, horrified to see men on the ground while a tiger was known to be within a few yards, shouted to them to get back into the trees and to their elephants, but alas! too late, as, with a roar, a tiger dashed out in hot pursuit of a flying shikari. Captain Wigram fired as it came on, but the beast was too near the man to aim, and with a wild leap the tiger bounded on the man, and as he and the man went down, I saw the great jaws close on the back of the man's head. I said to George, "The tiger has killed a man", but he had not seen it, and said "I think you are mistaken". In the meantime four seconds were passing while both man and beast were in sickening silence behind a rock. Then back came the tiger, slowly trotting, again Captain Wigram shot, and although the shot killed, the tiger got back to his cave. With great difficulty we got the mahout to move to where I thought the wounded man was. But this time everything was in roar and confusion, elephants coming up on all sides and nobody knowing what had happened. Slowly we lurched forward round the rocks, and there lay a man stone dead, his head half gone.

1902, August. *Kashmir*. 'The valley of Kashmir is the most fertile in the world. The crops were magnificent and the flowers beyond description, and round this mass of beauty like a protective wall rose the Himalayas, range upon range of peerless snow peaks from 10 to 29 thousand feet high. Through the valley, coiling like a silver snake, ran the Jhelum river. We drove to the banks of this about five miles above the town of Srinagar, and here the Maharajah met us with his state barge. This was a long houseboat entirely covered with Kashmir shawls. We sat on the roof in the setting sun and floated down the stream, with the help of a steam tug and enlivened by a flotilla of barges and boats of every description. Srinagar is like an Asiatic Venice, built entirely on the river and canals. The houses are too picturesque, built of brown brick with windows of lovely carving and roofs covered with flowers growing gaily. Every inch was packed with people gazing at our state entry, and the Maharajah and I sat like two great effigies in two big chairs. The Maharajah is about 4 ft high and addicted to opium, which he takes at one o'clock and is under its influence until about 7. As he came to meet me at 5, he was in a very torpid condition and he had only the energy to point me out the Hindu temples. I never in my life enjoyed anything so much as the sail down the beautiful canal in the evening light.'

1902, November. *Udaipur*. 'In the afternoon we went to a wet garden crowded with fountains and had tea, and the Maharajah came and shed distinction on us. We drove home on the edge of lovely lakes walled in by high Italian hills, crowded with palaces behind which the sun went down in a glory of red fire, and the moon came up and silvered the other side of the world. We had only time to dress quickly for a banquet in the Maharajah's palace, which was now wholly silvered by the full moon. Outside the palace was absolute romance and beauty; inside English horrors were rampant: velvet chairs, mirrors galore, blue and red glass balls hanging dissipatedly from the ceiling, and cheval glasses in every corner reflecting plaster figures and musical clocks and mechanical toys. The reincarnation of Vishnu [the Maharajah] looked a deity out of his frame in these surroundings, but he seemed proud of his gimcrack collection. After dinner we walked to a terrace overlooking the lake, and here we sat in another marble pavilion. All the palace (which is enormous, rising out of the lake in which it was reflected) was picked out with lights; so were the marble palaces on all the islands; so were the banks of the lake; and so were the hills surrounding. Nothing could exceed the beauty of it. Hundreds of fire-balloons floated about in the still moonlight, and the lake gave back the reflections of all the brilliancy. We sat in speechless delight. We descended to the water's edge and were rowed about, looking first at the shores, then at the moon, and then at one island of light after another. It was cold, and someone whispered chills and fever, which made us hurry back.'

1902, November. *Jodhpur.* 'It is a desolate desert, with an immense grim red fort towering up on a central hill, and when the sun goes down and turns the gigantic fort scarlet, and the desert into blood red space, and the streams of camels into rich red monsters, it is imposing enough. The Maharajah lives for horses, and the stables are vast. Outside my palace is a pit full of tigers and lions – the noise is diabolical, and I thought in the night that they were all in my room. I thought I felt the fur of a tiger's chest against my cheek, and while I lay in terror other tigers leaped over the chairs and tables. When I woke I heard an odd commotion, and in the early morning light beheld an immense tortoiseshell cat sitting on my table lapping milk out of my cup!...

'The inside of the fort is crammed with ghastly rubbish, old brass and glass beds, broken-down furniture, mirrors with spotty faces, marble tables with broken legs, pictures upside down, huge gilt flower-boxes broken in two – the only fate fit for it all was a bonfire. It was all so incongruous in the beautiful carved rooms.

'In one of the beautiful halls I was received by the Maharani, who

[135]

had come up to the palace from her house in the sand below. She received me in the centre of a white marble courtyard, surrounded by her women waving yaks' tails, and attended by eunuchs wearing the peculiar pear-shaped hat that these creatures wear. She took my hand and led me into the pillared hall, where a row of dingy cretonned chairs was stiffly arranged. She led me to the biggest and sat down beside me, and we sat on these magenta-roses cotton-tufted thrones. She was more gorgeously dressed than anyone I have ever seen. Her velvet and cloth-of-gold dress was a solid mass of embroidery, and jewels hung from her neck to her feet. Anklets of great weight dangled over her insteps, and emeralds the size of eggs were in chains round her neck.

'She is a handsome woman, and was born a Bundi princess; and she has great power with the Maharajah, as she has plenty of wits and a son besides. Her uncle was in the room and interpreted for her, but as a native woman cannot raise her voice in the presence of the only male relation she sees, the conversation was conducted in whispers on her part, and she kept her face covered by a gauze veil. Her two little girls of 3 and 5 in gold trousers were unruly and squeaked, and hundreds of blue sacred pigeons cooed and fluttered in the courtyard or flew into the room. A brass bed in the corner had only three legs, and the canopy over it had collapsed, so all the bedraggled surroundings made the splendour of the woman most incongruous. When the interview was nearly over, she rose and languidly hung garlands of wet tube-roses round my neck, and clapped attar of roses on to my reluctant handkerchief. I then shook her hand, heavy with rings and chains, and she vanished under a great leather curtain held aside by the eunuchs. George had been sitting on a beautiful marble balcony awaiting me. The contrast – he and I standing side by side looking over the battlements, and that painted jewelled female prisoner inside covered with emeralds, who has to receive her horrid little husband on the rare occasions he comes near her by placing her face to his feet – is really the contrast and dividing line between East and West.'

Mary found these expeditions the most enjoyable of all her Indian experiences. Everything was organized for her convenience and comfort. The Viceregal train was a travelling hotel of twelve coaches, of which she and Curzon had one each, hers divided into a saloon, a bedroom, bathroom, maid's room, box-room and lavatory. There was a staff of 100 officials and servants on board. Halts were made to take on fresh food and hot water; mail was delivered at main stations three times a day. ADCs went ahead to each stopping-place to make sure that the preparations conformed to protocol, and drew up a schedule for the Viceroy that told him in advance everything that would happen in a carefully timed order. He was supplied with notes on the people they would meet and briefed on the special problems of the district. Nothing was a surprise except accidents and the vagaries of local custom, or the strange tributes they saw displayed in their honour, such as the banner at Jaipur which proclaimed, by typographical error, A GAL A DAY. Mary knew what she would be doing and wearing, and almost what she would be saying, at any given hour on any given day, weeks ahead. But her progresses were never monotonous. How could they be, when India was the size of Europe, and its different principalities as varied in tradition and landscape as Europe's own? It was like travelling by Oriental Express from Paris to Constantinople, with the difference that the train's schedule was theirs to command, and that in every capital they stayed in the royal palace for two or three days as the most honoured guests it had ever received.

Yet India was not Europe. The Rajahs were richer than most crowned heads, and their subjects poorer and more adoring. Princely extravagance was unresented; there was no political protest. Their women never appeared in public. Though some of their palaces might be decrepit, their jewels were untarnishable: though their conversation was sometimes halting, their entertainments repetitive and their manners ungainly, there was always the chance of discovering a character of unusual charm or eccentricity, or a palace which caught the breath by its barbaric splendour or the beauty of its setting.

Mary floated through India like a rare butterfly. Her first appearance in a new town excited wonder; her departure left a gasp behind. She satisfied every hope of what a Vicereine should be, never grumpy, never awkward, able to break through

the stiffness of protocol by a spontaneous gesture or an un-
ceremonial laugh, enhancing the expected by the unexpected,
and her beauty of face, figure and carriage by the loveliness of
her clothes.

She took immense pains with her trousseau, knowing that she
must match the magnificent jewels, uniforms, turbans and saris
of her host and hostess, and how much importance an oriental
people attach to outward appearance. She must be ultra-
feminine when the men were ultra-masculine. She must not
give offence by adopting the Indian style, but pay tribute to it
by discreet reminders that she knew what it was. She had special
materials woven in India to her designs; embroidered Parisian
clothes with Indian motifs; bought costume jewellery in
Calcutta bazaars. Many of her clothes survive in the costume-
museum at Bath, a few displayed on dummies in the exhibition-
hall, the remainder carefully stored in the original trunks in
which she brought them back from India. There, seventy years
later, I was allowed to unfold and handle them. They were still
in perfect condition. Evening dresses, garden-party dresses,
trains, morning gowns; silks, satins and brocades; padded,
boned and upholstered. She had a taste for slithering materials
which changed colour as she walked, or crisp ones which
rustled (sound has gone out of modern clothes, to their loss),
and for lace edgings which would have dirtied within an hour
had she not taken the greatest care. Almost every dress was
made by Worth of Paris, and on most were stitched Indian
designs of flowers, or whorls following the skirt-hem or caressing
the neckline, strengthening the flowing silk or satin with encrusted dragons or insects unknown to entomology. She preferred glowing colours, rich reds and purples, imperial colours,
but pink was her favourite. In the daytime the dresses were
loose and flowing, or tightly waisted. In the evening, her splendid shoulders emerged candlelike from the tight socket of her
gown. Her beauty complimented the materials and jewels,
her wearing of them the designer, and all combined to satisfy
her desire, her obligation, to be the loveliest.

She was a success. She knew instinctively that she had two

main roles in India: to comfort and support her husband; and to compensate for the fear and awe that he inspired. In private she was his lover and confessor, the recipient of all the grumbles he could utter to nobody else. She was his only consoler, his co-adjutrix. In public she was the charmer, the sweetener, the Vicereine. In each role she used every ploy. She was alternately playful and queenly, teasing and solicitous, and soon discovered that what pleased Curzon, pleased his staff and the Indian nobles, too. Her father had been right: there was no need to act out of character. In fact, the more she remained herself, the easier it was to break down the stiffness of others. It seemed to her at times that she was the only white person in India who was able to behave naturally, she who was in the most artificial position of all. If she grumbled, other people felt able to grumble too; if she teased, they could tease back; if she yawned, the yawn could end in a laugh. Some of the older men, she knew, were half in love with her, and Curzon, who knew it, too, did not mind. There was no threat.

She found a strange community of feeling between herself and the Rajahs. Their wives were dummies, child-bearers. She was the only woman privileged to join in men's talk, to speak above a whisper, to initiate topics of conversation and suggest entertainments, and to propose that it was time that everyone went to bed. Curzon watched her growing assurance with amusement and delight. At a banquet they would catch each other's eye in the shorthand of a glance. She could make some excuse for sitting down, as he could not, when she saw him growing tired with standing. She could create conversational diversions, or with pretended innocence ask the question which he could not ask without arousing suspicion.

When they were alone together after a late party, they shed their weariness with their clothes. Mary never criticized him, knowing that an ounce of reproach might tip the delicate balance of his reserve, and that even with her he could suddenly turn silent. The most important service that she could do for him was to reassure him, never adding to his annoyance even if it meant sometimes deceiving him and herself, allowing him to have his say, however repetitive, without argument or rebuttal. She knew that he was not a conceited man, for conceit implies a self-assessment beyond deserts and of that he was never guilty, but he was lonely in his eminence, isolated by his gift of leadership, and to her alone could he confess his fears and occasional despair, his sense of inadequacy or impotence.

She wondered whether she might not have a third role, hitherto neglected. She had done little to fulfil her resolution to reach out beyond the British to the Indian people. She was known to all of them, and had been seen by millions, and her manner and appearance had touched their hearts. But that was not the same as knowing them. Apart from the Indian princes, she had never talked to Indians, and had done nothing for them directly, as Lady Dufferin had done by her nursing Fund. It was not easy. The Indians looked on the British Raj as omnipotent, all-pervading, benevolent for the most part, but 'capricious', as Sir Walter Lawrence had said, 'a deity of many shapes and many moods'. The British saw it as their role in India to promote the welfare of 300 million people, to prevent corruption and tyranny, to build roads, railways, dams, to fight famine and pestilence, but not to encourage the Indians to think that they could do any of these things for themselves. There was no social contact between the two races. So Mary's possible initiatives were very limited. She could, and did, preside formally over the Lady Dufferin Fund. She could, and did, help Indian artists by commissioning their work. But she felt that her growing popularity offered growing opportunities. She must involve herself in Indian life at its most humble level, by concerning herself with the welfare of the poor. It was to this that she would devote the second half of her Viceregal term.

In March 1901 Mary took her children to England for a six-month holiday. By convention the Viceroy could never leave India during his five years of office, but he could send his wife for her recuperation, and to explain to people at home his plans and difficulties more easily and intimately than was possible by letter or telegraph. Thus Mary found her fourth role, as an emissary and conciliator. She did not have a trained political mind and was ignorant of detail, but she had known as friends for many years the men who were now high in government, and she knew better than anyone the tensions to which her husband was subject, could dispel false rumours about his health and popularity, and could bring back to him opinions and advice which nobody would care to give him in writing. She was trusted as sensible, understanding and tactful. She was a dove from a storm-tossed ark, who would fly back to it.

The tedium of her journey home from Bombay was relieved only by writing daily letters to 'Darling, darling Pappy'. She felt 'so utterly lonely and friendless and away from all I love, that I had best be serene, as no one can help me but myself'. In Simla he felt the same, 'indescribably lonely. It is like living in a great sepulchre.' On board ship people stood in rows to stare at her as she paced the deck, and at meals she was sandwiched between a heavy judge and the yarn-spinning Captain. She disembarked at Marseilles for a short holiday with the children near Nice, and arrived in London on 4 May.

Her first shock was the prevailing ignorance about India. 'It is the great unknown: The moon seems nearer to the great majority.' People imagined that she and Curzon went everywhere on the backs of elephants, when the Viceroy did not possess a single one of his own. Did she have a horse and carriage? In what city did they live? When they travelled by train, were compartments reserved? Was Buddhism the religion of India? When Parliament debated the India Office budget, the House was almost empty. 'But there isn't a person I meet who doesn't speak of the great work you are doing. They don't know what it is, but they know that it is something.... Their affection and delight at seeing me is absolutely touching, and I am ungrateful to be critical.' She stayed with Lady Miller at her house in Grosvenor Square, and was invited out to every meal, and for weekends to Blenheim, Hatfield and Wilton. Slowly she began her defence of Curzon's policies, retailing to him in letters every nuance of the reaction, every piece of gossip that could be of the slightest use to him. If there was a fault in her loyalty, it was its blindness. She told him what he wanted to hear, and in many of her letters there is an echo of his own prejudices – his dislike of soldiers, for example, his contempt for the ignorance and insipidity of politicians, the unchallengeable rightness of his own judgments:

Last night I dined with the Gullys [Speaker of the House of Commons]. Delightful. Chamberlains, Consuelo, Roberts, Vincents, Tweedsmouths. Arthur Balfour [Leader of the House] took me in, and we talked straight through dinner, until his conscience smote him into putting on his glasses and looking at Lady Roberts on the other side and introducing me to her. His chief interest in India is Afghanistan, and what your plan of operations is to be in case of the Amir's death. He is really keen on this, and had read an alarmist Russian book on what Russia would do. I think if you have planned what you will do after proclaiming Habibullah it would be well to write to him for future use in the Cabinet. I chaffed him about all the letters he wrote to us. He said, 'I never write, but I love George.' It was so simply said, and I could have kissed him, but didn't. . . . You ought to hear Arthur on officers in His Majesty's Army.* He says they are the most corrupt jobbing lot of men he has ever known. He says, 'What are you to do with a lot of men who have no sense of honour, and more disloyal to one another than the weakest of the female sex, and have no brains to balance their defects?' He said: 'Look at that little man over there (Lord Roberts). I love him, but he cares for nothing but jobbing dukes into the Army.'

George Hamilton [Secretary of State for India, and Curzon's immediate superior] came to see me yesterday. He complained how in the Indian Civil Service mediocrity came to the front. It was not so when he entered public life. I gasped assent, but felt that he was the crowning illustration of his own theory. He grudges you praise; speaks of *his* policy for the frontier. I never knew such a hopeless dotard or such a small-minded ferret-faced roving-eyed mediocrity. He took the line that it was such a mistake for you to talk of your program of 12 reforms, as then everyone's back rose in hostile anticipation. I buttered the idiot by saying that you appreciated his capital letters. He was delighted.

* Queen Victoria had died on 22 January 1901.

Lord Salisbury [Prime Minister] said to me: 'George is having a very great career in India. His frontier policy will keep us in India 50 years longer than we should have kept it otherwise. It is a very difficult problem. We are always trying to balance a pyramid on its point.'

Winston told me that you should not serve your full five years, as you would be missing opportunities at home. It was 'unselfish' of you. Lord Milner said it was 'bad luck' that the South African war had diverted attention from India. I replied hotly that on the contrary, you could get on with your job without foolish criticism. But there is a lot of silly talk about our 'foolish formality'. St John Brodrick [Secretary of State for War] asked me if you would exchange your best troops for the 'spent and faded men of South Africa', but they would not press it on you if you felt it to be unwise. I said you would, I thought, go as far as you could to help the Empire.

Her letters to Curzon were of great length, one of them sixty-four pages long, written over a period of four days, but her handwriting was large and flowing, a word like 'innumerable' snaking across an entire line. She found herself treated once again as a novelty in London, and was subjected to much flattery on her own behalf and Curzon's, but slowly she became aware that his despatches had aroused misgivings about the pace of his Viceroyalty and his growing impatience with Ministers who appeared to believe that they could rule India from London. There were also many gentle hints that his grand style of living at Calcutta was inappropriate at a time when Britain was at war. She became his champion, and to an increasing extent his spokesman. There was nobody of whom she was frightened, not even of the King. She wrote from Windsor on 30 May:

Lady Gosford came to fetch me, and I, all in black and long sleeves, went with her to the green drawing-room. At 8.45 the King and Queen came in, unannounced and unpreceded by anyone. I felt ill but played up, and did my best to talk to the King who lost no time in condemning your ukase about the Princes* in the strongest terms. I asked

* Curzon had insisted that the Indian princes should pay more attention to their duties, and must not travel abroad without his permission.

if he had seen the Maharajah of Jaipur's letter. He said No, and was most surprised that any Indian prince should take that line, and he wished a copy of the letter sent him by you. So I said that I would write to you about it. His informant is evidently [the Prince of] Baroda, whom he cracked up to the skies. I mentioned the mortality of the famine in Baroda, also that the great man was not such a pattern prince as he thought. . . . He said no other word of your work, and only thanked you for the pretty sandal cabinet. He mentioned the huge sums you had got for the [Queen Victoria] Memorial, and expressed surprise that you should need so much.

After dinner the Queen came up and talked to me, and I didn't find her very deaf or difficult to understand, and she looked quite heavenly. Her conversation is of an infantile order: 'Journey home'; 'Children' etc, and quite unlike the old Queen, and neither King nor Queen know anything about India. I asked the King if he thought he could come out to be crowned. He wants to, but said he felt he couldn't, but he would not positively say No. He said quite pathetically that he was all alone. His only son was in the Antipodes, and his brother in Ireland, and he had no one to do for him what he had done for the late Queen, which is quite true.

Next day Mary drove with King Edward and Queen Alexandra to picnic beside Virginia Water, the three of them alone. There was much fuss about the seating arrangements in the carriage. The King wanted them to sit three abreast, facing the horses' rumps, with Mary in the middle, but she would not hear of it, insisting that she should sit opposite the royal pair, and preferred to travel with her back to the engine. After tea, the King took her sailing on the lake, smoking and spluttering, she said, but there was no wind and they lay becalmed, talking about the scenery when the subject of India was exhausted. There was one tangible result of the visit. Queen Alexandra commissioned Mary to order her Coronation robe and three other dresses in India, leaving the designs to her. It was an imaginative tribute to the Indian Empire, and to Mary herself. The commission occupied much of her time after her return, and the dresses were held to be of extraordinary beauty.

As was natural, the Mary-Curzon correspondence often

dwelt on the loneliness of their six-month separation, and contained much mutual commiseration on the poverty and stagnation of the company they kept. For Curzon at Simla there was 'no society but that of the boys [ADCs]: no talk but cricket, polo, racing and chaff. You cannot imagine the unutterable tedium of the whole thing.' Self-pity was often uppermost in his mind:

Poor Pappy gets so downcast sometimes in all this whirl-wind of calumny and fiction. No one to sustain him. Grind, grind, grind, with never a word of encouragement, on on on till the collar breaks and the poor beast stumbles and dies. I suppose it is all right and doesn't matter. But sometimes when I think of myself spending my heart's blood here, and no one caring one little damn, the spirit goes out of me, and I feel like giving in. You don't know, or perhaps you do, what my isolation has been this summer. I am crying now so that I can scarcely see the page. But it has always been so. The willing horse is flogged till he drops, and the world goes on. Darling, your letters are my only solace.

Mary responded in kind:

I want you, beloved Pappy, so desperately, and rebel against this separation. I do love you – but what is the use of a loving woman 4,000 miles away from your arms? I do feel in my heart that in our life there is a sense of comradeship almost as great as love. A man can know a woman well, because her life (consequently the interests which mould her mind and conceive her thoughts) are more or less simple. A man's life is so complex and much of it lies outside the woman's sphere, and his mind is so spiked with hundreds of magnets pointing to different possibilities that she may never know him in his entirety – but what is within her grasp is the power of making him truly happy. But take her away from it all and give her a blank six months in search of health, and she must feel that she has lost her anchorage.

For Mary London's social life was brighter and more varied than Simla's, but she could not conceal, and perhaps for his sake exaggerated, the mediocrity and triviality of the people whose company she had once enjoyed. 'Everyone is doing the same old thing – just flirting, and dining, and dawdling':

Bron Herbert asked me at lunch today what I thought had most changed since I went away. Of course it is the Queen. Reverence has gone out of people's lives. There is nobody who stands apart, and up aloft in your heart and mind. 'Edward the Caresser' is only made fun of, and there is a new story of him and Favorita [Mrs George Keppel] every day. The whole scandal is public property.

The politicians came off no better. 'Arthur [Balfour] is wizzened, worried and exhausted; Henry Asquith obese and hopeful about his political future, and Margot revelling in a garrulous selfish grief which gets on everyone's nerves. Then Asquith's amorous interest in various people, and his reckless consumption of champagne, and his loss of that old granite sense of right and his abomination of the disreputable. He is said to be in love with Pamela Plowden and goes to her room at night. Can you conceive of anything more grotesque than Henry as a lover of girls?' The central message of her letters to Curzon was that nobody at home was a match for him, in ability, imagination, decency or vigour. When he returned from India, the leadership of the Conservative Party was his for the taking. It was contemptible that meanwhile these effete men should seek to thwart his work as Viceroy, and she had no hesitation in telling them so.

Her spirited advocacy of her husband had its effect, but not always what she intended. St John Brodrick tells in his autobiography that she took him to task for the Government's 'hostility' to Curzon. He replied that the Cabinet had allowed him to have his way in nineteen cases out of twenty, and a senior Minister at home was often persuaded by his colleagues to change his mind on matters on which he was expert. 'Lady Curzon, who had no experience of the give and take of English politics, evidently thought, and said, that as they were only representing offices, and George was representing an Empire, the comparison did not hold!' The exclamation-mark was Brodrick's.

One man, however, in spite of what she wrote about him, seems to have captivated her, and she him: Arthur Balfour, who was to succeed Lord Salisbury as Prime Minister in the next year. A man of fine discernment, placid, fastidious, the most admired of the Souls, a philosopher by nature, an intellectual aristocrat by habit, blending art with politics, finding in women, though he never married, a necessary catalyst for a masculine society, he rediscovered Mary Curzon during these summer months of 1901, adored her, perhaps loved her. The evidence is in Mary's letters, guarded, anecdotal, flattered, amused; and in Curzon's unworried replies: 'Oh dear, it seems to me that you have fairly bowled over Master Arthur. However, he is a tepid though delightful lover. So Pappy does not feel seriously afraid.'

The incidents that provoked this response were these. On 31 May Mary spent a weekend with Willy and Ettie Grenfell. 'Such a heavenly party. A.J.B. [Balfour], Milner, Asquiths, Vincents, Cranbornes, Winston, Wyndham, Elchos. At dinner A.J.B. sat by me again. He will be relieved when I have gone, I fear, though he will hear no lamentations for him on my part when I deplore the frequency with which he falls to my lot.' He took her motoring next day, the first time she had ever been in a car, lending her a black balaclava hat to shield her hair against the wind, and they started off alone together to the cheers of the house-party, 'and for an hour we flew up hill and down dale, faster than a train. I was nearly swept away by the wind, the roar, the speed. It was like being a girl again, and I felt like a Madonna. Poor humble old Kinkie. I have gone away now on the crest of a wave.'

A month later they were fellow guests again at Wilton, Lord Pembroke's house. Mary Elcho, George Wyndham's sister and Balfour's current inamorata, took Mary Curzon to her room. '"I suppose you know that Arthur is very fond of you", she said. I said, "I don't think he is at all. I am only in the galère with his other friends, and, after all, you, Mary, are the only one that matters with A.J.B. in the least." "No", says she, "I know when he is interested, and he loves being with you." "Of course", I said, "this is nonsense."' Behind this sweet interchange was intense jealousy on Lady Elcho's part, as the sequel was to prove. Mary described it fully for Curzon:

[147]

On Monday I was standing in the hall [at Wilton] when he came in and said, 'What are you going to do today?', and I said, 'Motoring with you to London, and meeting you at dinner.' Arthur: 'But why not lunch at Willis's Rooms, and Lady Elcho will come too.' So I said Yes, flew off to collect my clothes, and left Arthur to invite his Mary. We started off in his motor, he, Mary and I. The lunch at Willis's was referred to, and time settled. Well, at 2 I went to Willis's. There was Arthur – no Mary – so we sat on a sofa to wait for her. And Arthur said, 'Where shall we sit for lunch?' I said, 'There – for there are no mirrors, and at that table I cant see my profile from 18 points of view.' A. said simply, 'I should then prefer that seat, as anything more singularly perfect I have never seen.' 2.10 came, and no Mary. So he said, 'Let's begin', and we did, and got all through lunch and forgot Mary, Arthur saying from time to time, 'I love this tête-à-tête, but it was unexpected.'

After coffee, I said, 'I am worried about Mary, and I shall go to Cadogan Square to see what has happened to her.' So he said, 'Very well, we will go together', so off we went to 62 Cadogan Square. Once there, we asked for her, and the footman went off to fetch her, while we waited in the library. Suddenly Mary appeared, wild-haired in a *filthy* dressing-gown, and for two seconds we all stood quite still. Then Arthur said, 'Well, why didn't you come?' 'Come where?', said Mary. 'To lunch', said A. 'You never asked me', cried Mary, and hurled herself on a sofa. Arthur said, 'You must be mad.' Then Mary said, 'Don't you think I would have come if I had thought you wanted me? Would I miss an hour when I could be with you? I have suffered agonies to think you didn't want me, and you had promised to lunch alone with me.' A. said, 'I am dazed. All was arranged, and time settled, and as you didn't come, Lady Curzon and I came to see if you were ill.' I said, seeing her on the verge of tears, 'It was all a mistake. I must fly away. I will take your hansom, Mr Balfour, and you can get another.' Arthur was quite stern and cold with his poor trembling wild Mary, and he said, 'Yes, I will go back to the House directly, but let me understand clearly (with a smile) that you and I meet for dinner tonight at the House of Commons.' I hope for Mary's sake that she flew into his arms and repented of her aphasia, for it can only be a succession of reasons that made her think she wasn't asked.

On each side, there was a sudden, short-lived, intense attraction. A month later she wrote to Curzon about him: 'When the

sun shines and women smile, he is a picturesque, rare, enchant-
ing creature. In times of stress he is, I think, harsh and just a
little selfish.' Mary relished the admiration of distinguished
men, and enjoyed describing it for the man to whom she was
pledged by marriage, to make him proud of her more than to
make him jealous. London had recreated for her what Calcutta
and Simla seldom could, a consciousness of her attractiveness to
other men, a reminder of her youth. In London she could talk
on equal terms with equal men, and among them Balfour alone
seemed to have a distinction and power commensurate with her
husband's. She was being lionized in circumstances of luxury
and tradition quite different from India's, more natural, less
adulatory, and she could enjoy a freedom, a challenge, which
she never knew there, holding her own because she was what
she was, not a Vicereine, but a lovely young woman who had
made her mark, not just a wife on holiday, but a woman of
ability, usefulness and charm. Balfour summed it up when he
called her 'intoxicating, delicious and clever'. She may have
responded to him because she felt their intimacy might be more
helpful to Curzon than agreeable to herself. Balfour was to
become Prime Minister: Curzon was to remain Viceroy. Each
needed a new link with the other. She was that link. Or it may
have been a little more.

Mary took breaks from London, in Munich and in Scotland.
She went to Munich at Curzon's suggestion, to have her portrait
painted by Franz von Lenbach. He was sixty-five, the most
fashionable portraitist in Europe. He was primarily a painter of
men of strong character, the Emperor William I, Wagner, Lizst,
Gladstone. But he had a romantic side too, and beautiful
women entranced him. When Mary first entered his studio, 'he
quite raved about me', she wrote to Curzon, and she was fascinated by his charm and genius. 'He could hang beside Titian
and Velasquez.' His manner towards her was elaborately flattering: 'Overjoyed to see me, he kissed my hand, and led me
through his lovely rooms with Titians smiling off the walls.' He
first had photographs taken of her by an assistant, from twenty
angles, while he stood to one side adoring her, murmuring,

'There is an angel-light in your eyes, and sunshine in your heart.' He made a first sketch, which he showed her when she returned next day, and by which she was 'dumbfounded, for there was I smiling in a white frock, leaning on my hand laughing, just as I had done at all his compliments. The rest of the face was quite grave, but the fun with which he had made the eyes dance was wonderful' (fig. 23). On her next visit she found that he had done five more sketches from the photographs, 'some smiling, one adorable: he had just caught a fleeting little half-smile and painted it with a few strokes'. She asked him how long he wished her to stay in Munich. He replied: 'If I had to say, it would be a whole lifetime, and then I would paint 10,000 pictures of your supreme beauty.' The portraits would be the greatest work of his life. 'Every line of shoulder, neck, nose, eyelid, and Lord knows what, has been glorified in sketches.' Mary was deceived by his flattery. Curzon was not. Of the twelve finished sketches, he sent back all but two, one now at Kedleston, the other, here reproduced, owned by Mary's youngest daughter. 'With the remainder,' Curzon said, 'he seems to have made a miserable failure. What a pity, considering his genius and your trouble.' Mary was hurt by this judgment. Lenbach had captured what even photographs concealed, her mischievousness. She was not a Vicereine here, as Curzon wanted, but a sprite. Normally she suppressed her merriment: Lenbach had discovered it. She wished to attract men; she attracted him. She was fastidious, but fastidiousness needs challenge: he challenged it. The Lenbach portrait remains the most truthful of all her likenesses, because it is unreverential.

Mary's second expedition was to Scotland. In August she took a lease of Braemar Castle, a property of the Farquharsons, lairds of Invercauld, which lies beside the Dee only a few miles from Balmoral. It is basically a seventeenth-century keep, rebuilt in the eighteenth, to which are attached a drum-tower containing the staircase, and turrets that hang like wasp-nests from the upperworks. Inside it is comfortably furnished, and some rooms even grand, but the charm of the castle increases as you mount to the upper floors, which break into little rooms with circular chambers off them, and from where the views over the valley and the mountains expand. Mary was delighted:

It is quite the most amazing and fantastic erection I have ever seen ... standing out in the open like a slender white exclamation mark against the pines beyond – windowless, turreted, charming. I thought King Lear might have built it up in a moment of melancholy. Cork-screw stairs. The house is exactly like a hyacinth, if you think of the stem as the stairs and unexpected rooms growing off it at the sides. 6 steps up came a big smoking-room: 6 more, a charming red-papered dining-room; another few, and a large low charmingly furnished sitting-room; then a succession of bedrooms with such low doors that you must crouch in and out; until at the top of the hyacinth, I found the little girls [Irene and Cynthia, who had been staying at Kedleston] in such pretty bright nurseries, both in bed. I have never been so completely fascinated by a building. I climb about from room to room, never in the least knowing which I am in, laughing the whole time.

Mary's mother joined her there, and for a few days so did her American journalist friend, G. W. Smalley. Visitors came over from Balmoral, among them St John Brodrick. But there was little to do but 'breathe air and look at heather hills and laugh at this absurd house', and search the newspapers for Indian news, of which there was little. One of her last letters summed up her experience and message:

If you keep your health, as I pray God you will, you have the whole future of the Party in your hands. Arthur will not take the trouble to lead. St John isn't inspiring enough. George Wyndham is a senti-mentalist, and hasn't the hard sense to do strong things. So who is there but my Pappy? No one has anything like your vigour, and there is an apathy in London about everything and everybody. It was illustrated by Arthur saying of bridge, which he now plays the whole time, 'I like it because it saves the effort of conversation'. Inertia seems to have attacked them all. They will need you to come back and wake them up. Great as your work is in India, it will be even greater in England, where the party is slipping down the well of indifference and incapacity. So don't wear out your great big brain. Keep it young, and let it go to bed at 12.30. And angel, take sulphonal as little as possible.

She returned to England to see Queen Alexandra once more about the Coronation dresses, and started her return journey to India on 26 September 1901. She and the children were reunited with Curzon at Simla on 15 October.

FIVE

DELHI

THIS book is only marginally concerned with Curzon's
immense achievement as Viceroy. It has been fully
recorded by Lord Ronaldshay in his three-volume biography and by David Dilks in his two-volume *Curzon in India*.
Mary's contribution to that achievement was threefold: in
keeping her husband as happy as he was capable of being when
parted from his friends; in pleasing people better than he could
please them himself; and in acting increasingly as his adviser
and intermediary.

As we have seen, whenever there was a serious clash of
opinion between the home and Indian Governments, Mary
always took Curzon's side. It required of her no effort to align
her views with his, mainly from admiration, love and loyalty,
but partly because there was a certain intellectual weakness in
her. She did not easily form her own judgments, and had
neither the knowledge nor the strength to challenge his. All her
energy and courage went into sustaining and defending him.
No wife, and certainly no woman except a wife, could have persuaded Curzon to change his mind in what he regarded as the
most important work of his life, and Mary, from the moment
she married him, and even earlier, bolstered his self-confidence
by her sympathy and approval, and by ridiculing the attitude
of his critics and opponents. Occasionally she slipped in a gentle
argument that there might be something to be said for their
point-of-view (having heard it from them privately), or that
Curzon might get his way more easily if he were not quite so

lapidary, not quite so quick to anger, rebuttal or contempt. But these occasions were rare.

Her first attempt to change his nature by persuading him to reduce his hours of work failed totally. She corresponded with Bishop Welldon of Calcutta about Curzon's 'self-immolation', telling him that even when Curzon was ill in bed, he would take no rest from his daily toil, but rather increased it, for he need not waste time dressing and undressing, and his bed became a monster desk. Together she and Welldon conspired to distract him, by taking him for walks, by arranging small dinner-parties at which he could relax. It did no good. After a short trial, Curzon refused the walks, and sulked at the dinner-parties because he felt guilty that 'more important people' were not there to hear him expound his views. Never did Mary make the slightest impact on his working habits. Once she crept downstairs at 5 a.m. to beg him to come to bed. He looked up from his desk, annoyed at the interruption. He said he had an important document to finish, and it must be done before morning. She crept away. But even on this subject, about which she felt most deeply, she defended him. At Windsor in 1901 Lord Salisbury begged her to use her influence to save George from killing himself by overwork, not knowing how hard she had already tried. He said it was a form of selfishness. 'Not at all', Mary replied, 'for George work is a form of recreation and relaxation', an argument which she did not wholly believe herself, and which left the Prime Minister puzzled and in despair.

In London she had made or re-made friendships with ministers who were ultimately Curzon's masters, and they made her an unofficial channel of communication. Lord George Hamilton (Secretary of State for India) wrote to her frequently; so did St John Brodrick, who was to succeed Hamilton in 1903; so did Balfour when he became Prime Minister. All repeated arguments which they used in their official despatches to the Viceroy, but qualified and simplified them for her understanding, appealing to her not to allow Curzon's pride and self-assurance to override his duty to take instructions from the Cabinet in the last resort. Here is one example, a letter from Lord George Hamilton written in June 1902:

Dear Mary, I fully appreciate your motives in writing to me, and am grateful to you for so writing. George in his last letter to me wrote strongly on what he described as the hostile and suspicious attitude of the [India] Council here, and gave what he considered to be a summary of their hostile actions. Now to be quite frank with you, I am sure that he would not have written his complaints in such forcible and disturbing language if he had not been unwell and suffering from overwork and the strain it imposes. I do not always agree with the decisions of the Council, and from my constant communication with George I can better appreciate his objects than those who only see his official despatches. But George has had his way more than any Viceroy of modern times, and when you consider the magnitude of his reforms, and the inevitable personal antagonisms that such changes arouse, it is marvellous that the instances in which he has been checked have been so few ... I have a deep and growing admiration for your husband's talents and force of character. But in public life you must give as well as take. The Council here are the final authority on all Indian matters. They are mostly distinguished and experienced men and they cannot be expected to acquiesce in everything suggested to them without comment or query.

Try to get George to give himself a little more rest and holiday. It is the isolation that aggravates his sense of being checked and unsupported, and the activity and power which makes him forgetful of the duties and responsibilities of mundane bodies such as the India Council. . . .

Women can at times mould and change the whole aspect of things. I know of nobody more capable of performing such a feminine duty than yourself.

These letters were usually sweetened by social gossip and affectionate teasing, but in each there was the core of a political message which the writers wished her to pass on in her own voice. Pass them on she did, qualified by her own opinions, and gradually Curzon came to discuss matters of policy with her more freely, and she to study some of the state documents that poured ceaselessly from his pen:

I have become a sort of necessary companion to statesmen, [she wrote to her father in June 1903.] I talk to George literally by the hour about every one of his political plans; and the other Sunday, Kitchener [now Commander-in-Chief, India] sat in the garden and talked business with me for $3\frac{1}{2}$ hours. It is only after vast study and reading that women can become good companions, but it is a far greater satisfaction than frivolity.

She was not the influence she could have been, not quite the interpreter her friends hoped for. Her replies repeated the opinions they had already heard from Curzon. But she was still worth cajoling, even worth flattering. She might be a chink in an otherwise impenetrable wall.

Mary had another level of correspondence. She continued to write regularly to influential men she had met in America, like Henry Adams, G. W. Smalley and Cecil Spring Rice, and to the wives of leading men in England. All wrote to her. Mary's had become a name to drop. It was flattering to receive a letter from her, self-important to write one back, especially if one were permitted to address her as My Dearest Mary (Pamela Plowden, Jennie Churchill, Consuelo Vanderbilt), or Darling Mary (Sibell Grosvenor), or even Mary Darling (Ettie Grenfell). This extensive correspondence is still physically as fresh today as when it was written, the thick embossed notepaper differently coloured, differently scented, bearing at the head of each letter the address of one of the most historic houses in Britain, and at the foot one of its greatest names. They were written in the intervals of busy, pampered days, in bed after breakfast, while half-dressed for dinner, in the train to Paris, and the handwriting is sometimes cramped, sometimes flowing, sometimes crossed (a strange economy), and the page is often thickly bordered in black for the Queen's death, or for a son killed in the South African war. They told her the gossip ('The one subject of conversation is Sophie Scott's elopement with Mr Algy Burnaby'), but they contained political news too, half-digested fragments of husbands' talk, and literary allusions ('I have just read *Adam Bede* for the first time: we were not allowed to read it as girls'). The letters grew less trivial as the war took its toll, and girlish titter was replaced by something more genuine and nobler, sorrow for the absence of young men and fear for their safety, and many reveal a guilty awareness that war was somehow necessary once in a generation to justify the self-indulgence of their lives, and to raise the level of their emotions above the small demands of the hunting-field, the poker table, the ball-room and the bed.

In her replies Mary seldom complained of her lot. On her return from England she was not unhappy. After they had spent two weeks together in Simla, Curzon left her to tour Assam, and she joined him in Burma, going by sea from Calcutta to Rangoon, and thence by train to Mandalay. She told him ahead of their reunion that she felt 'vulgarly well', and the heat of Burma did nothing to spoil the enchantment of this the most pleasurable of all her tours. After Mandalay they floated lazily down the Irrawaddy in a golden barge escorted by paddle-steamers and canoes, landing at different riverside towns. At Paghan Mary was carried ashore by forty men on Thebaw's portable throne, and it began to rain: the parasols sagged, and the crimson lining of the throne stained her clothes. Mary, who could be driven to frenzy by the incompetence of a London foot-man, was at her best on such occasions. She insisted that the bearers complete the planned route in the downpour, laughing at her discomfiture, turning a disaster into a farce. So they came down again to Rangoon, to endure another four-mile cere-monial drive between packed thousands, halting at intervals under specially erected arches to receive addresses of welcome and bouquets. The strain at last began to tell: 'I am hot and tired. The heat takes it out of me terribly, but I keep up, though India saps every ounce of strength.'

In February 1902 she was allowed a respite. She went with the children to Darjeeling. For most of the day she read – Macaulay, John Addington Symonds on the Italian Renais-sance, Kinglake's *Eothen* – and busied herself with Queen Alexandra's coronation dresses. It was also the period when she began to concern herself seriously with her main practical legacy to India. Queen Victoria had expressed the hope that she might do something for the medical training of Indian women, since taboo was so strict that many a woman would not allow herself to be touched once in a lifetime by a male doctor. The training of women had been started by Lady Dufferin, and Mary continued her work, founding 'Victoria Scholarships' for the training of nurses, midwives and female doctors at various centres throughout the country, financed by the Appeal which Mary organized in the Queen's memory. From the Princes and Maharanis she soon collected £50,000. Great difficulties of caste and taboo hampered the scheme, but she pressed it forward tenaciously to success. In 1903 she extended it to the European community as well, convening at Simla an organizing committee of which she took the chair, and consulting personally all the local Indian governments which would be affected. The scheme was accepted in 1904 by Curzon's Council, who forwarded it to London, where certain changes were proposed by St John Brodrock, particularly to the financial provisions. Mary reconvened the committee during her last year in India, and they had recast the scheme to the point just short of practical action when Curzon's term ended. It was carried out by Lady Minto, her successor as Vicereine, and to Curzon's intense annoyance was thereafter known as 'Lady Minto's Scheme'. Thus Mary's idea, and her successful persistence with it, went unacknowledged except by very few.

The American newspapers in 1902 carried several reports that her health was breaking down. She asked her parents to deny them. From Simla in the summer of that year she wrote to her father:

George never does any social functions of any sort and they all devolve on me. I do them all. He has not gone out once since he came back, so I go through all the endlessly long list, bravely making his excuses and telling no one how he suffers and works. Duty is a wonderful incentive, and I have inherited my devotion to it from you, and I know it is a great help to G. to make the effort for him. So I go out to races, parties, concerts, weddings, prize-givings, polo-matches and the Lord knows what. It is all work and very little pleasure.

[158]

To her mother she wrote:

No one knows how I loathe Simla and its cruel climate. I never feel
well here. . . . You simply cannot know how I long for my darlings in
this life of formal greatness.

But she was always restored by a new experience, by exchanging British society for the Indian. Her visit to Kashmir that
year was one example. Another was the journey she made with
Curzon to the north-west frontier, to Malakand and Peshawar.
Her diary-letter (April 1902) begins:

I am sitting in the fort of the Malakand! We were met in the plain
by officers and officials and a crowd of Swat tribesmen with beards of
vermilion and wildfire eyes. We set out in a carriage to climb the pass,
up the new metalled road. We had a strong escort of cavalry, and the
hills were picketed by men at 200 yard intervals to prevent the over-
fanatical Pathans from shooting at us. We swept round a corner, and
there, hundreds of feet up stood the Malakand fortress – towers, walls
and blockhouse commanding the Pass with indomitable strength. At
the base of the rocks we left the carriages and found Sir Bindon Blood
waiting for us. Then on ponies we climbed up to the Political Agent's
tiny mud house inside the fort where we are to live.

She was the first white woman to visit the Malakand, and
from it she descended to the smiling Swat valley, which until
1895 no European had seen since Alexander the Great, protected by the cavalry and by the tribesmen's respect for her sex.
It was the same a few days later when she went to Peshawar at
the entrance to the Khyber Pass:

A vast picturesque mud town, endless, mysterious. It is the camping
ground of the worst ruffians in India, and a greater variety of mankind than you see anywhere else – Afridis, Afghans, Central Asian
tribes and Orakzais swarm through the Khyber on the two days it is
open to caravans. . . . It is a hotbed of rumour and flaming reports, and
the bazaars are alive with every lie imaginable about this visit of
George's and the Durbar he is to hold tomorrow. Representatives of
all the wild tribes have been invited to attend, and thousands have
swarmed in, goaded on by curiosity and the love of a show.

The Durbar was held on 26 April. The Curzons drove in state to a tent pitched on the race-course, and sat enthroned on a dais before a crowd of ten thousand while the chieftains filed past. Curzon made a speech which was translated into Pashtu, and then walked slowly through the ranks. 'To their amazement,' wrote Mary, 'I came behind, and they stared like things possessed at a woman coming at all.'

With the excitements, the novelty and the danger of these tours came experiences of a kind which made her detest India and long for home. In November 1902 she wrote from a prince-dom in central India:

We are staying in a horrid dirty house belonging to a general. Rats fight all night by my bed and huge lizards cling to the folds of my mosquito net, and every known animal from a grasshopper to a flea inhabits my bed. It is like a mediaeval prison, and I suffer agonies of fright at night. Last night rats knocked off all the things on the table beside my bed, while I shivered with terror. I cant eat the filthy food, and live on Benger's food and chocolate in our rooms.

In compensation, if it was that, she could look forward to the most spectacular event of her years in India, the fortnight which made all her sufferings seem worth while. In January 1903 she presided as Vicereine at the greatest Durbar the East had ever staged, the Coronation Durbar in Delhi.

The Durbar was a brilliant spectacle, an affirmation to the world that British rule in India was not only permanent but willingly accepted. Its main purpose was to acclaim King Edward as Emperor. The King could not come in person to be crowned without provoking all his other Dominions to demand that they be equally honoured. He much wanted to come, Jennie Churchill told Mary, but was dissuaded by his Ministers: 'He is a bit jealous of George and you, but he agrees that too many cooks can spoil the broth.' His Viceroy must act for him. It is true that he sent his brother, the Duke of Connaught, to attend the ceremonies, but the Duke, on Indian soil, was subordinate to the Viceroy, and therefore his Duchess to the Vicereine. Curzon was the central figure of the Durbar, its inspirer, its master-organizer, its focus and its philosopher. It gave him on the largest scale the opportunity that he most relished: to stage a magnificent ceremony every detail of which he conceived and organized; to recreate the pageantry of the ancient kings of India to the glory of its new rulers; to demonstrate in the manner most acceptable to Indians the unity of their country.

Powerful empires existed in India [he exclaimed in one of his Delhi orations], while Englishmen were wandering painted in the woods, and the British colonies were a wilderness. The British Sovereign has been able to do what Alexander never dreamt of, what Akhbar never performed, namely pacify, unify and consolidate the grand mass into a single homogeneous whole.

When Kitchener proposed that the hymn *Onward Christian Soldiers* be sung at the Durbar service, Curzon vetoed it on the grounds that the two lines,

> Crowns and Thrones may perish
> Kingdoms rise and wane,

might spoil this happy image.

The Durbar was criticized for its extravagance, but not in India. It was said that Curzon staged it more for his own glory than the King's. The New York *Journal* rushed in as champion of 'the starving Indians who had asked for bread and been given a durbar. Such extravagance is a shameful manifestation of the cruelty of Lord Curzon's craze for imperialistic display. It is reported that the expenditure of many of the native princes will bring them to the verge of bankruptcy. This unparalleled show will cost considerably over $5 million.' The sum was greatly exaggerated. When the final accounts were published, Curzon was able to show that the net cost had been £180,000. 'Is there anyone,' he asked, 'who will tell me that this is an excessive charge upon a population of over 280 millions for celebrating the Coronation of their Sovereign?' He might have added, what was undoubtedly true, that it would seem to any American a paltry sum for the pleasure of seeing *their* Miss Leiter ride into Delhi on the back of an enormous elephant and take her place beside her husband on a golden throne.

It was not the cost, but two other controversies, which slightly diminished the glory of the Durbar. The first was the refusal of the home Government to remit the salt tax. This concession had been proposed by Curzon as one which could well be afforded, and would satisfy oriental expectation of some such gesture to accompany so great an event. The Cabinet insisted that it would create an unfortunate precedent, and they would only allow Curzon, after he had threatened resignation on the issue, to announce a guarded intention to reduce taxes in the future. The incident wounded Curzon deeply. It was yet another example of the iniquity of allowing a group of ignorant men, sitting 7,000 miles away in London, to impose their judgment on the Viceroy and carry their foolish objections to the point just short of his resignation on the eve of an event which the world would watch with awe, rather than bow to his wishes. Mary wrote to him that she was 'lost in amazement. The whole point of view of the Government is very narrow, and their willingness to sacrifice you, after the magnificent work you have done, for a mere scruple, is incomprehensible. My poor Pappy is learning the bitter lesson of how home Governments break the hearts of their absent workers.'

The second incident was constitutionally less important, but more dramatic in its impact because it led to a public demonstration of Curzon's unpopularity. It was the affair of the 9th Lancers. The regiment was one of the smartest in the Indian Army, and its officers had aristocratic connections at home which they did not hesitate to exploit when the scandal broke. On the very night when they arrived back in India from the South African war, 9 April 1902, they held a party with the Black Watch at which a native cook named Atu was beaten up by some drunken troopers. A few days later Atu died. A court of inquiry, on which nobody but officers of the regiment sat, reported that they were unable to identify the culprit. Curzon was furious. He was convinced that this was yet another cover-up of ill-treatment of the natives by British troops. He expressed himself in the strongest terms:

I know that as long as Europeans, and particularly a haughty race like the English, rule Asiatic peoples like the Indians, incidents of *hubris* and violence will occur, and that the white men will tend to side with the white skin against the dark. But I also know, and have acted throughout on the belief, that it is the duty of statesmanship to arrest these dangerous symptoms and to prevent them from attaining dimensions that might even threaten the existence of our rule in the future.

He was moved not only by the threat of Indian reaction, but by his innate, burning sense of justice, and those who condemn Curzon for being the haughtiest of 'a haughty race like the English', should remember the courage with which he stood against the entire Army in insisting that Atu's murderer be found and punished:

I will not be a party to any of the scandalous hushing up of bad cases of which there is too much in this country, or to the theory that a white man may kick or batter a black man to death with impunity because he is only 'a d——d nigger'.

The 9th Lancers never admitted that any of their men was responsible for Atu's death, nor for the murder within their lines of another coolie a week later. A second inquiry produced the same result: no evidence could be found against any individual. For Curzon this was not good enough. He determined to punish the whole regiment, and in this he was supported by the Commander-in-Chief (Sir Power Palmer, before Kitchener's arrival) and by Lord George Hamilton at home. All officers and men of the regiment on leave in India were to be recalled, and no more leave would be granted for six months. General Palmer further proposed that the regiment be forbidden to take part in the Delhi Durbar, and although Curzon vetoed this added disgrace, he refused Lord Roberts's request to announce a remission of the other punishment at the Durbar itself. The damage was done, not to the regiment which deserved it, not to the Commander-in-Chief who had authorized the punishment, but to Curzon. The Viceroy's name was execrated throughout

India: he was freely denounced as a nigger-lover in Army messes and civilian clubs; it was said that he was trying to win popularity with the Indians at the cost of Britain's prestige. When the 9th Lancers marched into the arena at the Durbar's military parade, they were greeted with ecstatic applause by all the Europeans present, including Curzon's own guests who had come from England, and its meaning could not possibly be misinterpreted. Curzon did not flinch.

As I sat alone and unmoved on my horse [he reported to Hamilton], conscious of the implication of the cheers, I could not help being struck by the irony of the situation. There rode before me a long line of men, in whose ranks were most certainly two murderers. It fell to the Viceroy, who is credited by the public with the sole responsibility for their punishment, to receive their salute. I do not suppose that anybody in that vast crowd was less disturbed by the demonstration than myself. On the contrary, I felt a certain gloomy pride in having dared to do the right.

History must be overwhelmingly on Curzon's side in this affair. The British were in India not only to rule but to set an example of fair play. As their power resided ultimately in the military, the soldiers must be even more careful than the civilians to set that example. But they were the least capable of setting it, being the most conceited, the least far-seeing, the least humane. They saw the Lancers' public disgrace as a weakening of British prestige; Curzon saw it as manifest justice, an essential ingredient of that prestige.

Suspecting that some such demonstration was in store for him and angered by the Government's refusal of tax concessions, Curzon set out for Delhi without pleasure. Mary was waiting in the wings at Dehra Dun, where her mother and Daisy joined her, clutching bags of diamonds for Mary's greater brilliance at the Durbar. She wrote to Curzon:

Every bit of my vitality has gone, and I am iller than I have ever been, and simply cant get back to life somehow. I hope the poison has not killed my spirit. My hand weighs a ton, and I cannot write or think but do think of a miraculous cure before you come: it *must* come! I

[164]

21 Curzon and Mary with their daughters Irene (left) and Cynthia, in 1903

22 Mary dressed
by Worth of Paris
when she was
Vicereine

23 *Above* Mary Curzon,
painted in Munich by
Franz von Lenbach, in
1901

24 *Right* Coming ashore
in the Persian Gulf,
autumn 1903

25 Arthur Balfour, Prime
Minister while Curzon was
Viceroy, with Winston Churchill

26 Lord Kitchener,
Commander-in-Chief, India

27 Alexandra Curzon, aged 2,
with her bodyguard at Simla in
1905

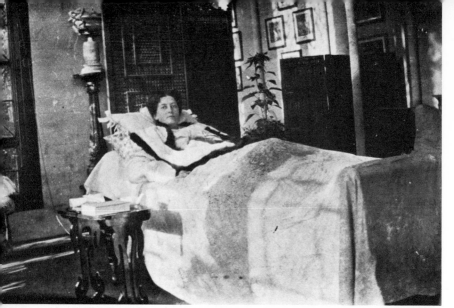

28 *Above* Mary
convalescing at
Highcliffe Castle,
Hampshire, after
her serious illness in
1904

29 *Right* The
tomb of Mary and
George Curzon in
Kedleston church

know it will! I believe absolutely in my power of 'coming up to time' or answering my ring, as an actor does. Some day though, the bell will go and I shall not appear, as India, I know, slowly but surely murders women. Bring back a magic cure for poor broken Kinkie!

The celebrations at Delhi lasted two weeks. There had never been such a show, not even Lord Lytton's Durbar of 1877, when Queen Victoria was proclaimed Empress, and not even King Edward's coronation at Westminster the year before. It began with the State Entry. In brilliant sunshine the Viceroy and Vicereine advanced slowly along the processional route, mounted on the largest elephant that India possessed, the same unaging beast, loaned by the Maharajah of Benares, as that on which Lord Lytton had ridden in 1877. Its vast flanks were covered by a cloth of gold embroidered with lions rampant and the sun in glory, its patient face and trunk hung with ropes and chains. On the elephant's back rested a silver boat-shaped howdah, and here Mary and Curzon sat, shielded by the umbrella of state, slight figures for so unstable an eminence and for so august a role. The outsize animal, absurd were it not monumental, awkward did it not appear in a curious way serene, humiliated more than adorned by its trappings, conveyed with dignity the two people, man and woman, who at that moment represented the highest degree to which mankind aspired. It was not easy for them to maintain attitudes worthy of their role when with each slow pace the howdah swayed from side to side. But the vast crowd saw in the clumsy movement India's noblest stride, and acclaimed them, the Viceroy because he was sovereign, the Vicereine because she was beautiful, and both of them because they jointly represented authority and compassion, and the consummation between East and West. Mary, her headache forgotten, the precariousness of her perch ignored, entered Delhi like an Empress. It was ridiculous; it was splendid; it was immensely enjoyable; it was the most wonderful moment of her life.

The celebrations continued, day after day. There was the great march-past of British and Indian troops, led by the veterans of the Mutiny. The armed retainers of the Indian princes might have marched in the army of Xerxes. There were men clad in mail from head to foot, and Nagas, half-naked, who engaged in single combat with long curved swords. Others were mounted on camels, elephants and stilts. One Prince sent his gold and silver cannon, drawn by white oxen. The parade passed in waves of colour, brilliant with jewelled turbans. The silver bells of the elephants tinkled as they strode, and their great feet raised clouds of dust which floated like golden spray in the sunshine. On succeeding days came the Investiture, and a great assembly at which Curzon proclaimed his Sovereign as the new Emperor. At intervals there were polo-matches, receptions and dances, varying in scale like the muted and exalted passages of an opera. Inevitably Mary was the centre of attention. A display of authority was the purpose of the immense jamboree, but glamour was its inspiration, and she supplied it. Each night she wore a lovelier dress. Each day she floated between the tented compounds where her guests were lodged. Never had there been so supreme, so calm a hostess. To the English visitors who had known her shy and withdrawn in London, she seemed transformed. There were 160 of them, including the Marlboroughs, the Portlands, the Derbys, the Crewes, the Elchos, and on their return home they gave her the credit she deserved. She embellished every occasion. Her mother and sister stood aside, amazed.

The climax was the State Ball. It was held on the last day of the Durbar in the Diwan-i-Khas, or Private Hall of Audience, of Delhi's Moghul palace, the supreme creation of Shah Jehan, a many-pillared hall which he built as a pleasure-house to the greater glory of man. The hidden electric bulbs, installed to Curzon's order and to his careful design, suffused the cusped arches with a glow as soft as candlelight, and irradiated walls of pure marble inlaid with agate, amethyst, malachite, onyx and lapis-lazuli. The hall and neighbouring supper-rooms contained nearly 4,000 guests, including fifty Princes in full regalia. They parted to form a lane down the centre of the hall when the Viceroy and Vicereine arrived. Mary was dressed in a cloth of gold embroidered with a pattern of tiny peacock feathers stitched in metal thread, an emerald filling each eye, the skirt trimmed with white roses and the bodice with lace. (The dress, which is preserved, less its emeralds, in the Museum of London at the Barbican, was a reminder of the peacock throne of the Moghul kings which had once stood at the far end of the Diwan-i-Khas.) As she moved up the hall with Curzon in white-satin knee-breeches at her side, there was a stir in the crowd. 'You cannot conceive what a dream she looked', wrote one eyewitness; and when she reached the marble podium and turned to greet her guests, her radiance caused another to exclaim, 'Such beauty is not given to one woman in a million.' Among the company was Pearl Craigie (John Oliver Hobbes), who in her book *Imperial India* analyzed more subtly the indelible impression which Mary made that night:

The woman who presented the most romantic appearance and embodied the romantic ideal was Lady Curzon herself. A perpetual reason for this lies, no doubt, in the fragile beauty of her countenance; it does not follow, however, that the possession of beauty makes, in the modern, for romance. Lady Curzon suggests this rare sentiment, because she does not smear her face with red-and-white washes, nor disfigure her head by the pyramids of curls, pads, fringes, tulle and ribbons, which pinned on without regard for proportion, balance, or line, alter many handsome members of English society until they resemble the ignoble advertisements of fashionable wig-makers. . . . Lady Curzon always wears elaborately woven or embroidered materials, but she never overloads them with ornaments.

The ball ended the Delhi celebrations, and Mary went back to Dehra Dun exhausted. She and Curzon exchanged mutual congratulations:

The Connaughts were no more than an extra gargoyle to a most intricate and wondrous building [she wrote to him], every stone of which had been carved and placed by you. Neither of them have personalities – he has a most exquisite manner, but she is only a German hausfrau. The 9th Lancers gave them a flash of glory, as they were supposed to espouse their cause. But now that all is over, every civilian in India knows to whom the credit is due, and your position today in India is stronger than any man's has ever been.

He wrote to her:

As you say, it was a great success, and if ever the policy of doing everything oneself down to the smallest detail was justified, it was here. But after all, I was responsible merely for the ceremonial side. For the splendid triumph of the social side, yours is the credit. Your beauty, your charm, your absolute unselfishness in looking after others, and your sure and unfailing tact – these it was that carried through the whole camp life, the dinners and parties, on the crest of an unbroken wave of success, while to all the public ceremonial you lent a grace and distinction the more marked from the utter inability of even the smartest and the most beautiful of our English ladies to contest it.

The year 1903, which began in Delhi, continued in Calcutta and then in Simla, where Mary suffered a reaction. 'I do not see a living soul day in, day out, and have now been flat on my back in bed or on a sofa for one whole month. I sometimes wonder if I am the same person who lived through the gaieties of Delhi as I lie here in the silence which no one disturbs unless I ring a bell or the children come dancing in.' When she recovered her strength she spent much time in the tented camp at Naldera, where Kitchener was a constant visitor. 'A fine character with a perfect scorn of popularity', Mary described him to her mother. 'He and George both have indomitable wills, and it is frequently my diplomacy which keeps them great friends.' She sang for them both to the accompaniment of a hidden band while the rain drummed on the canvas roof. The monsoon always cleared her head as it did the air, and by the autumn she was well enough to undertake another tour, though now pregnant with her third child.

They went by sea to the states bordering the Persian Gulf, escorted by four warships, and Curzon landed at intervals to hold a durbar or review the troops, while Mary usually stayed on board, cooled in the intense heat by electric fans, reading and sewing. A doctor and a nurse attended her, but she told her mother that she was in the best of health, and the only reason why she seldom went ashore was the difficulty of clambering in and out of launches in her condition. As the ship lay off Kuweit, she wrote: 'The air is divine here, a mixture of sea and desert. And I am very well indeed, and love the long peaceful days on deck.'

In December she was back at Barrackpore, and was excused most social duties. Kitchener was now her constant attendant, and his growing affection for her was reciprocated. Some of his letters to Mary were tender to the point of flirtation, while to her he was 'a rugged sort of companion. There is a sort of bracing north wind of resolution and strenuousness about him, and a gentle spot about a woman which a woman is always quick to find.' From England, early in 1905, she was to tell Curzon that those long hours with Kitchener were some of the happiest she had spent in India, 'as his utter dependence upon me appealed so strongly to me – more so because liking me as a woman, he talked to me as a man'. Having little small-talk, he spoke to her mainly of his work, but he could be attentive in a way that Curzon seldom was, and Curzon was aware of it:

I fear I do not lavish half enough attention on Kinkie. The reason is not, as you know well, that I do not feel it, but that I live at such high tension and am such a slave to work, so worried by it and stretched almost to breaking point. You must forgive me if I am not always sufficiently considerate or understanding or fond.

Their plan was that Mary would return to England early in 1904 for the birth of her child, and spend a few months in the United States during the summer, for she had not been in America since her marriage, nor seen her father since 1898. This plan was upset by Curzon's determination to continue his work in India for a second term. No Viceroy in living memory had prolonged his rule beyond the five stipulated years, and Curzon had been expected to leave India at the end of 1903, but his energy and achievement had been so exceptional that it was difficult for the Cabinet to refuse his request to supervize the completion of his many reforms. All he requested was a break of four or five months in England before returning to India for two final years, and this they were ready to grant him. Mary's wishes were not consulted. The prospect of another

Indian stint, even after a long holiday, appalled her. 'India suits him, and the air of the House of Commons never did ... He will come home next spring [1904], and if he accepts another term, I cannot stop him, but I shall tell him that I will not stay uninterruptedly as my health will not stand it.' To Pearl Craigie she wrote: 'I want him to go home and not come back, but if he decides to come back, I shall never let him know how much I regret the decision.'

The decision was made. Mary returned to England in January; Curzon was to follow in May; both were to return to India in September and remain there till 1906.

Mary's welcome in London was a repeat of her triumph of 1901. She was able to stay for the first time in her own house 1 Carlton House Terrace, and one of her first visitors there was the King:

He appeared at 5, and I met him at the door with the two little girls. He was most affable. I gave him tea off your silver service and he stopped 1½ hours, and he talked about Bushire. Tibet he was very hazy about. He spoke in the warmest terms of your work and your letters, and hoped that St John [Brodrick] was behaving properly. He asked me when I was to be laid up, and said I must take great care as I looked very frail.

Her almost daily letters to Curzon were designed to comfort and reassure him, but also subtly to influence him, as far as she dared, to reconsider his decision to remain in India, by hinting at the even more glittering opportunities that awaited him at home:

You do loom so great and big and strong out there in India, away from the miserable muddles here, where each day seems to add to the failures of your friends. ... Austen Chamberlain is an admitted failure; AJB hopeless; and Joe [Chamberlain] run away from the muddle he has landed them all in. You are so out of it – untouched by the strange ill luck that pursues the party. . . . Here you are looked on as a giant – and a frightening one.

On 7 March, only two weeks before the birth of her baby, she lunched alone with Balfour, the Prime Minister:

He was full of enquiries about you, and then said, 'Now I am coming straight to the point – I wish to God George were here at this moment. First because of my affection for him which has never and never will waver; and secondly because I want a better understanding between the English and Indian Governments – the two *must* be one – instead of what they are at present. I fear I think the Indian Government desires to be treated like the Government of a separate country, and we are always wasting time and temper over argument on paper. I want G. *here*. The differences are of a nature which the sight of him – dear old boy – would put right.' He looked fearfully worn and aged and suffers terribly from neuralgia at night. He was amazed at how well I looked, kept putting on his glasses and saying, 'You look quite astonishingly well.'

Curzon briefed her by letter so that she should never be at a disadvantage in discussion with ministers, and she represented his views to them with unshakable loyalty. She echoed from London the phrases he wrote from Calcutta. This letter, for example, might have been written by either of them, but was in fact Curzon's:

St John continues to show the most abject ignorance of India, and is at the mercy of any one of his Councillors who happens to disagree with us. It is truly maddening on all things where we are unanimous, to have objections, obstacles and obstructions, almost always resting either on prejudice or on ignorance.

How little did he understand that by always taking his side, she was doing him no service, and by always speaking with his voice she was throwing away her gifts and influence. He wrote:

I feel so happy and proud when I see you run after, admired and adored. You hold a really unique position in this respect. For what other woman in London combines great beauty with exceptional intelligence as well as a tact which is an inspiration? There is no limit to the influence which you can exercise at home, as you have done in India, smoothing down those whom I ignore and offend, and creating our own atmosphere of refinement and devotion.

Their baby was born in London on 20 March 1904. Another girl. They had longed for a son, but as the chances were still equal, he had prepared them both for disappointment: 'Darling, it doesn't in the least matter if sweet Nalder is a girl. Don't fuss about that. Girls are very loveable.' But not quite so loveable as boys: 'I pray in these same words every day: "May she bear a child to thy honour and glory and to the good of thy kingdom, and may it be a male child."' When the news reached him by telegram, he wrote at once to console her:

Darling, I felt how miserable you would be, and though of course I too was somewhat disappointed, I really felt it much more for you than for myself. However, I think we must entirely attribute it to me! You will remember that months ago we discussed and contemplated this, and that the name Naldera was arranged in consequence. So we will be content with our little Naldera and postpone Irian-Dorian till some future date. After all, what does the sex matter after we are both of us gone?

The child was given two names, Alexandra after the Queen, who was one of the godparents (St John Brodrick was another); and Naldera after the camp near Simla where she was probably conceived. But from a very early age she was known to her family and friends as 'Baba' (the Indian servants called her 'Baba Sahib' – 'Viceroy's baby'), a name which she still thinks absurd but which has done nothing to diminish the affection in which she has been universally held ever since.

Curzon returned home as planned in the middle of May, leaving Lord Ampthill, Governor of Madras, temporarily in charge at Simla. Mary met him at Dover. At first he seemed miserable for want of work, wandering round the house muttering, 'What am I to do? What am I to do?', but Ministerial conferences soon absorbed his time, and he received the Freedom of the Cities of London and Derby, and an Honorary degree at Oxford. One honour specially pleased him. He was offered and accepted the position of Lord Warden of the Cinque Ports in succession to Lord Salisbury. He enjoyed the ceremony of his installation at Dover, for it was a change from the sycophancy of India to assume the ancient office in the presence of friends like George and Sibell Wyndham and St John Brodrick, and to be greeted with homely speeches, the town band, and 'forty members of St John's Ambulance Brigade, Dover division, under the supervision of Superintendent Lawes'. Curzon made a speech at a luncheon in the Town Hall, saying with flattering hyperbole that the Viceroy and the Lord Warden had this in common, that both were required to see to the defence of the realm. The appointment was for life (Churchill later held it for twenty-four years), and its duties and privileges were officially described as 'The Office of Governor of Dover Castle, Warden, Chancellor and Admiral of the Cinque Ports, together with all wreck of the sea, flotsam and jetsam, within the liberties of the Ports, together with Walmer Castle as a dwelling place'.

In fact no executive function was required of the Lord Warden, and the office carried no salary, but Curzon welcomed it for its historic associations and innocent anachronism, and because it was an honour which famous men had held in the past, including the Duke of Wellington (who died at Walmer Castle), and two previous Viceroys, Dalhousie and Dufferin. Walmer would make a perfect country residence when he was in England. Mary had been to see it before he returned. 'I simply loved it,' she reported to him. 'I gazed at Wellington's wash-basin and his boots; the former was very small and the latter very big, and I thought of the great man as I sat on the edge of his bed. I slipped along the corridor and peeped into all the rooms, and rested in the lovely big drawing-room, full of dear grimy dilapidated furniture. I heard the caretaker, so hid in the corner where Pitt said farewell to Nelson. Then I crawled on to the ramparts, and dragged out a chair and watched the Channel fleet do foolish manoeuvres in the deep blue sea. I shall be very happy there.'

Her first impressions, as of Kedleston, did not last long. Walmer Castle was highly inconvenient, and crumbling to decay. There were twenty-two bedrooms, but only one sitting-room, and when Lord Salisbury had attempted to use as a study the bedroom where the Duke of Wellington died, he was forced to abandon it by cries of protest from Walmer town.

There was no electricity or heating, and the furniture consisted in cast-off pieces from the Cecils' minor houses, and the incoming Warden found that he was expected to buy this trash for £1,500. But the greatest drawback of the castle was its sanitation. Every corner seemed to contain a broken-down water-closet, and the drains which linked them were clogged and lethal conduits. Gwendolen Cecil, Salisbury's daughter, was not the only past inhabitant to denounce the place as a death-trap, 'families of microbes of ancient descent still flourishing in the homes of their mediaeval ancestors'. Before the Curzons could move in, it was essential to renovate the Castle, and temporarily they rented a house opposite it, Walmer Place, while the Royal Engineers ripped the old sewers apart.

It was while Mary was supervising these restorations that she heard of her father's death on 9 June at Bar Harbor, Maine, a house rented from the Vanderbilts. She had not seen him for nearly six years. 'My love for him was almost the strongest part of my life', she wrote to her mother, and her sustained correspondence with him confirms it. Different though their temperaments were, Levi Leiter had been to her what Curzon became, a man to whom she gave unreservedly all her love and admiration, and his death snatched away one of the two pillars of her happiness. She could not reach America in time to attend the funeral, but begged her mother to come to England, offering her Walmer Castle as a home when she and Curzon returned to India. No expense would be spared to make her comfortable, and Mary could now say this with confidence. She had become a great heiress. Her father's legacy would yield an income of at least £20,000 a year, and more when her mother died.

During the early summer of 1904 Mary had intermittent illnesses, and at times complained of great weariness. But she was socially active, spending most weekends at country-house parties, two of them at Windsor. In August the Curzons moved into Walmer Castle, now declared habitable, but when the King asked her about it, she replied cheerfully that it was 'a rotten, tumble-down old place'. Soon after moving in, she had a miscarriage, and although she seemed to make a quick recovery, complications, which Curzon blamed on the doctor, caused a temporary relapse, but not serious enough to postpone their preparations to return to India on 23 September. On the 20th, when all their baggage was being moved from Walmer to catch the boat which they were to join at Marseilles, she went for a drive along the Kent coast, and although she returned home feeling cold, there was no indication that she would be unfit to travel.

During the night she was seized by intense pain, which the doctors diagnosed as peritonitis, complicated by phlebitis. The cause was never satisfactorily explained, but it was probably a combination of the effects of her miscarriage and infection from the effluent of an old drain immediately beneath her bedroom window. The engineers had bungled their job.

Within a few hours Mary was on the point of death. The first bulletin, on 21 September, told the world that her condition was critical, and she had two operations which seemed only to worsen it. For many days she wavered between coma and brief intervals of lucidity, and Curzon was warned to face the probability that she would not recover. The successive bulletins still arouse the pity and terror with which her friends in three continents heard of her struggle: 'Still critical'; 'Grave relapse'; 'A change for the worse: her condition is exceedingly grave'; 'Serious anxiety'. The last of these was dated 15 October, more than three weeks after her first attack, when pneumonia had been added to her other sufferings.

For Curzon the ordeal was terrible. 'I am worn out with anguish and suspense', he wrote to Brodrick. And to King Edward, who inquired after her daily: 'Hope is sinking lower and lower within me, and the cloud of darkness seems to be settling down.' While he remained as punctilious as ever in replying to the flood of telegrams and letters which reached him at Walmer, he spent hours on end at Mary's bedside. When he believed her to be dying on 22 September, he kept by him a pad of paper on which he scribbled in pencil every word she whispered, and some years later added to the thirty-four sheets this heading: 'These are the notes made by me at Walmer Castle in

September 1904 when my darling lay dying, and when she gave me her last instructions and bade me farewell.' Seldom can so moving a document have been made and preserved. It is printed exactly as written:

3.40 am. Thursday Sep. 22 Great pain into the night. Eyes.

8.15 am. I'll do my best.

(1)   Pain gone to the other side.
       Pulse better. Only 110, it was 130.
       Cable to my people; they ought to know. I have peritonitis.
       How are the little children?

(2)   All right. Would you like to see them? No.
       My tongue is quite dreadful. It is cracked right across.
       The wind continues dreadful.
       Peeling clothes off like very doz. [deuce?], but no idea how bad.

(3)   Asked about Champneys and Barlow [doctors].
       knew going to be operated on
       said she knew it would kill her
       said I must not say anything to make her cry
       What little things life turns upon. If only they had let me stay in.
       I knew I could not get up. I felt so cold on that drive.
       Curtains for Queen's room. Queen's bed.

(4)   What o'clock is it? 10.50 am. Only that?
       What day. Thursday.
       Sickness. right to head of bed.

(5)   Sickness again
       Going to give food of injection
       Have you heard from Barlow
       Did you say Champneys for consultation?

(6)   2.20 pm. Try and keep up. Make a good struggle. Keep your strength.
       I haven't got any
       My darling, my beau. Dont make me cry.

(7)   3–8. From 3.30 to 5.30 things were at their worst. During this time she was thrice nearly gone. Her hands and arms and extremities became cold. I rubbed her arm and hand with brandy and hot water bottles were put under feet and legs, even up to her thighs.

       She was most reluctant to believe that she was going and said that she did not want to see the children till the end.

[176]

At intervals she gave me instructions about everything.

(a) I was to see that a sum of £750 or £800 which she was to have spent out of Mr Phipps donation on an operating table should be paid back to the [Indian nurses] fund.

(b) I was to tell Boucheron not to reset her necklace but to put back the old stones.

(c) I was to give

> diamond bird given her by the Argies to Mouche [Lady Ulrica Baring]
>
> also a black heart badge in same box as Chinese butterfly
>
> also presents to Alice [Keppel?], Mrs Craigie, Evie Kelly, K [Kitchener].
>
> also tea-service to Matron and present to Nurse
>
> also donation to Deal Hospital
>
> also present for Ida from Irene Carrington

She said several times, 'You are to have all my jewels. But give the pearls to the children when they grow up'.

and repeatedly, Tell Joe [Leiter] as my last wish that I wish him to carry out what he wrote to me

She wished to write to Syis [?] a paper to this effect. But I would not allow her.

She said, I leave everything to you

She said, See that the little children are treated kindly.

Dont let any governess or servant treat them unkindly.

Dont make Irene work too hard at her lessons. I have loved them so dearly and Irene loves me so much. Never let Sibley [children's nurse] leave the children (when Sibley entered the room she made her promise this). Give her a house at Kedleston and never let her go.

Dont let the children remain here. It is too cold for them

Dont stay here after I die (I promised not to).

Dont take them to India. Ask Mama as my last wish to come and take them to some warm place and look after them.

I asked her if she died whether she would wish to be buried at Kedleston.

Yes I should love it.

Here she said, Dont put me in the ground. I have a horror of being put in the ground (and at another time: I have a horror of being buried alive.) Put me in the vault.

I asked her if she would wish any of her friends invited at the funeral. No, she said, it is too far. Only your father and Frank and specially Lilian.

She said, I give Lilian [Curzon's youngest sister] £50 a year, and I promised to continue it.

She took off her rings and gave them into my hand, and said, Keep the sapphire brooch and the silver mirror. I said I would not keep the latter but would keep the former because it was the last thing she had worn.

At one time when she thought she was going she asked me to read through our favourite psalm, 'Lord who shall dwell in thy holy tabernacle or who shall rest upon thy holy hill' and I read it through in floods of tears. She repeated the first two sentences after me.

Then she asked me to read Tennyson's Crossing the Bar, and I repeated the first verse. She said, 'But you must not mourn for me'. At one moment when she was nearly going she said, Repeat the Lord's Prayer, and I repeated it and she after me.

She said, Do not have a funeral service for me in London. But when I answered that all her friends would want to be present, she said, Have it then in the Chapel Royal, St James's.

At intervals when she asked to be alone with me and at other times, she said, 'Bless you' and 'Sweet Pappy' and 'I love you dearly'. I asked her if she had been happy and she said, 'Very, very happy'. She apologised for not having been nice to me sometimes this summer, eg. at Bexhill, but said that it was due to her health and she had not meant it. At one time she said, 'I have suffered so much, so much. I must surely go to Heaven'.

About 5.30 she asked to see the sea, and the outer shutters were unbarred and the inner shutters folded back, and she looked out upon it.

Then she said I always had a presentiment about Walmer. From the first I knew that it would mean misfortune. I knew it again when a little robin came in at the window and settled on the back of the chair. That is an omen of death. The little nurse saw it and I said so.

Between 4 and 5 when we thought she was going, the children were brought in. She kissed each tenderly and said something to them about presents. Irene was to give her present to Ida.

She said, When I die, let no one come into the room but the nurses and you.

From 3.0 onwards she began eagerly to count upon the arrival of the doctors. She was disappointed that Dr Cheyne could not come till 3.15, and when she heard he could not arrive till 6.15, she said, 'I will fight it out. I will be alive to see him'. As the time drew near she began to revive and hypodermic injections of strychnine and brandy and milk kept her going. She kept asking the time every 10 or 15 minutes eagerly awaiting the 6.15, enquiring about the motor and how quick it could come. Then when he came she wanted him to examine and operate at once. 'Can I live?' 'Is there a chance? What are you going to do?' At one time she said, 'Oh I dont want to go. Why should I have to go? I want to stay'. We encouraged her to battle and struggle and she did so with indomitable courage, and from the moment that Dr Cheyne arrived she began to rally. Her temperature improved and her pulse descended from 135 to 120, 118, 112, and she said she meant to fight her best.

Nevertheless Dr Cheyne at first came into my room and told me that there was no hope, and that if operated upon she would never survive the anaesthetic, and that there was nothing to be done.

Her condition however continued to improve, until Dr Barlow arrived about 9.30.

Curzon's notes were interrupted at that point, and he resumed them three days later, after Mary had had her first operation:

She had heard me say that she had fought a splendid fight, and she was glad of that. But now it was over, and she must go.

She was now perfectly tranquil and began to talk to me about our love and our life.

Oh how happy we have been. You have been my only love. I have loved you intensely and you have made me utterly happy for 10 years. We have done a great deal together, George. We have succeeded. It has been a wonderful time. Religion, she said, has not been very much to me. But I have always tried to do that which is right and good from an instinctive sense of duty, and I die happy and without alarm.

She said, You must go back to India to your work there. Work will be the only thing for you. I want you to promise me to do it.

But she said, You must not take back the children. You must leave them with Mama.

Then she sent again for the children and bid them each good-bye. She sent for the doctors and thanked them for their care and devotion and she thanked Sibley and the Matron.

I asked her whether in another world, if there was one, she would wait for me till I could come. Yes, she said. I will wait. When I said that we had loved each other long and been all in all to each other, she asked that that might be inscribed on her tomb. She asked that we might be buried side by side with a marble effigy of each of us looking towards each other, so that we might one day be reunited. She said, Keep the feathers [Peacock dress?] picture of me – that is the best – and get all the Lenbachs. I promised to do so.

Over and over she murmured, My darling, my sweet Pappy, and she said that the thing that had touched her most was my letters from India at the birth of our last child when she was in England.

She said our love letters have been wonderful and who that read them could doubt that ours had been a wonderful love. We talked of our marriage day, and of her look at me and mine at her as we stood side by side on the steps of the altar and the lovelights shone in her eyes.

After a while she grew more composed and presently asked to see the doctors again. Her wound was again dressed without pain. This cheered her a great deal: and she asked the doctors if it was worth while making another fight. They encouraged her, and with set lips she said, Well then, I will.

Soon after she settled down to rest, and as I left the room her last words were, My darling.

The bulletins repeatedly despaired of her life, but slowly she began to regain her strength from 17 October onwards, when she was moved at her own request from Walmer Castle to the nearby house, Walmer Place, which they had rented earlier. Nothing, Curzon said, would induce him to sleep another night in that 'charnel house' of a castle. 'I assure you it is uninhabitable', he wrote to Sir Schomberg McDonnell, secretary of the Office of Works. 'I am clearing all my own things out now, and having the place disinfected.' Mary begged him to give up the office of Lord Warden, and he needed little persuasion. He resigned after holding it only a few months, and nobody was greatly offended or surprised.

By the end of October she was out of danger, but clearly she would need a long period of convalescence. Should Curzon return to India? Should she follow him there when she was fit to travel?

Almost any other man would have stayed. His extraordinary record of her dying words and his response to them is evidence of his profound emotion, and of a love for her as deep as a man can feel for a woman. She would be desperately lonely without him, and he without her. She might have another relapse at any moment. He himself had suffered acutely from backache while he was in England. There was no pressure on him to return to India. Only one other Viceroy in 130 years had returned for a second term. Although many small and some larger policies had gone astray in his absence (Lord Ampthill being nervous of taking initiatives as deputy to so formidable a chief), nobody would have thought the less of Curzon if he had asked Balfour to release him from his promise and send out his successor at once. After a few months he could have accepted a high position in the Cabinet, and his Viceroyalty would have been recorded as one of the greatest in history. But Curzon was not like any other man. He saw it differently. He would not allow a new Viceroy to complete his reforms. Several urgent crises, in Afghanistan, in Tibet, had blown up in his absence, and he believed that they could not be handled by anybody but himself. 'I felt it a duty to the Government of which I had been the head for so long not to desert it in the hour of trial', he said in a public speech, 'but to sacrifice all personal considerations to the necessity of fightings its battles.' Mary would understand; she had always understood. He wrote to her from Marseilles on 24 November as he embarked on the ship that would take him back to India:

All the way through I have thought of Kinkie only – Kinkie through all the phases of her fearful illness, Kinkie's courage, her beautiful and unparalleled devotion, her resignation, her patience, her combat with all the foes of evil and death, her serene and conquering love for poor Pappy, her darling face with the bandage round it, her smile, her kisses and endearments, all the movements of poor hands and limbs. It is with a sad and miserable heart that I go, leaving all that makes life worth living behind me, and going out to toil and isolation and often worse. But it seems to be destiny, and God who has smitten us so hard must surely have better things in store. . . . We have been drawn very close by our companionship in the furnace of affliction, and I hope that it may leave me less selfish and more considerate in the future. To me you are everything and the sole thing in the world, and I go on existing in order to come back and try to make you happy.

As he approached Bombay, he wrote:

I am getting old and played out, and the fire in me is not what it was. My sole claim, I think, is that I love my darling and want to make her happy in this life to which she has been won back by her courage and the mercy of Providence.

The Governor of Bombay, Lord Lamington, who had been his best man, proposed his health at a dinner on the night of his arrival, 'with such apposite and touching reference to you, that I broke down most discreditably in my reply. I literally could not proceed, and it must have seemed a very painful exhibition. You see, I have been stretched nearly to breaking point and any reference to you destroys my balance at once . . . And now my coming back to this rack of duty, all alone, with you still at home, excites such poignant contrasts and emotions in my mind that I feel at times quite unhinged and it will be some time before I recover complete command.'

One service he had been able to do for her before he left England. He rented Highcliffe Castle, a large and beautifully furnished house near Christchurch in Hampshire, where she could spend her convalescence with the children. She was taken there by special train in the last week of November, a day before Curzon's departure. His brother Frank spent some time with her, and as she grew stronger she was visited by many of their friends. Her mother, who had darted across the Atlantic when Mary was dying, now returned to Washington for the weddings of her other daughters, whose bridegrooms were both British officers who had been Curzon's ADCs. Nancy married Colin Campbell on 29 November, and Daisy the Earl of Suffolk on Boxing Day. Each was the other's best man. 1904 had been quite a year for Mrs Leiter. Within six months she had lost her husband, nearly lost a daughter, and staged the weddings of the other two.

Curzon had never expected Mary to rejoin him in India. He had steeled himself to endure a two-year separation, and put no pressure on her to return to him except by constant, irrepressible reminders of his loneliness: 'I have not dared to go into your room for fear that I should burst out crying,' he wrote from Calcutta. 'And indeed I am utterly miserable and desolate. Nobody to turn to or talk to, memories on all sides of me, and anxiety gnawing at my heart.' Daily telegrams punctuated his daily letters: 'How is angel?' 'So glad beloved.' 'What news beloved?' 'Flourishing when sweetheart flourishes.' 'Overjoyed progress.' He was careful to tell her that he would not let her run any risk, and would be willing 'to chuck my hand in to-morrow' and return to England if she became seriously ill again or found her isolation intolerable. 'The first and only factor, in the front rank, is you.'

His astonishment and delight at the news that she intended to return to India broke down all his reserve. It was her decision, not his. He heard it by telegram on 25 January 1905. 'I could hardly credit it, and I went dancing off to the Belvedere Ball (usually the most hateful of functions) in a most indecent state of glee. I told everybody, and they were in a wild state of exalta-tion. K. [Kitchener] looked a new man, and the room was one vast smile.' Mary told him that her doctors had recommended her to go partly for medical reasons, partly human, partly political: 'They both agreed that I should never get well alone without my Pappy, and old Cheyne thought it my duty to go out and sustain you in your great work, and he feared you might return if I did not go out, and so your return in March might be credited to poor Kinkie . . . I would not come unless I felt I had strength enough. I feel that the Indian heat could do no more harm than the gnawing pain in my heart and my anxiety about you.'

When she wrote this, she could not move around her bedroom without the support of a nurse's arm, and when she was strong enough to descend to the Highcliffe garden, for weeks it was in a bath-chair. The pain in her 'phlebitis leg' was still agonizing. The smallest effort led to quick collapse. Her feet and hands did not function properly, she told him: 'They refuse to bend.' But India would not necessarily worsen her condition. Curzon even persuaded himself 'that this wonderful climate will help your recovery'. Warm days at Simla in champagne-like air would do her the world of good. The doctors agreed, and for Curzon's sake she was willing to believe them.

She had never told him how unhappy she had been in India, just as she had never told him of her misery in England after her marriage. If she had died at Walmer, he would never have known about it, and he was too absorbed in his work to notice it. Now that some light was visible at the far end of the tunnel, she felt able to speak to him more frankly. By looking forward to the years when both of them would be freed of India, she could hint that all along it had been a purgatory to her, and in this she knew that he would sympathize, for in a different way it had been purgatory to him too. In future, she hoped, but without great conviction, he might become less of a slave to his work, and because they would have more privacy, they would be happier.

Her illness had brought them very close. Mary was not a deeply religious person, but she believed that happiness was purchasable only by pain, and that her recovery was a prize for her devotion to him. In winning his love she had won a new lease of life. Through weakness she had discovered strength. By parting with him she had increased their togetherness. It was a happy chain of paradox.

If she felt hurt by his return to India before she was fully recovered, she did not admit it even to herself. Another woman might have pleaded with him to stay with her. But she, while not begging him to go, recognized that his devotion to his work (it could no longer be called ambition, for it was dedication) was an impulse so strong in him that to thwart it would be a crueller blow to him than his departure was to her. A protest might wreck her marriage, the foundation of her existence. She had noticed in recent years how her mother had drawn apart from her father. She believed her sisters' marriages to be thin, shallow-rooted, social affairs. Hers was quite different. It had started in undeclared loneliness, been preserved and deepened by tribulations (her failure to bear a son was not the least of them), and almost ended in premature death. All this time her love for Curzon had grown through her life like a plant, and so had his for her. To preserve it was worth every sacrifice, every effort. Curzon's struggle to rule India, and her struggle to rule herself, were complementary duties, mutually sustaining.

So she determined to rejoin him in India. There was a certain glory in it, a defiance of fate, a gesture which would cap the miracle of her recovery, and Mary was not indifferent to the effect it would create. If she had not wholly fulfilled herself in India, which she felt at times, her return as if from the dead would exhilarate an entire continent and justify her role. It would be her most magnificent contribution to Curzon's career, at a moment when he was under severest pressure, and when he needed her most. She would not need to stay there more than eighteen months. She would be excused much that was previously assumed. Her return was what mattered, and her continuing presence. If she were to die, it would be better to die in India than in some rented English house, with Curzon beside her, instead of alone in terror.

She embarked at Tilbury on 9 February 1905, on the same ship, SS *Arabia*, which had taken her to India six years before. Her three little girls were with her, with two nurses, one for Mary and one for the baby, and a live cow in the hold to supply Alexandra with fresh milk. Nancy (now Campbell) saw her off from Highcliffe, and Daisy (now Lady Suffolk) from Tilbury, and touching messages awaited her on board from the King and Prime Minister. At Bombay Curzon was on the pier to greet her.

There, and a few days later in Calcutta, she was acclaimed by the crowds with a delight that no woman in India had experienced before. The streets were lined with the British and American flags, ships in the harbours decorated overall, and bouquets were tossed into her carriage as she passed. At Government House a thousand people, including Kitchener, lined the lawns and steps. She entered the Throne Room in a new white dress, 'looking beautifully well', said an eyewitness, 'bright and cheerful as one could wish to see, with no trace whatever of her recent illness'. When Perceval Landon, correspondent of the *Daily Telegraph*, said to her that she seemed as one risen from the dead, 'she turned towards me with that direct and level glance which was one of her most attractive characteristics, and answered, "Yes – but one may not do those things twice."'

SIX

SIMLA AND KEDLESTON

WHEN Dalhousie, after seven years in Calcutta, prepared to hand over the Viceroyalty to Lord Elgin in 1856, he wrote to a friend: 'If Elgin cannot properly bring his wife to India, he will be a fool if he comes without her, and a maniac if he runs the risk of bringing her after all.' Dalhousie's own wife had died at sea three years earlier, when he sent her home to recover her health. Curzon quoted the letter in his *British Government in India*, at the end of a melancholy catalogue of the sufferings of his predecessors. 'Over the Viceregal throne there hangs not only a canopy of broidered gold,' he wrote, 'but a mist of human tears.' Then he allowed himself to add this reminder of his own anguish, though anonymously: 'A later Viceroy lost the partner and main author of his happiness in India a few months after they left the shores of that country, to whose climate the recurrence of the illness which terminated her life was largely due.'

He believed that India killed Mary, and she too had long felt a premonition that she would end her days there: 'The bell will go, and India will kill me as one of the humble and inconsequent lives who go into the foundations of all great works, great buildings and great achievements.' Both on Curzon's part and on Mary's it was a pardonable dramatization, which no doctor ever confirmed. Mary did not die in India, and she did not suffer in India any illness which so weakened her that she perished like a withered plant on her return home. Her accounts of her many official tours already quoted in this book show that she stood the heat and monsoon without great strain, and was in fact most animated when constantly travelling and most on show. She sturdily followed Curzon even on his hunting expeditions. 'We had such a delicious day,' she wrote after one such foray into the mountains near Simla. 'I trudged about with George from one beat to another ... The little Maharajah who hovered near us kept begging me to get into his dhoolie. He could not understand a woman who walked all day behind guns.' That does not conjure up the picture of an invalid. Mary's illnesses in India usually coincided with the periods when she had nothing much to do, at Simla particularly, and she was apt to blame on the climate the lassitude induced by loneliness and depression, and on the altitude the exhaustion caused by minor social duties. She had recurrent migraine and occasional attacks of dizziness, but she escaped all tropical diseases, and her life in India was never once in danger through sickness. After her near-mortal illness in 1904, India was actually recuperative. The doctors, and her own inclination, were proved right. The long sea-voyage had greatly helped her convalescence, and during the few weeks she spent in Calcutta, people were amazed to see how energetically she took her part in entertainments which they had assumed would be beyond her. Even Simla, where she went in March, now seemed a rest-cure:

I think the summer here without care will be my salvation, [she wrote to her mother]. I could never have got well in England, badgered and worried by a great house. Here at least I have peace of mind and everything done for me. In all my years in India I have never suffered such atrocious ills as I did during my year at home. My heart is very tender towards India, and I shall do my best to get well here. I am practically all right, and only want a little more strength to make me fit, and you know that I have all your strength of will.

She was excused all but a few functions, and spent long hours reading in a corner of Curzon's study while he worked. The children were a great joy to both of them, and smoothed away his tension and irritability. 'In his daily life,' wrote Lord Ronaldshay, 'for all his seeming strength and self-sufficiency, he was extraordinarily dependent upon others for his happiness.' Stealing a moment from his work, he would write for the little girls notes of touching whimsy and affection, folding them in the complicated manner, latticewise, he had learnt at Eton, and sent them round to their rooms by a servant. One or two happen to have survived, and here is an example from a slightly later date: 'My darling little Baba, I am so pleased to see your precious dimple again. Is there a rabbit inside it?'

The happiness of their family life, and the dry Simla air, restored Mary to complete health. Curzon reported to Mrs Leiter later in the year, 'I truly believe that she is far better now than she would have been had she spent the last 6 months in England. Barring the headaches, she is splendidly well.' By the early summer, in fact, she was in a better condition than Curzon himself. He was forced to spend a whole month in bed when his leg became too painful for him to walk even to his study.

However, death did nearly come to Mary in India, from an earthquake. On 3 April 1905, when Curzon was at Agra supervizing the restoration of the Taj Mahal, Mary was at Viceregal Lodge with the children. At 6 o'clock that morning, when she was still half-asleep, she felt her bedroom swaying like a cabin on a heaving ship. Immediately afterwards she heard a heavy fall of masonry, and ran into the great hall fearing that the tower had collapsed on the children's wing. As she paused there, the skylight fell in pieces around her. She took refuge in the smallest of the sitting-rooms, crouching in a corner, for it seemed that the whole house was about to collapse. An ADC came to tell her that the children were safe, but they must all leave the house at once. She flung some clothes over her nightdress, gathered the children, and while the building was still rocking, ran with them back through the hall and into the garden. The tremors continued for about an hour, and when they appeared to subside, Mary took the girls into a relatively undamaged part of the house, as it was too cold to remain outside. They spent the rest of the day and the next night huddled on the ground floor. There were fifteen smaller shocks which further weakened the structure to a point which made it a death-trap, and they moved into a smaller house nearby, where they were so cold that they ate in hats and fur-coats and slept fully dressed. The children, Mary told her mother, were as good as mice, 'and little Sandra smiled sweetly in the general pandemonium'.

Next day she went to inspect the damage. The main tower stood intact, but the house was uninhabitable, and its rebuilding was to take 300 men three months work. A twenty-ton stone chimney had collapsed and broken through the roof and ceiling of the room immediately above her own, and but for the chance that the rubble and masonry fell on a thickly mattressed double-bed in that room, she would have been killed instantly, as her own bed lay directly beneath it. As it was, the walls of her bed-room bulged menacingly, and only a very strong girder had prevented them from falling inwards on top of her. Her escape was greeted as further evidence of a charmed life. One thousand five hundred people died in the earthquake at Simla and in its neighbouring province. Curzon returned as soon as he could, and moved his family to Naldera, where only the mosquitoes disturbed their peace.

The last few months of Curzon's Viceroyalty, which should have put a seal of honour on his achievement, were scarred by quarrels, treachery and the destruction of some of his closest friendships. He resigned his office, and returned home a humiliated and embittered man. Throughout this shattering experience, from which his spirits and career took some ten years to recover, his mainstay was Mary. Never had he been in greater need of her support and consolation. If she had only once been critical or disloyal to him in the past, he would have suffered silently in this supreme crisis of his life, being too proud to risk her disapproval a second time. But because she had shown over and over again that she was unshakably at his side in everything he undertook, he was able to turn to her with complete trust and certainty. The crisis spanned the period when they were together at Simla, and there are few letters to record how much he owed to her at this time. But in the spring of 1905, he composed for her this poem, which summed up all his gratitude for what she had become:

> I would have torn the stars from the heavens for your necklace,
> I would have stripped the rose-leaves for your couch from all the trees,
> I would have spoiled the East of its spices for your perfume,
> The West of all its wonders to endower you with these.
> I would have drained the oceans, to find the rarest pearl-drops,
> And melt them for your lightest thirst in ruby draughts of wine:
> I would have dug for gold till the Earth was void of treasure,
> That, since you had no riches, you might freely take of mine.
> I would have drilled the sunbeams to guard you through the daytime,
> I would have caged the nightingales to lull you to your rest;
> But love was all you asked for, in waking or in sleeping,
> And love I gave you, Sweetheart, at my side and on my breast.

The causes of the crisis will be explained later, but it is first necessary to say something about the change that had come over Curzon during his six years in India, for his character, both in its strength and its weakness, contributed to his downfall. To many of his staff, particularly to those closest to him, he was not only a genius, but a loveable genius. When his Secretary, Sir Walter Lawrence, left India in 1903, he wrote to Curzon: 'I feel absolutely broken and dejected at the idea of leaving you. Whatever the future may hold – and it seems dreary and empty enough now – I shall never have a chief whom I shall admire and love as I have admired you.' Another of his staff, Sir Evan Maconochie, said that he was 'the greatest Indian Viceroy of our times – possibly of all times – fearless, creative, ardent, human . . . His were great days, and to us who knew and served under him they are a treasured memory.' These are tributes normally paid only to great Captains in war. It is impossible to imagine them addressed, even sycophantically, to Viceroys like Elgin, Curzon's predecessor, or Minto, his successor. Curzon was not only great in his courage, his industry, his oratory and strength of will, but great in his feeling for history, his insistence on impartial justice, his noble concept of imperial duty. One example is the trouble he took to save from utter decay the monuments of India's past, the Taj Mahal, the Red Fort at Delhi, Fatehpur Sikri, the Pearl Mosque at Lahore, the palace at Mandalay, the ruins of Bijapur. Let us pause here (for it is not irrelevant to his character) to quote his reply to a mean-minded critic who said that it was no business of a Christian Government to restore pagan monuments:

Art and beauty, and the reverence that is owing to all that has evoked human genius or has inspired human faith, are independent of creeds. . . . What is beautiful, what is historic, what tears the mask off the face of the past and helps us to read its riddles, and to look it in the eyes – these, and not the dogmas of a combative theology, are the principal criteria to which we must look.

He would not be dismayed to know that today he is remembered in India with more affection than any other Viceroy, not for his reforms, not even for his courage, but for reminding the Indians of what most of them had forgotten, that India had had a past as great as Britain's before the British came, and for saving the memorials of it for posterity.

It has been said that in the loftiest political sense he lacked imagination, because he would not admit that one day India would wish, and be entitled, to govern itself; that he was too deeply involved in the administration of the vast country to comprehend that the system which he strove so masterfully to perfect was based upon an unjustifiable premise. The Indians comprised about one-fifth of the human race, but they had no say in how they were governed. Once Curzon was asked to appoint an Indian, any Indian, to his Council. He replied shortly that none was qualified for it. When the President of the Indian Congress asked to see him in order to present its Resolutions, he refused. None of his predecessors had ever done so, and he did not wish to set an unforutnate precedent. David Dilks quotes another instance in his *Curzon in India*. One day the owner of a leading Indian newspaper said to Walter Lawrence: 'We do not ask for Home Rule now, nor in ten years, nor in twenty, but all we ask is that the Viceroy will not shut the door of hope upon us. Ask him to say that perhaps in fifty years India may be self-governing.' Moved by his earnestness, Lawrence repeated his words to Curzon, who thought long before he replied: 'No I will say nothing, for it might embarrass my successor if I raised any hopes or expressed any opinion as to when self-government will come.' When Lawrence said that it must happen some day, Curzon answered, 'It will not come in my time and I cannot say what may happen in the future.'

The British were in India to benefit the Indians, he believed, and if the Indians tried to interfere, the only result would be chaos. They must be convinced that the British, 'the speck of foam upon a dark unfathomable ocean', knew best. He made no protest against the social ostracism of even the most highly educated natives. He never had a close Indian friend; nor did Mary. His attitude reflected what every Englishman then believed. If he had proclaimed a policy of gradual emancipation, he would have been denounced immediately at home and lost the confidence of all the British in India. He did not for one moment believe Lawrence's warning (in his autobiography) that British rule 'rests on an illusion of infallibility and invulnerability'. To Curzon it was no illusion, but a fact of life, a God-given and beneficial fact, that the strong were destined to rule the weak, and he was appointed to control the strong. In 1903 he had written to Lord George Hamilton: 'All my policy and my acts tend to rivet the British rule on to India and to postpone the long-for day of emancipation. I am an Imperialist, and Imperialism is fatal to all their hopes.' His finest exposition of that creed was contained in almost the last speech he made in India:

Let it be our ideal to fight for the right, to abhor the imperfect, the unjust or the mean, to swerve neither to the right hand nor to the left, to care nothing for flattery or applause or odium or abuse, never to let your enthusiasm be soured or your courage grow dim, but to remember that the Almighty has placed your hand on the greatest of his ploughs, in whose furrow the nations of the future are germinating and taking shape, to drive the blade a little forward in your time, and to feel that somewhere among these millions you have left a little

justice or happiness or prosperity, a sense of manliness or moral dignity, a spring of patriotism, a dawn of intellectual enlightenment or a
stirring of duty where it did not exist before – that is enough, that is the
Englishman's justification in India. It is good enough for his watch-
word while he is here, for his epitaph when he is gone. Let India be my
judge.

Curzon lived up to these high ideals without faltering, but he
failed at the two levels where he might have been expected to
succeed more easily, his relations with his own people at home
and in India. He broke with the home Government by his
reluctance to admit that the ultimate source of his authority lay
in Whitehall; and he antagonized many of the British in India,
those most remote from him, on whom the execution of his
policies depended. The Army continued to hold against him
incidents like the disgrace of the 9th Lancers. The junior officials
were annoyed by his constant intervention in details of administration, and by his determination to challenge and change
established practices. A lesser Viceroy could have won popularity
by tacit consent. Curzon would never consent without interrogation. He wanted to improve, and improvement meant distur-
bance. It is the problem faced by any strong-willed Minister
confronted by any conservative Civil Service. Things were running smoothly, which meant normally; an inquisitive and determined Viceroy created roughage. Therefore such a Viceroy, the
argument ran, must be a bad Viceroy. Curzon possessed the
capacity to persuade but not to conciliate. His bearing was aristocratic and alarming; he could be petulant and scornful. He
seemed anxious to confirm his reputation as 'a superior person'.
'The world saw him as a caricature', wrote Lawrence, 'and
unfortunately he was apt to play up to the caricature'. His most
unattractive quality was his self-pity: his conviction that he was
badly served, that his colleagues betrayed him, that his load of
work was due entirely to the incompetence of his staff. His temper was exacerbated by the strain he put upon himself, and by
the climate. The charm to which his intimate friends, particularly women, all paid tribute, was not evident in his dealings
with his subordinates. Margot Asquith despaired that he

would never allow 'his affection, gaiety and native kindliness to expand'; and in *Great Contemporaries* Winston Churchill wrote:

The contradictory qualities which dwell in the characters of so many individuals can rarely have formed more vivid contrasts than in George Curzon. The world thought him pompous in manner and in mind. But this widespread and deep impression, arising from the experience and report of so many good judges, was immediately destroyed by the Curzon one met in a small circle of intimate friends and equals, or those whom he treated as equals. Here one saw the charming, gay companion adorning every subject that he touched with his agile wit, ever ready to laugh at himself, ever capable of conveying sympathy and understanding. It seemed incredible that this warm heart and jolly, boyish nature should be so effectually concealed from the vast majority of those he met and with whom he worked.

An office was a fountain of commands, not a place for the exercise of charm. He was the commander. As rapidly as he mastered every detail of administration, his authority grew more imperious and was increasingly resented. So he failed to create in the middle levels of British India an affection which would have sweetened the admiration they could not possibly withold. He did not establish a base there, and when the crisis came, he lacked a ground-swell of local support.

In his dealings with the home Government he threw away by petulance all the advantages with which he started: the respect of the House of Commons, his intimate friendship with leading men in Government and Opposition, their conviction that only Curzon was capable of reforming Indian administration from top to bottom. The one misgiving which was expressed on his appointment, that his pugnacity might draw Britain into a war with Russia, had not been realized. Throughout his term, apart from Younghusband's expedition to Tibet, there was no serious fighting on the frontier, and India itself remained quiet.

All these advantages crumbled to nothing because he quarrelled with Whitehall on the degree of independence he should be allowed. He was bound ultimately to lose this argument, since the Constitution was quite clear: the Viceroy is in the last resort subordinate to London, and he can be overruled, like any Minister, by a majority in Cabinet. Curzon did not challenge this principle, but he believed that it was being misinterpreted. The Viceroy's views should be disregarded only on the rarest occasions and on the highest issues of policy, on peace and war, for example, or the financial strategy of the Empire. In all other matters he should be left to govern India as he thought best. That was why only men of outstanding ability had been selected for the post, and why it was regarded as the greatest overseas appointment in the gift of the Crown. He disputed the argument that the Viceroy was in the same position as any senior Minister at home. Calcutta was 7,000 miles from London; the journey took seventeen days; so did the mails. Most members of the Cabinet had never once visited India. The Viceroy, moreover, was not responsible for a single department like Education or Health. He was his own Foreign Minister, Defence Minister, Chancellor of the Exchequer, everything. His position in India was like a President's, a Regent's, a Prime Minister's, rolled into one. But he was not a Dictator. For all his decisions he must gain the support of his Council, a small group of leading executives each with his own department but collectively responsible, like a Cabinet, and if he failed to carry them with him, he must either succumb or resign. Surely that was sufficient control on the Viceroy when it came to matters which affected India alone?

In London there was another India Council, which advised the Secretaty of State. It was composed for the most part of retired ex-India officials of distinction, but their information was out of date. How could they judge the rightness of a policy without having heard the debates in the Council at Calcutta, and without having read a tithe of the documents? Curzon's indignation was increased by his mounting authority within India itself. His Council, while in theory composed of equal and independent men, was little more than a sounding-board for the Viceroy's ideas. Few Councillors dared question his judgment: he was the fount of local promotion, and his disapproval could wreck a senior career. The Viceroy was responsible to no elected

Assembly in India, as a Minister was to Parliament. 'He alone', he wrote to Sir Arthur Godley, head of the India Office, 'is the Government in its personal aspect; and from his lips the Indian people look to learn how and wherefore they are governed.' The reverence with which he was regarded, the many formal occasions at which he appeared in state, placed him so far above the rest that he seemed to them, and inevitably to himself, in all but name a Monarch. To have his opinions questioned by old and ignorant men at home, after he had studied the matter deeply and gained the support of his chief advisers in India, infuriated him.

Curzon's pride became increasingly offensive to his friends at home, and his visit to England in the summer of 1904 did nothing to improve their relations. The whole Cabinet, St John Brodrick wrote in his autobiography, had become convinced that 'despite Curzon's ability and knowledge and service, his continuance in India in 1905 was a danger to the Empire'; and Balfour admitted retrospectively that it had been a major error to allow him to return. It was not simply his current dispute with Kitchener about the Army's administration that worried them. There had been Curzon's threat to resign if he did not get his way about taxes at the time of the Delhi Durbar. There had been disagreements between Viceroy and Cabinet about his policy in Afghanistan and Tibet. Curzon's partition of Bengal had caused deep resentment in India. But the main trouble was psychological, the increasingly angry tone of Curzon's despatches, which led the Cabinet to believe that he was claiming for the Indian Government a predominance, as Balfour commented, 'which would raise India to the position of an independent and not always friendly power'.

Curzon's irritation focused on St John Brodrick, Secretary of State for India. He looked to him, because of their linked offices and long friendship, for unqualified support in Cabinet. As far as he was able, Brodrick loyally gave it, to the point where one of his colleagues, Alfred Lyttelton, remarked, 'You have put the case and fought it well for Curzon, but the Cabinet will stand no more.' Brodrick did not pretend to a quarter of Curzon's ability, but he was, after all, the Minister responsible for Indian affairs, and resented Curzon's assumption that he was no more than his London spokesman. Relations between the two men rapidly deteriorated, and almost their last gesture of friendship was Brodrick's acceptance of Curzon's invitation to be godfather to Alexandra. After his return to India their correspondence became acrimonious and cold.

The immediate issue between them was Kitchener's demand that the administration and control of the Indian Army be placed wholly in his hands. It seemed a not unreasonable request for a Commander-in-Chief to make. But in India the system had always been one of dual control. The Commander-in-Chief was responsible for manoeuvres, the distribution of troops, intelligence, discipline and promotion, and if war came, he would take the field in supreme command. Army finance, ordnance, stores, supply and transport were controlled by the Military Member of the Viceroy's Council, who also had the right to criticize and veto recommendations of the Commander-in-Chief, and had repeatedly done so. In Kitchener's first two-and-a-half years nearly a hundred of his proposals had been turned down. As the Military Member was an officer of junior rank, Kitchener found this system intolerable. It might have suited his ineffective predecessor, Sir Power Palmer, but he, the most famous British soldier alive, the hero of Omdurman and the South African war, was determined to be militarily supreme. He wished to abolish the post of Military Member completely, and absorb his staff into his own headquarters.

Curzon's reply was that if this happened, the burden on the Commander-in-Chief, even a Kitchener, would be too great for one man to bear. He would be overwhelmed by administrative detail, when he should keep his mind free for great issues of strategy and his time free for visiting troops. Since arriving in India Kitchener had been able to carry out extensive reforms, and alter the Army's entire disposition, without any interference from the Military Member. But if the post were abolished, the Viceroy would lose a valuable second opinion on military matters. The Commander-in-Chief might be away, perhaps on campaign, and who would be left in Calcutta and Simla to advise him? The concentration of power which Kitchener proposed would make the Commander-in-Chief as important as the Viceroy himself. When the argument grew more heated, he accused Kitchener of an ambition to subvert civil supremacy in India. He wrote to Mary while she was on her way back to Calcutta:

I regard K's proposals as a positive menace to the State. He proposes to set up the C. in C. as an absolute military autocrat in our administration. The scheme if accepted would collapse within a year of his leaving India. I do not see why we should revolutionise our constitution to humour him.

Kitchener, too, put his case to Mary, in a letter dated 19 January 1905:

I am sorry to say that the Viceroy told me the other day that he had decided to give his support to that effete Military Department and reject my proposals. I told him that in these circumstances I felt it to be my duty to the Army to resign, and this he has accepted as the natural consequence. There will be a few formalities, possibly a commission sent out from home, but I fear the final result, with Curzon's position and ability against me, is a foregone conclusion. Poor Army! Poor soldiers! I do think it is hard that they should be sent to fight the battles of the empire all unprepared and without leaders to guide them. It is next door to wholesale murder. Well, it cannot be helped, and I shall at least have the comforting thought that I have done all I could for them, so I am starting my packing-up.

The dispute was carried on in India by courteous memoranda and interviews between the protagonists, and at an increasing level of acrimony by telegram, letter and personal emissaries to London. Both Kitchener and Curzon threatened resignation. The Cabinet (and the country, for the controversy soon became public) were asked to come to a decision on a highly technical matter, which became acutely political and dramatic because of the fame, characters and mutually antagonistic attitudes of the two men. A decision in favour of one of them would mean the resignation of the other. Both staked their careers on the outcome. Curzon had the advantage that he was Viceroy, senior to the Commander-in-Chief; Kitchener the even greater advantage that he was a national hero, which Curzon never was. At a moment when Russia was threatening India's northern frontier and war might break out, public opinion tended to regard the Commander-in-Chief as less expendable than the Viceroy, and, by and large, Kitchener's arguments seemed to ignorant people to make more sense. While the Viceroy should certainly have the right to overrule the Commander-in-Chief on financial and political matters, it was absurd that a junior officer should be able to countermand his instructions on matters which vitally affected his operations. How could any British General be expected to fight a war without full control of his administration and supply? They overlooked the fact that every British General, from Marlborough to Kitchener himself, had done so, because the War Office had played almost exactly the same role in supporting its Armies as the Military Department did in India.

Kitchener won the support of lay opinion at home by skilful and at times unscrupulous manipulation of the press. Through one of Curzon's former ADCs, Major R. J. Marker, who had once been jilted by Daisy Leiter and was now Private Secretary to the Secretary of State for War, he leaked to *The Times* and other newspapers confidential documents which supported his own case, and when questioned on the rumour that he had done so, flatly denied it. Moreover, he wrote weekly to Lady Salisbury, knowing that his letters, which were replete with disparaging comments about Curzon, would be passed on to her husband, a member of the Government, and by him to Balfour. By this channel he revealed top-secret documents and plans, and details of the controversy which Curzon regarded as wholly confidential. Curzon's position at home was being rapidly undermined. The Cabinet became convinced that Kitchener had the better argument, and that Curzon, if necessary, must be sacrificed to restore peace.

In India their relationship was still outwardly cordial. In Mary's absence they had spent Christmas together at Barrackpore, and together they visited the battlefield of Plassey. After her return, Kitchener continued to seek her company, though now they avoided mentioning the controversy. He was a strange mixture of arrogance and gentleness, of the rough soldier and gracious host. 'He did not ask to be loved,' wrote his biographer, Philip Magnus; 'he wooed nothing except opportunity; and he was perfectly content so long as his strength was feared and admired.' But when he became famous 'he relished the society of great ladies, and relaxed in the congenial warmth of great country houses'. It was the same in India. Although a bachelor, he spent vast sums of public money on reconstructing his two official houses at Calcutta and Simla in a palatial style worthy of the lovely women he wished to entertain. Like Curzon he adored pageantry, beautiful objects, beautiful people and surroundings, and took an almost pathological interest in domestic arrangements. Like him, too, he had a passion for work, cared little for the susceptibilities of others, and was intolerant of failure and inefficiency.

Kitchener had come to India at Curzon's own request, as the only British soldier worthy of his Viceroyalty, the only man with the drive and prestige to remodel the Indian Army with a zeal equal to Curzon's own. Few other Viceroys would have risked the competition of so formidable a colleague, and the tension was bound to be greater in their case, for Curzon despised soldiers and Kitchener despised politicians. But when Lawrence suggested that a clash between them was inevitable, Curzon laughed at the notion that he would be unable to handle him.

Mary wrote to Kitchener soon after his arrival in India in November 1902: 'Do please take the Army and all the military straight into your heart. It will be a wonderful load off George ... I suppose you know that the prayer of the soldiers has been that the two giants would fall out, and it will be a great grief for them to see you work in harmony, and to know the intense satisfaction it is to George to know that you are here at last.' Kitchener replied in the same friendly tone, and for eighteen months his affection for Mary did much to mitigate his growing animosity towards her husband. While she was convalescing at

Highcliffe, Curzon wrote: 'If you were here you might be able to exercise some influence over this wayward and impossible man. At home A.J.B. & Co. are all frightened to death of him. Here no one but his subordinates are on his side. There was never a greater shock to him than when I came back to India, for he had laid all his plans to strike his final blow, and get what he wanted as soon as I disappeared from the scene.'

The dispute had now passed the point where an exchange of compliments and dinner-parties could diminish the rivalry between Viceroy and Commander-in-Chief. Curzon, who for five years had never quarrelled with any member of his Council, was now landed in a bitter controversy with his nominee. In June 1905 the Government attempted a compromise, drafted by St John Brodrick. The Military Department was to be retained. But the present Military Member, General Sir Edmund Elles, must go. He would be replaced by a more junior officer who would be renamed Military Supply Member, and would control only stores and transport. He would no longer give expert opinions on military questions, nor would he be allowed to veto proposals put forward by the Commander-in-Chief. He could advise the Viceroy on 'general policy' (which was left undefined), but not on strictly military matters. Although he would normally be an officer, his job was in effect civilianized. Curzon saw this proposal as a defeat for himself, 'although a disembowelled Military Member has been left to prevent me from resigning'. Kitchener, with a political dexterity that compels admiration, established his *bona fides* by saying that he would resign himself rather than allow Curzon to resign, knowing that the Cabinet would never let him go.

Mary put the situation to her mother in a letter of 27 July:

There has never been such feeling in India as there is now against St John, and the populace longs for his blood, and no one is more indignant than Lord K. St John was so anxious to give Lord K. all he wanted and more, that he formulated a wild scheme that is unworkable and which can only break down. The civilians are wild and the soldiers furious, and Lord K. has been censured by Indian opinion for bringing about such a state of things. Altogether it is a fine row, and

no two opinions are held about the unstatesmanlike action of St John.
I do long to leave India, and be out of reach of his bludgeon which we
feel daily in an insulting telegram, order or letter. He is a public
disgrace. There has never been any disagreement between Lord K.
and G, and they are on absolutely friendly terms, but I hope he may
never have to speak to St J. again as long as he lives.

Her letter does more credit to her loyalty than to her knowledge of what was going on. The 'populace' had probably never
even heard of St John Brodrick, who was in any case acting as
little more than the agent of the Cabinet. Lord K. was certainly
not indignant: he was delighted by the way things were working out. The scheme was not 'unworkable': it was put into effect
as soon as Curzon left India. In claiming that opinion in India
was unanimous in condemning both Brodrick and Kitchener,
Mary was just thinking wishfully. Although the Council supported Curzon, the Generals supported Kitchener almost to a
man, and the lower ranks of the civil service were divided between them, indifferent to which of them resigned. The Indians
simply watched with consternation the white man's quarrel.
Nor was it true that by this time Curzon and Kitchener were 'on
absolutely friendly terms'. Describing to Lady Salisbury his
interview with Curzon on 16 July, Kitchener wrote: 'He was not
very pleasant; no more was I, as I had to speak to him pretty
straight.'

Curzon was feeling utterly dejected. 'I am really quite willing
to go if you would like to,' he wrote to Mary. 'India has long
ceased to give me any pleasure, and if the Cabinet at home want
someone to lie down to lick the hand that chastises him, I have
no doubt plenty of suitable animals will be forthcoming.' Mary
advised him to play for time. If the entire Indian Council
threatened to resign too, would that not force the Government's
hand? 'Resignation and political shipwreck are the same terms
nowadays. And your future is too important to wreck it for
ever.'

The only way in which Curzon could retrieve his position was
by persuading the Government to accept modifications to the
compromise plan which would leave the status of the Military

Member virtually untouched. Some moves were made in this direction during July, and Curzon claimed publicly that 'we have very considerably strengthened the guarantees for civil supervision and control', an interpretation which was immediately challenged from London. In a letter to the King, Balfour described the speech as 'deplorable in taste and temper ... No such public exhibition of disloyalty to the Home Government has ever been made by an Indian Viceroy.'

The breaking-point came over Elles's successor. Curzon wished the Government to appoint General Sir Edmund Barrow, who commanded the Peshawar Division and had been one of the few Generals to take Curzon's side. Kitchener at first preferred General Egerton. The very suggestion made Curzon laugh. He was 'an elderly apoplectic General with no administrative experience'. Why did Kitchener not take him as his Chief of Staff? 'Oh no,' replied Kitchener, 'I don't want a duffer.' Nothing could have revealed to Curzon more clearly Kitchener's concept of the revolution he had brought about. The matter was referred to London. Brodrick refused to appoint Barrow, and redefined the role of the Military Supply Member in terms which showed that it would be nugatory. 'Two hours work a day', commented Curzon. It was the last straw. He telegraphed to Brodrick on 12 August:

In these circumstances my ability to act with advantage as head of the Indian Government has ceased to exist, and I beg you again to place my resignation in the Prime Minister's hands.

His resignation was accepted in a telegram from the King ten days later, and the formal announcement was coupled with the appointment of his successor, Lord Minto, who had recently been Governor General of Canada.

Mary wrote to Pearl Craigie on 16 August:

I am so thankful that I came back when I did, as we have been involved in perpetual crisis for months with Mr Brodrick who is deaf and blind to the vital interests of India. I fear it must result in our going, as it is simply impossible to endure the methods of that amazing

Minister. He has set India ablaze with indignation at his tactics. I have
never known such unanimity or intensity of feeling. . . . I have been
wonderfully well. G. has been constantly ill. I have been an untiring
and anxious nurse and never left him. Life would be intolerable had
we not the comfort of each other.

And to her mother on 24 August:

G's resignation has come, and now the home government are bent
on kicking him out with as little delay as possible. . . . The great
mistake which G. made was in ever coming back to India. But as you
know, nothing would dissuade him. The strain of all this has been
terrible and my solitude has been cruel. I feel sometimes that I shall
go out of my mind if I have to bear much more strain and worry. The
whole of life seems sacrificed to this thankless public life.

They were obliged to remain in Simla under notice for two
further months, and the messages of sympathy which reached
them from all parts of India did something to alleviate the pain.
The Civil and Military Services combined to give Curzon a
magnificent farewell ball, and the people of the town dragged
their carriage through the streets. They left Simla on 23 October. Kitchener was persuaded to take part in the final farewell,
'only to stop people talking', he told Lady Salisbury, 'although
it was not very pleasant to shake hands with a man who has
called you a liar. However I consoled myself by the consideration
that it was the Viceroy to whom I was saying goodbye, not
Curzon.' The ceremony of departure was very painful. A Guard
of Honour was drawn up on the lawn of Viceregal Lodge, and
next to it stood Kitchener in full uniform, surrounded by his
staff. Curzon shook his hand in silence. Mary said just one word,
'Goodbye', and then walked on. 'When we had made the
round,' she told her mother, 'we turned and faced everyone and
I bowed right and left. G. stood with his hat off. The band
played God Save the King. Then we got into the postillion
carriage escorted by the Body Guard and the whole crowd
cheered and cheered. Lord K. never moved. He raised his
white helmet and stood like a sphynx as our procession moved
away, and we left Simla and its troubles behind us for ever.'

Then she added with characteristic fierceness, but uncharacteristic bitterness: 'For years I have succeeded in keeping him [Kitchener] from the most awful mistakes and kept him on friendly terms. Now I feel no hesitation in telling what I know of his lies – and let the King as well as everyone in England know what he is, and we shall ruin him if it is in our power, as he is bringing the Indian Army to the verge of mutiny by his evil stupidity.'

For a few days they went to Dehra Dun, and then to Lahore and Agra, playing out time because the King had insisted that Curzon remain to welcome the Prince of Wales at the start of his Indian tour. On 10 November they greeted him on board HMS *Renown* in Bombay harbour. Mary was disappointed: 'I found the Princess in a little common white muslin like Sandra's, with a narrow blue sash and a little blue ribbon round her neck. This for her great public entry into India! I think people were taken aback by her appearance, for there was no cheering at all.' The Mintos, who arrived in Bombay a few days later, were even less exciting. He seemed to Mary 'like a little grey mouse'. Their reception at Bombay was almost perfunctory, and Mary asked forgiveness for contrasting it with her own arrival six years before.

On 18 November the Curzons sailed for home.

They arrived in London on 3 December 1905. Not a single member of the Government was at the station to greet them. Although the King had asked Balfour and Brodrick to be there, both had found excuses for refusing, and not one of their colleagues, not even George Wyndham or Alfred Lyttelton, two of Curzon's oldest friends, not even Lord Lansdowne, a former Viceroy who had been one of Curzon's few supporters in the Cabinet, made a single gesture of welcome. 'Other old friends of a lifetime,' wrote Mary, 'were mute.' When Curzon called on Margot Asquith, his first words were, 'Beloved Margie, are you a St Johnite, or a Georgite?'. She had to tell him that she was a St Johnite. But the press were generous in acclaiming the totality of his achievement in India, and several public men like Winston Churchill spoke out warmly in his defence. The Government maintained an attitude of cold aloofness, and when a public banquet was proposed in Curzon's honour, it was abandoned at his request because no Conservative ex-Minister would attend.

The Liberal Government under Campbell-Bannerman, which replaced Balfour's on the very day after Curzon's return, was equally distant. Curzon was refused the Earldom which had been given almost automatically to past Viceroys on their retirement, although the King had personally requested it, and indeed promised it to Curzon in 1904. The outgoing Prime Minister, Balfour, feared that the honour might be regarded as a repudiation of Brodrick and Kitchener. The incoming Prime Minister, Campbell-Bannerman, did not feel able to reward a man who had been cold-shouldered by his own party, when Liberals, too, 'had not always viewed with sympathy the methods and actions of Lord Curzon.' His humiliation was complete. He was invited by several constituencies to stand as a candidate in the forthcoming General Election, but he accepted none of them, because Balfour, in a painful interview, refused his active support, and Curzon's health was not good enough to stand the strain of a contested election.

After less than three weeks in England, he and Mary went to the South of France to join their children, who had remained there on their way back from India when London was thought to be too cold. They stayed first in a hotel at Cap St Martin, and then, because the rooms were too expensive and the food bad, they moved to another hotel near Cannes. Curzon was occupied with editing some of his Indian speeches for publication, and Mary with her children and her books. They saw few people whom they knew, and avoided those they didn't, reading the *Daily Mail*, two days in arrears, to discover what parties they had been fortunate enough to miss. Their only excursions were daily drives. They did not return to England until March 1906.

During this period Mary's health fluctuated no more alarmingly than it had at frequent intervals in India. When she first arrived at Cap St Martin she had influenza and a cough 'which shook my bones to pieces', and her heart was giving trouble. At the least exertion, she told her mother, such as dressing or going upstairs, she became breathless. She consulted a specialist who assured her 'that I am good for many years of life with care', and Curzon wrote to Mrs Craigie, 'Mary is wonderfully well, but has a little leg trouble'. These various symptoms caused him some anxiety. Mrs Craigie saw her in London in April, and reassured Mrs Leiter that 'Mary is looking splendidly – you would be delighted by her appearance', but this was not the whole truth, because Mrs Craigie wrote to Curzon after Mary's death: 'I had forebodings even when I saw her apparently so well in April. I *knew* that she was not herself – that unconquerable will was doing the work of her physical strength. I said nothing. I am sure I betrayed nothing of my inward sorrow. I came away in profound distress.' Curzon himself, only a few days after her death, wrote to Schomberg McDonnell, 'I had seen it coming, and dared not avow it to her or even to myself.'

On 12 June Mary wrote to her brother Joe, 'I sometimes fear and feel I shall never be well again', but in the same letter she told him of her plan to come with Curzon to America to discuss financial matters, and she continued to be quite active socially throughout the early summer, though still suffering from 'devilish ills', which she did not specify. The words occur in the last letter she wrote to Curzon, on 7 July. They were both at 1 Carlton House Terrace, and she put the letter on his pillow:

You have, I know, in your patient and generous heart forgiven me for being so naughty yesterday, but I can give you no conception of how much more I hurt myself than I hurt you. But yesterday was one of those rare days that I felt I was going out of my mind and I really reached the lowest ebb of misery. That is why I kept so still when you came in before dinner. I didnt want to break down. But when you had gone out, I collapsed and cried the whole night. I was awake when you opened the door, but it was better that you should think me asleep than see the depths I was in. I wont let my nerve go if I can keep it, but what causes me such acute agony is that I should be a burden to you whom I worship, just when I would give my very soul to be a help.

I will be brave, beloved, and when I am naughty, you will know it isnt your Kinkie but all these devilish ills! There is plenty of hope and light ahead, and I wont always add to the shadows in Pappy's life, but pray that I may yet bring him the sun in all its glory. Love. M.'

Curzon also preserved his reply:

Precious darling, When I came up, I found Kinkie's loving letter which sent me crying to bed. I had forgotten all about Friday. The only wonder is that with all you have had and have to go through, you keep such a wonderful courage and such a sweet temper. I think of nothing but getting you right so that we may both lift our heads again and go ahead. Nothing else matters but to make my darling well again, and then if she is happy, my cup will brim over. Ever loving Pappy.

Ten days later, on 18 July 1906, she died at Carlton House Terrace. She was thirty-six years old.

She had had a restless night, Curzon told Mrs Leiter, and her health and spirits were so low that he spent the whole day at her bedside, watching her strength ebb. The doctors kept her alive with oxygen and injections of strychnine, but her breathing collapsed in the late afternoon, and her last fierce struggle was unavailing. She died just before 6 p.m. of a heart-attack, the bulletin said. Curzon's arm was around her in the final moments. The room was locked, and nobody, not even Curzon, re-entered it until she had been placed next day in her coffin, his photograph in her hand and a single flower on her breast.

She was buried at Kedleston, as she had requested when she lay ill at Walmer, and in the same hour a memorial service was held in London at St Margaret's, Westminster, attended by all her friends. At Kedleston her coffin had lain all the previous night in the Marble Hall. The only people at the funeral were Curzon himself, his three daughters, his father and brothers, Mrs Leiter, Daisy Suffolk, and Bishop Welldon who conducted the service. Among the many wreaths were tributes from the King and Queen and the President of the United States.

Curzon received over 1,150 letters of condolence, and replied to most of them in his own hand. For many days it was his only occupation and consolation. All the letters expressed the writers' sense of shock. They had not known that Mary was so unwell. Her recovery in 1904 had seemed to them not so much a warning that she would die young, as evidence of her indomitable strength. Of her nature, most of her friends wrote that she was above all deeply sympathetic. Her beauty, grace and charm were known to all. But that she was loving too was a quality which took time to discover, for she was intensely reserved. Pearl Craigie, who was herself to die a month later aged thirty-eight, put it best: 'You can always know that Mary's life brilliantly fulfilled her hopes for you and for herself. Her absolute devotion to you was the first cause of my loving her; afterwards I loved her for herself also. To me she was the most precious and beloved of my women friends. There was never anything but a most exquisite generous tenderness and understanding in her.' Ettie Grenfell wrote: 'She was the best and most beautiful of all. There was no one like Mary. She had that innate dignity of nature that seems to set certain people quite apart, and one was never with her without feeling better and happier.'

Many others recalled acts of kindness: to a daughter lonely in India, to a woman in childbirth. The word 'noble' was often used, and people wrote of her 'beautiful light presence', and how she lived her life 'radiantly'. There can be no question of the genuineness of their grief and admiration. One does not write eulogies of a man's dead wife which will strike him as absurd. If there is no emotion, the easy refuge is in formal sympathy. Curzon received many of that character, but all the letters from people who had known her well still convey the sense of the writers' missed heart-beat when they heard of Mary's death. 'What a world of sunniness has gone', wrote Evan Charteris. And Henry Adams: 'I cannot talk of her. What you would say, I would only repeat. Some visions are too radiant for words. When they fade they leave life colourless.'

All this was true of Mary Curzon, as it was true of Mary Leiter. Proud and reserved as she was, she was never contemptuous or austere. American she remained at heart, but through her husband she came to respect the British. She wanted, deserved and fulfilled a great role in life, and her enjoyment of it was earned by her sustained effort to survive its tribulations. She was not a brilliant woman. If she had been, she would never have suffered three years of misery, loneliness and frustration in London after her marriage. Later she would have left a deeper mark on the politics and intellectual life of India. Mary lacked dominance; and to some extent, as I have tried to show, she lacked judgment. When she was given a role, as a debutante in Washington, as a Vicereine in India, she played the part to perfection. Without it she was apt to falter.

The purpose and triumph of her life was to be loved by such a man as George Curzon. If I have read the evidence correctly, he did not love her deeply when he proposed to her, nor when he married her. The fullness of his love came in India. There he needed someone, as Lord Ronaldshay has said, to whom he could bring the spoils of victory. Still more, when failure dogged his footsteps, must he have someone to whom he could lay bare his soul. In India, where other intimacies were denied to him, he turned with increasing dependence and delight to the one source of comfort which was open to him. She responded with a warmth and solicitude which was totally unforced. 'There is no happiness so great to a woman,' she wrote, 'as the admiration she can feel to the depths of her heart for her Belovedest.' When he heard that she was returning to him from Highcliffe, he sent up a shout of joy which still echoes: 'This will be like beginning life again after a hideous interlude and all my efforts will be directed to make the new life happy and sweet – happier and sweeter if possible than the old. Every night and morning I thank God that you are coming out.' It is impossible to judge this difficult, complex man correctly if one ignores his capacity for joy and love, which Mary, more than any other woman in his life, awoke in him.

It took Curzon many years to recover from her loss. On the day after her death, he wrote to Mrs Leiter: 'There has gone from me the truest, the most devoted, most unselfish, most beautiful and brilliant wife a man has ever had, and I am left with three little motherless children and a broken life. Nothing however can take from me the memory of 11 happy and loving years, and somehow her spirit is watching over me and doing me what good she can. I owe to her all the happiness of my life.' A year later he wrote to a friend, 'I am conscious of no courage, only a sort of mute endurance.'

He determined to honour Mary's memory in the most monumental way he could conceive, to perpetuate their love in emblematic and indestructible form. What else was the Taj Mahal? He built as an annex to the church at Kedleston a chapel in which they would lie side by side in marbled placidity, her hand clasped in his. He visualized, with a religious faith curiously simple for a man so intellectually mature, their actual reunion in Heaven. Meanwhile, like his medieval ancestors around him, but in his own lifetime, he and Mary would lie in effigy, imperishable when their bodies perished in the crypt below, she in her youthful beauty, he in his Viceregal robes. The sculpture by Bertram Mackennal, and the surrounding embellishments of the chapel – a floor of green translucent quartz, an iron grille which Curzon designed himself, the stained-glass window, the works-of-art which he purchased or had copied from originals – took five years to assemble and complete. When it was finished, he placed on a shield within the chapel this inscription:

Mary Victoria
Lady Curzon of Kedleston
Born May 27 1870. Died July 18 1906
Perfect in love and loveliness
Beauty was the least of her rare gifts
God had endowed with like Graces
Her mind and soul
From illness all but unto death
Restored, only to die.
She was mourned in three continents,
And by her dearest will be
For ever unforgotten

EPILOGUE

URZON's life was blighted by the two almost coincidental blows to his career and happiness, the torment of his last months in India, and Mary's death. 'I am not fit for society', he told a friend, 'and desire only to hide my head.' He remained out of public life for nearly ten years. For much of this time, when he was not at Carlton House Terrace, he lived at Hackwood Park, the great house near Basingstoke in Hampshire which he rented from Lord Bolton, and there, with the help of their faithful nurse Sibley* he brought up his daughters. Later, he took a lease of the Elizabethan house, Montacate, in Somerset. He had three main occupations. In 1907 he became Chancellor of Oxford University, and devoted to its problems far more time and care than did any of his predecessors or successors. Secondly, he was President of the Royal Geographical Society. Thirdly, he purchased the ruins of two great monuments of Britain's past, Bodiam and Tattershall, and restored them with infinite skill, bequeathing both to the nation at his death.

He longed to re-enter politics, but not through the House of Commons. His chance came in 1911 when he at last received his Earldom (elevated in 1921 to a Marquisate). A second period of important public service was about to open before him. In the Coalition Government of 1915 he was Lord Privy Seal. When

---

* Miss Sibley was engaged to an Englishman in India, who owned a chain of haberdashery shops. On Mary's death, she broke off her engagement, and remained with the children until she died in 1915.

Asquith's Government fell in the next year, he became a member of Lloyd George's inner Cabinet as Lord President of the Council and Leader of the House of Lords. At the Armistice, he was put in charge of the Foreign Office in the absence at the Paris Peace Conference of Arthur Balfour, the Foreign Secretary, and in 1919 succeeded him, retaining the office for five arduous years. Such was his success, particularly at the Lausanne Conference of 1922, that he had every expectation of succeeding Bonar Law as Prime Minister when he resigned in 1923. This ultimate ambition was not realized. Stanley Baldwin was appointed instead of him. Loyally Curzon remained Foreign Secretary under him, until early in 1924. On 20 March 1925 he died, aged sixty-six, and was buried beside Mary at Kedleston, which he had inherited from his father in 1916.

He married a second time, in 1917, another American, Grace, daughter of Joseph Hinds, formerly United States Minister in Brazil, and widow of Alfred Duggan of Buenos Aires. She was a beautiful woman of great charm and vivacity, and during her marriage to Curzon Carlton House Terrace became a centre of brilliant social and political gatherings. But she never took Mary's place in Curzon's heart, and she knew it. The two effigies lying side by side in the chapel at Kedleston symbolized her exclusion from the deepest level of his emotions. Not long after Curzon's death, she related in her autobiography, she went down to the vault to gaze at his coffin. On one of the shelves she saw a postcard bearing in his handwriting the words, 'Reserved for the second Lady Curzon'. Mary's coffin, she cannot fail to have noticed, lay centrally beneath the chapel beside Curzon's own. Grace was to lie to one side, in a niche. She was the second Lady Curzon in more senses than one.

Curzon's daughters (there were no children of his second marriage) grew up to be young women of exceptional loveliness. Irene, the eldest, who inherited her father's secondary title as Baroness Ravensdale, devoted much of her life to women's emancipaton, social causes, music and travel. She never married, and died in 1966. Cynthia married Sir Oswald Mosley, and died at almost the same age as her mother, in 1933. The youngest daughter, Alexandra, who married Edward Dudley Metcalfe, Equerry to the Prince of Wales, has been an untiring champion of children's welfare throughout the world. The love she has for her mother, who died when she was only two years old, has been the inspiration of this book, and to her it is dedicated.

INDEX